AI: American Innovation and the Economic Recovery

Graham Turner
Demetris Pachnis
of GFC Economics

2QT Limited (Publishing)
Lancaster, United Kingdom LA2 8RE
www.2qt.co.uk

Cover images: Adobe Stock

All our charts have been created with Macrobond and/or Thomson Reuters Datastream

Printed by CMP (UK) Limited

A CIP Catalogue record for this book will be available from the British Library

ISBN 978-1-910077-89-4

Table of Contents

List of Tables

Chapter 7 – US inequality and the NAIRU

Chapter 8 – New technologies driving the economy

List of Charts

Chapter 1 - Introduction

Chapter 2 – Cheap, but tight is working

Glossary

Cheap, but tight money – A monetary framework where credit or lending is cheap (i.e. available at low short- and long-term rates of interest), but the growth in credit or lending is simultaneously constrained.

Complementarities – Arise when technology augments the productive capacity of workers. Rather than substituting machines for workers, employers find it more beneficial to increase the intensity of both inputs in the production process.

Core consumption deflator – This is a chain-type price index from the Bureau of Economic Analysis that measures the rate of inflation, excluding food and energy, for personal consumption.

Core inflation – Inflation excluding food and energy (see also *core consumption deflator*).

Creative destruction – Process of economic transformation by which old companies or industries are destroyed, leaving space for new, fast-growing businesses.

Credit Crunch – A sudden downturn in lending precipitated by distress at financial institutions. Credit Crunch was the name widely given to the sub-prime mortgage crisis in the US and the run on banks, from 2007 onwards.

Debt deflation – High levels of debt leading to a decline in asset prices. It may also lead to falling consumer prices or negative inflation.

Debt trap – Attempts to pay off outstanding loans leading to a higher real debt burden, as a result of the negative impact on prices.

Dotcom recession – Collapse of the speculative bubble in the Internet and technology sectors from early 2000 onwards.

Forward rate guidance – A monetary policy tool where the central bank provides guidance for the likely future path of short-term interest rates.

The Federal Open Market Committee [FOMC] – The monetary policymaking body of the Federal Reserve System.

Federal Financial Institutions Examination Council [FFIEC] – The Council is a formal US government interagency body that includes five banking regulators - the Federal Reserve Board of Governors (FRB), the Federal Deposit Insurance Corporation (FDIC), the National Credit Union Administration (NCUA), the Office of the Comptroller of the Currency (OCC), and the Consumer Financial Protection Bureau (CFPB).

Great Depression – Economic collapse in the US from 1929 onwards.

Great Inflation, The – A period of spiralling inflation that officially began in 1965 and ended in 1984.

Great Recession – Economic recession starting with the failure of the investment bank Bear Stearns in March 2008 and accelerating after the collapse of Lehman Brothers in September 2008.

Hedonic pricing – A statistical technique that controls for quality change when constructing price indices

Hysteresis – Deterioration in the skills of workers that have been unemployed for long periods of time. This can potentially increase the natural rate of unemployment.

Intellectual property products – Defined as the sum of investment in software, research & development, and entertainment, literary & artistic originals.

m/m – month-on-month.

National Bureau of Economic Research [NBER] – A private, non-profit organisation dedicated to conducting economic research and to disseminating research findings among academics, public policymakers, and business professionals.

Non-accelerating inflation rate of unemployment [NAIRU] – Rate of unemployment above which inflation tends to slow and below which inflation tends to rise.

Non-investment grade corporate bonds – Also known as high-yield, or 'junk' bonds, they bear greater risk than their investment-grade counterparts. These bonds are rated below BBB- (S&P) or Baa3 (Moody's).

Online-to-offline commerce – Business model that uses the web-based market to attract e-customers into physical stores.

Productive investment – Defined as the sum of investment in intellectual property products and equipment.

Quantitative easing – A monetary policy weapon where a central bank buys assets – normally government bonds, but can also include agency debt and mortgage backed securities – to influence the yield and borrowing costs across the economy.

Secular stagnation – Term used to describe a period of negligible or no economic growth. Advocates of this theory points to an imbalance between excessive savings in the private sector and insufficient investment that depresses economic growth. The current low level of interest rates is often seen as a vindication of this theory. However, such claims are inconsistent with the strong growth in investment and employment in the technology sector. Low interest rates also reflect the effectiveness of cheap, but tight monetary policy.

Treasuries – US Government debt.

US Bureau of Labor Statistics [BLS] – The principal fact-finding agency for the US Federal Government in the field of work economics and statistics.

US Bureau of Economic Analysis [BEA] – A US government agency that provides official macro-economic and industry statistics including the gross domestic product of the US.

y/y – year-on-year.

GFC Economics

About the authors

Graham Turner

Prior to founding GFC Economics in 1999, Graham worked in the City of London, establishing himself as an expert on the Japanese economy. He has produced consistently accurate research on five of the major global economies: the US, the Eurozone, Japan, China and the UK. With 30 years' experience as an economist, *AI: American Innovation and the Economic Recovery* is Graham's fifth book.

Demetris Pachnis

Demetris joined GFC Economics in 2014 as an Economist and is now Head of US Research. After reading Politics, Philosophy and Economics at the University of Warwick, Demetris completed post-graduate studies in Economics at Birkbeck, University of London. This is Demetris's first book published with GFC Economics.

About the research team

Guillaume Derrien

Guillaume is Head of Research for Asia at GFC Economics. Previous to joining GFC, Guillaume worked in the department for Business Innovation and Skills (Regional Growth Fund) at the Civil Service. He has an MSc in Economics from Nottingham University.

Stephen Jones

Stephen graduated from Keele University with a BA in History and Politics in July 2014. He joined GFC Economics as a research assistant.

About GFC Economics

GFC Economics is a London based macro-economic research consultancy established by Graham Turner in 1999. It has grown to be a well-respected and highly regarded source of quality independent research. GFC accurately predicted the collapse of the dotcom bubble in 2000 and in 2006 warned that the US (and the West) was headed for a hard landing.

GFC Economics adopts a 'top down' integrated approach towards its analysis and seeks to identify long-term strategies arising from its economic projects. GFC Economics has enjoyed a consistent track record in calling economic and market trends as well as providing fresh, independent and timely research.

The company continues to attract interest from a wide range of asset managers and hedge funds.

If you would like to know more about GFC Economics, please visit our website at www.gfceconomics.com or contact: info@gfceconomics.com

Books

The U.S. Economic Recovery, Graham Turner.
Published by 2QT Limited (2014)

An optimistic analysis which argues that the economic upturn underway in the US can be sustained. The book offers a critique of monetary and fiscal policy since late 2008 in response to the sub-prime debacle, and provides a thorough case for investment-led growth and a positive outlook for the US economy.

***No Way To Run An Economy: Why The System Failed And How To Put It Right*, Graham Turner.**
Published by Pluto Press, London (2009)

GFC Economics recommended aggressive measures, such as quantative easing, in early 2008. But the action taken came too late. *No Way To Run An Economy*, dissects policy errors including Obama's fiscal stimulus and the obsession of central banks with the red herring of inflation.

***The Credit Crunch: Housing Bubbles, Globalisation and the Worldwide Economic Crisis*, Graham Turner.**
Published by Pluto Press, London (2008)

The Credit Crunch examined the pitfalls within globalisation that led to the 2008 global financial crisis. When it was published, *The Credit Crunch* warned that central banks and governments were underestimating the potential difficulties that lay ahead. It examined the parallels with Japan and argued for a more urgent policy response to "prevent debt deflation taking root".

***Solutions to a Liquidity Trap: Japan's Bear Market and What It Means For The West*, Graham Turner.**
Published by GFC Economics (2003)

An in-depth analysis of Japan's long bear market that examines in detail the policy mistakes made by the Japanese authorities, as they battled against more than a decade of deflation.

Preface

It is not easy to find an optimistic assessment of the economic outlook today. When stock markets fell in the early weeks of 2016, predictions of an imminent recession were hard to ignore. Once again, commentators were warning that a repeat of the 2008 financial crisis was close at hand. *AI: American Innovation and the Economic Recovery* offers an alternative perspective. It builds upon the framework outlined in a book published in July 2014, *The U.S. Economic Recovery*. This book had detailed the correct policies needed to secure full employment and underpin the economic upswing in the US.

Twenty months on, the US is still creating jobs at an impressive rate. The global economy is fraught with risks, both economic and political. Nonetheless, the popular narratives of the US economy are too pessimistic. Technological progress is creating opportunities for the US to enjoy a long economic expansion. The US has a strong global lead in technology. Some groups of workers will lose out: technology can be destructive. However, the correct response to the challenges posed by the present rapid pace of innovation is to recognise the importance of education and skills. Investing in human capital, and not protectionism, provides the only sustainable route towards higher standards of living.

AI: American Innovation and the Economic Recovery documents how investment in key areas, such as information technology, is driving the creation of new jobs. It offers a detailed critique of the relevant statistics. Taking the economic numbers at face value can be misleading. It is important to dig deep and understand the limitations of the official data, which are wrongly being used by some economists to argue that the US is suffering from secular stagnation. We do not claim to have all of the answers. Many of the data issues remain unresolved and will need to be explored further. This book highlights the areas that need to be examined more closely. The impact of technology on the US economy has been deeper than perhaps many economists are willing to acknowledge. It is important to consider how the current economic cycle is different from the periods of boom and bust that have dominated the last forty years.

The structure of the book is as follows. Chapter 1 revisits the *cheap, but tight* framework initially set out in *The U.S. Economic Recovery*, to show how this has spurred innovation and jobs growth in the current cycle. However, risks will emerge. Chapter 2 highlights why the US was able to sidestep the market turmoil in early 2016, but also examines potential risks going forward. Chapters 3 to 8 include edited versions of six articles written by GFC Economics since the autumn of 2014. Each chapter has an updated section, examining the latest data, to see how many of the encouraging trends highlighted in the original articles have evolved.

Chapter 1
Introduction

At the time of going to print, the current cycle of economic growth in the US had officially stretched to 78 months.[1] Employment had increased for 65 consecutive months, the longest period of uninterrupted jobs growth on record (see chart 1a).[2]

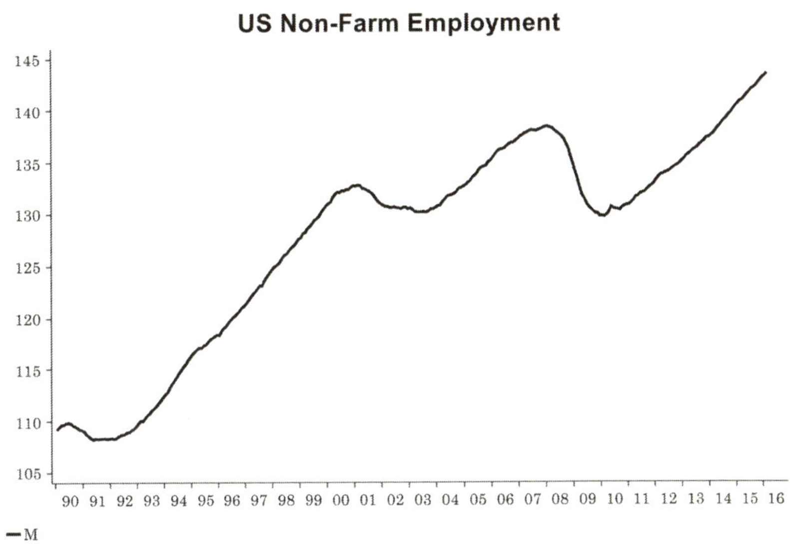

Source: GFC Economics

Chart 1a

1 Source: National Bureau of Economic Research (NBER), US Business Cycle Expansions and Contractions. The current economic expansion currently stands at 78 months (from the trough of June 2009 through to December 2015). This is the fifth longest economic expansion in US history (records began in 1850). The four longest expansions in ascending order are: June 1938 to February 1945 (80 months), November 1982 to July 1990 (92 months), February 1961 to December 1969 (106 months), and March 1991 to March 2001 (120 months). Note: "The NBER does not define a recession in terms of two consecutive quarters of decline in real GDP. Rather, a recession is a significant decline in economic activity spread across the economy, lasting more than a few months, normally visible in real GDP, real income, employment, industrial production, and wholesale-retail sales."

2 Source: Bureau of Labor Statistics (BLS), Current Employment Statistics (CES), National, All Employees, Nonfarm, Payroll. The latest data are for February 2016.

The US created 2.7m jobs in 2015 despite the slowdown in emerging markets and a rising Dollar.[3] The unemployment rate had dropped to 4.9% by February 2016 (see chart 1b).[4]

Source: GFC Economics

Chart 1b

Record job openings had drawn more individuals back into the labour force: the labour force participation rate was starting to rise again.[5] The key to any sustainable economic recovery and full employment lies with productive investment (see chart 1c).[6]

---

3 Source: BLS, Employment, CES, Nonfarm, Payroll, Total and FX Indices, Federal Reserve, Major Currencies Index (Nominal) and Broad Index (Nominal). Employment rose by 2.744m in 2015. This was down slightly from 3.015m in 2014, which was the highest annual rate of jobs growth since 1999. The trade-weighted Dollar appreciated 10.5% in 2015 (broad index). With respect to major currencies, the strength of the Dollar was even more pronounced, rising 11.0%.

4 Source: BLS, Unemployment, CPS, 16 Years & Over, Rate.

5 Source: BLS, Socio-Demographic Labour Force Statistics, Civilian Labour Force Participation Rate, Women & Men, 16 Years & Over. By February 2016, the labour force participation rate had rebounded to 62.91%, having fallen to a secular low of 62.42% five months earlier.

6 Productive investment is defined in this book as investment in intellectual property products and equipment. This is equivalent to non-residential investment less

Source: GFC Economics

Chart 1c

This increased rapidly in the US following the financial crisis of 2008. Rising investment in technology has been critical to the new jobs created during the subsequent recovery.[7] The dotcom boom of the late-1990s accelerated the development of the internet infrastructure. This in turn provided the platform for technology to generate a raft of new occupations in the services sector. Manufacturing has also been transformed, with US companies leading in the expansion of high-tech industries.[8]

---

investment in structures. Investment in intellectual property products consist of spending on software, research & development, and entertainment, literary & artistic originals.

7 This view is not universally shared. For a rather pessimistic interpretation of the reasons for falling unemployment, see *Rate rise belies frailties in US economy*, Financial Times, December 7th 2015. "JP Morgan economists have concluded that one of the main reasons for... lower than expected joblessness is because of falling productivity. More workers need to be hired because the output of each worker has dropped – not because the economy is so vibrant. It is not clear what the causes are, but the consequences are deeply disturbing."

8 See chapter 4.

The labour market is changing rapidly in the US because companies are innovating, pushing the frontiers of knowledge. Intellectual property products investment, which includes software as well as research and development (R&D), has hit record highs in Dollar terms and as a share of real GDP.[9] Despite the big increase in share buybacks, US companies are recycling profits into the economy. Moreover, there are strong reasons to believe that the official real GDP numbers are too low. Important work by one Federal Reserve economist in particular shows that the true level of productive investment is likely to be higher than currently reported by the Bureau of Economic Analysis (BEA).[10]

Treasury bond yields may be close to historic lows, but the secular stagnation thesis is wrong.[11] The falling returns on government debt "bear little resemblance to the returns on productive capital."[12] Indeed, "pre- and post-tax real returns on business capital and all capital have not been declining".[13] They dropped during the last recession, as would be expected. However, these returns "quickly rebounded and are now as high as they have been over the past three decades".[14]

---

9 See chapter 3.

10 See *Does the United States have a Productivity Slowdown or a Measurement Problem?*, David M. Byrne, John G. Fernald & Marshall B. Reinsdorf, Finance and Economics Discussion Series, Federal Reserve Board, 2016. The work of David Byrne is discussed extensively in chapters 3 and 4. This particular paper pulls together all of his research on technology mismeasurement. The deflators have been *overstated* for many high-tech investment goods. As a result, productivity has been *understated*. Ironically, the biases were even worse during the period of high productivity growth between 1995 and 2004. As a result, the productivity slowdown of today vis-à-vis that exceptional period appears greater.

11 See, for example, *U.S. Economic Prospects: Secular Stagnation, Hysteresis, and the Zero Lower Bound*, Lawrence H. Summers, Business Economics Vol. 49, No. 2, 2014.

12 See *Secular Stagnation and Returns on Capital*, Paul Gomme, B. Ravikumar & Peter Rupert, Economic Synopses, No. 19, 2015, p. 3. To compute the after-tax income from business capital, the authors "use the net operating surplus data in NIPA [National Income and Product Accounts] (value added minus depreciation and payments to labor) and modify the income flows and tax rates to subtract out the income generated from the housing sector." They also "attribute a fraction of proprietors' income to capital income (because the NIPA do not separate capital from labor income for proprietorships)."

13 Ibid., p. 1.

14 Ibid.

This has important ramifications for monetary policy. The Federal Reserve has been late in recognising the significance of the technology revolution. Interest rates have been kept low largely because the US central bank believed the economy had not fully recovered from the trauma of 2008.

The Federal Reserve has reluctantly revised down its estimate of the NAIRU (i.e. how far the unemployment rate can fall without causing inflation to accelerate).[15] Federal Reserve chair Janet Yellen has been slow to acknowledge the importance of the expansion in information technology.[16] The vice chair of the Federal Open Market Committee (FOMC), William Dudley, has also been guilty of underestimating the rapid changes underway.[17]

The West has become accustomed to goods deflation following China's emergence as a key manufacturer, and the broader trend towards globalisation.[18] This dynamic may be running its course, as the minimum

---

15 Source: Federal Reserve, Federal Open Market Committee, Meeting calendars, statements, and minutes (2010-2016), Accessible Materials. The central tendency of the FOMC's longer-run estimate of the unemployment rate has been revised down slowly during the recovery. The central tendency excludes the three highest and three lowest projections of the FOMC. Since April 2011, this central tendency has been revised down in the following FOMC meetings: September 2013 (from 5.2%-6.0% to 5.2%-5.8%); March 2014 (5.2%-5.6%); June 2014 (5.2%-5.5%); March 2015 (5.0%-5.2%); September 2015 (4.9%-5.2%); December 2015 (4.8%-5.0%); and March 2016 (4.7%-5.0%).

16 See *The Outlook for the Economy*, Janet Yellen, May 22nd 2015.

17 See *The U.S. Economic and Monetary Policy Outlook*, William C. Dudley, June 5th 2015. Mr. Dudley talked of the "weakness in capital spending".

18 See *The Credit Crunch*, Graham Turner, Pluto Press, 2008, pp. 60-62. The period of rapid globalisation in the 1990s was characterised by US companies shifting production abroad to take advantage of cheaper labour costs. In anticipation of China's acceptance into the World Trade Organization in 2001, capital flowed into China. This funded a surge in exports to the US. Indeed, the US trade deficit vis-à-vis China widened significantly after 2002. This trend has continued: the bilateral trade balance (12-month moving total) hit a record low of -$366.0bn in January 2016. Similarly, US investment poured into Mexico after the North American Free Trade Agreement was signed in 1993. The trade deficit with Mexico also deteriorated significantly, although the decline was abruptly halted in 2008. The flood of cheap imports placed downward pressure on durables prices. The y/y for the durables deflator has been in negative territory since September 1995.

wage rises quickly in China.[19] Nevertheless, technology is rapidly driving down the cost of services for businesses.[20] Cloud computing, for example, now offers sizeable economies of scale or savings for companies.[21]

Low short- and long-term interest rates are not a reflection of a weak economy.[22] On the contrary, they are a necessary pre-condition for a strong rise in productive investment. The purpose of low borrowing costs is not to encourage a rise in debt to fund investment. This merely creates the risk of another boom-bust cycle. Higher debt and falling profits are a toxic combination, as the dotcom bubble of the late-1990s demonstrated.[23] Rather, central banks have to enshrine financial stability

---

19 See *World's factory slowing down, but wages still rising*, Nikkei Asian Review, February 2nd 2016. Minimum wages have been hiked from between 8% to 28% in a number of provinces, many in the "hotbeds of manufacturing". Higher wages are symptomatic of China's shift into high-value manufacturing, and will also facilitate a transition towards services. Durables deflation eased sharply from 2.66% in January 2015 to 0.92% in January 2016, despite a rapid appreciation of the Dollar through this period. Source: BEA, Price Indexes for Personal Consumption Expenditures, Durable Goods, Index.

20 Source: BLS, Producer Price Index (PPI), Final Demand, Services. The final demand services PPI averaged 0.39% y/y in the three months to December 2015. It edged up to 0.91% y/y in February 2016 (3-month average). Nevertheless, this was still well below the average of 1.98% y/y recorded in the three months to January 2015. The PPI for 'management, scientific & technical consulting services' fell to an average of -0.67% y/y in the three months to February 2016. For 'cellular phone & other wireless telecommunications services', the y/y rate was -8.29% on a similar basis. Prices for internet access services had dropped to -0.54% y/y in the three months to February 2016.

21 See *Microsoft's Satya Nadella rethinks the cloud*, Financial Times, November 12th 2015. Mr. Nadella discussed the "massive scale efficiencies of the cloud – what he calls 'hyperscale'".

22 See *One tiny step on rates highlights America's hidden weakness*, James Grant, Financial Times, December 18th 2015. "You may remember the interest rates of yesteryear – sturdy integers such as 4 or 5 or even 6. They vanished with prosperity in 2008 [...] It is easy to forget that interest rates are prices, not – chiefly – knobs or levers on some infernal monetary policy control panel. Proper interest rates balance the supply of savings with the demand for savings." This view was echoed by Ben Bernanke, who claimed that low real interest rates would indicate that "investment opportunities are limited and relatively unprofitable." See also *Why Are Interest Rates So Low?*, Ben Bernanke, Ben Bernanke's Blog, March 30th 2015. This reflects a misunderstanding of how monetary policy operates in a cheap, but tight framework.

23 Source: BEA, Corporate Profits with Inventory Valuation & Capital Consumption

with effective controls over bank lending. This is the essence of a cheap, but tight monetary policy.

Low long-term interest rates in particular have an important role to play, bearing down on the required break-even rate for investment projects. They are also part of a culture shift, away from speculation towards a more productive deployment of capital.[24] When companies use retained earnings to invest, it reduces the systemic risks from a misallocation of capital.

Low interest rates do not eliminate the possibility that some investments will be misjudged. Some technology companies searching for the next big idea will make mistakes. The success rate of biotechnology research, for example, is uncertain. The recent investment surge in the oil sector has generated losses for some investors.[25] The payback from investment in renewables is potentially very long: some businesses may struggle to make the necessary breakthroughs to deliver sustainable energy that can compete with cheaper oil. Others may succeed.

It is important for companies to take a 'calculated' gamble. The pace of innovation will otherwise stall. Inventions are necessary to secure a higher standard of living and will be critical to tackling climate

---

Adjustments and Federal Reserve, Flow of Funds, Balance Sheet, Nonfarm Non-Financial Corporate Business, Liabilities and BEA, GDP, Current Prices. Profits from current production (i.e. profits with inventory valuation adjustments (IVA) and adjustments for depreciation charges (CCAdj)) peaked at $892.6bn in Q3 1997, before falling steadily to $803.3bn in Q1 2000. As a share of nominal GDP, corporate sector debt surged from 75.84% to 86.75% over this period, before peaking at 92.71% in Q1 2001.

24 See *The U.S. Economic Recovery*, Graham Turner, 2QT Publishing, 2014, p. 256. "A policy of cheap, but tight money would have the advantage of shifting the focus of investment away from financial to real assets. It would, Keynes argued, accelerate the 'euthanasia of the rentier'. In the early stages of an economic recovery, the rentier or the investor in financial assets will benefit perhaps disproportionately, as asset prices recover. However, this will be a 'transitional phase which will disappear when it has done its work. And with the disappearance of its rentier aspect, much else in it besides will suffer a sea-change'. The maintenance of low long-term interest rates combined with tight money will in short encourage a shift towards investment in productive capacity."

25 A potential misallocation of capital – for example, in shale oil – will be less damaging if the financial sector is well capitalised, and if the rise in debt is not systemic. For more on this point, see chapter 2.

change. It is only by taking risks that firms can hope to make scientific discoveries. The same is true whether research and development is driven by businesses or by governments.

The optimal balance between private and public sector investment is a matter of legitimate debate. In the US, the private sector is currently driving the strong increase in research and development.[26] That is partly because the US has secured a dominant position in the technology sector. According to a worldwide survey by PricewaterhouseCoopers (PwC), eleven out of the top 20 companies for research and development are from the US.[27] Of these, six are in the technology sphere. Another of these eleven US companies is leading the push for zero carbon emission vehicles. Strong profitability has, for some of these businesses, been the key to the rise in research and development. Nevertheless, it would be wrong to ignore the important, historic role of the public sector in allowing the US to secure its strategic advantage in technology.[28] Indeed,

---

26 See chapter 3.

27 See *The 2015 Global Innovation 1000: Innovation's New World Order*, PricewaterhouseCoopers (PwC), Issue 81, Winter 2015.

28 See *The Entrepreneurial State*, Mariana Mazzucato, Anthem Press, 2014, pp. 21-22. "The discovery of the Internet or the emergence of the nanotechnology industry did not occur because the private sector wanted something but could not find the resources to invest in it. Both happened due to the vision that the government had in an area that had not yet been fathomed by the private sector. Even after these new technologies were introduced by Government, the private sector still was too scared to invest. Government even had to support the commercialization of the Internet. And it took years for private venture capitalists to start financing biotech or nanotech companies. It was – in these and many such cases – the State that appeared to have the most aggressive 'animal spirits'."
Ibid., p. 13. "From the development of aviation, nuclear energy, computers, the Internet, biotechnology, and today's developments in green technology, it is, and has been, the State – not the private sector – that has kick-started and developed the engine of growth, because of its willingness to take risks in areas where the private sector has been too risk averse." In short, the state has in the past taken a leading role in directing future technological innovation."
See also *Where Does Technological Innovation Come From?*, Wall Street Journal, November 11th 2015. "The Internet had many origins, but the three most cited contributors are the invention of the TCP/IP protocol [Transmission Control Protocol/Internet Protocol] (funded by DARPA [Defense Advanced Research Projects Agency]), the invention of the World Wide Web (at CERN), and the creation of the Mosaic Web browser (at NCSA [National Center for Supercomputing Applications]/University of Illinois)."

the role of the public sector in the early stages of development has been critical, a point the UK government would do well to heed.[29]

Technology is disruptive. Automation in a swathe of manufacturing sectors and across services could lead to further significant job losses. Some groups of workers have already lost out. The gains from technological progress are not spread evenly across the economy. In the US, the real median income has remained under downward pressure, despite the significant number of new jobs created since 2009 (see chart 1d).[30] This is not inevitable. It is possible for technology to create jobs and protect the median wage. Governments have a key role to play. Nonetheless, there is strong evidence to suggest technology has been a net positive for job creation in the US (see chart 1e).[31]

---

29 See *Business Enterprise Research and Development: 2014*, Office for National Statistics (ONS), November 20th 2015. The UK's track record on research and development (R&D) remains disappointing, and a potential threat to its long-term economic prospects. Business R&D expenditures amounted to 1.1% of nominal GDP in 2014. The three sectors with the largest share of R&D spending were pharmaceuticals (19.7%), computer programming & information service activities (11.8%) and motor vehicles & parts (11.6%). The UK is falling behind in R&D spending vis-à-vis major competitors. According to the OECD, total UK R&D spending as a share of GDP was 1.70% in 2014. This was well below the OECD average of 2.37%. By comparison, US R&D spending was 2.74% of GDP (2013). Japan (3.58%), China (2.05%) and the EU (1.94%) also devoted a greater share of their economies' resources to R&D. South Korea topped the rankings (4.29%), followed by Israel (4.11%). The Scandinavian countries also scored highly. One important caveat: these crude measures do not reveal the quality of R&D, which is just as important as the quantity. See *Gross Domestic Spending on R&D*, OECD, 2016.

30 See chapter 7.

31 Source: BLS, Employment, CES, Professional & Business Services, Nonfarm, Payroll, Total. Since the 2008-09 recession, employment in professional & business services has accelerated, hitting 20.019m in February 2016. Payrolls in this sector were 10.9% above the previous cyclical peak in December 2007 (this compares with a 4.7% increase for total private sector employment over the same period). A large proportion of employment growth in professional & business services has been concentrated in 'productive' subcategories. Payrolls in professional & technical services totalled 8.806m in February 2016, 12.6% above the previous April 2008 peak. Within this, employment in computer systems design & related services had risen to 1.960m. This figure was 35.5% above the previous cyclical high of August 2008 (this industry includes a high proportion of science, technology, engineering and mathematics occupations). Employment in management & technical consulting services had also hit new highs, climbing to 1.308m in February 2016. This was up 29.0% since September 2008.

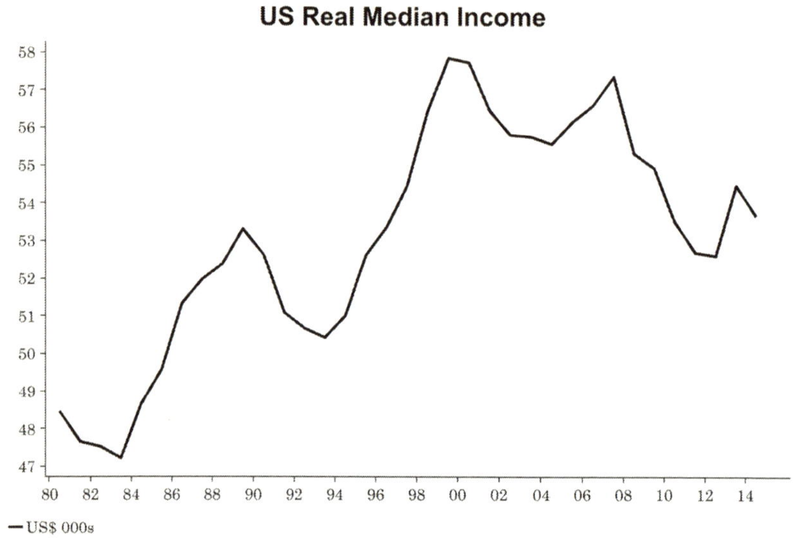

Source: GFC Economics

Chart 1d

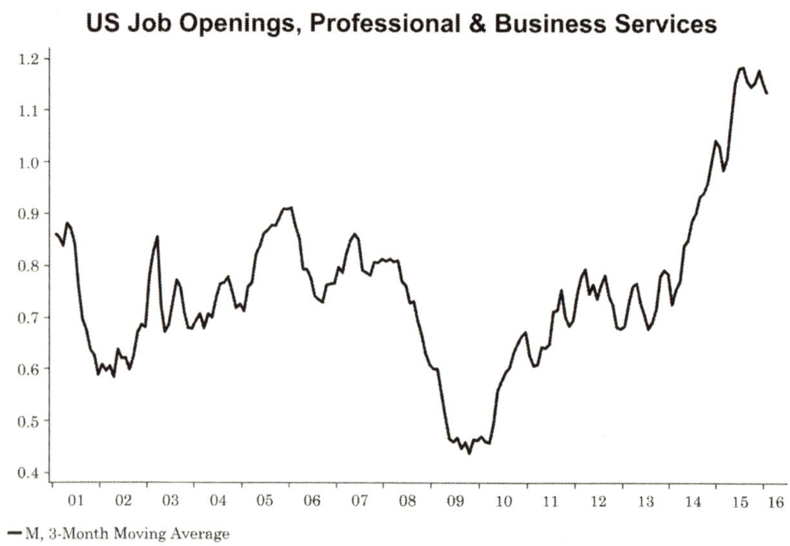

Source: GFC Economics

Chart 1e

It is important not to lose sight of the complementarities or compensation dynamics.[32] Complementarities refer to the inherent economic value embedded in automation or any other labour saving innovation. In the short run, a company that introduces robotics, for example, may shed jobs and will certainly reduce its costs.[33] That said, the robot will produce a larger surplus for companies. Any rise in unemployment should prove short-lived. Prices may well fall, stimulating demand for the company's product, as well as for other goods and services.[34] The larger surplus enjoyed by companies will be redeployed, leading to higher investment, larger dividends and share buybacks.[35]

---

32 See *Labour's Share*, Andrew Haldane, November 12th 2015, p. 7. "There are two opposing effects at work. The first is the substitution or *displacement* effect. Labour-saving technologies displace workers, almost by definition. Capital substitutes for labour, machine for man. If there is a 'lump of labour' to be allocated across a fixed pool of jobs, technology will raise unemployment, other things equal. This being the real world, other things are of course never equal. As cheaper capital displaces labour, goods and services become cheaper, raising real incomes across the economy. That boosts the demand for *new* goods and services and new industries to supply them. To complete the loop, displaced labour then switches to meet this new demand, lowering unemployment. These are the income or *compensation* effects of technological progress. They are what make the 'lump of labour' a fallacy."
See also *Polyani's Paradox and the Shape of Employment Growth*, David Autor, p. 2. David Autor argues that "journalists and expert commentators overstate the extent of machine substitution for human labor and ignore the strong complementarities that increase productivity, raise earnings, and augment demand for skilled labor."

33 See *Machines set to take over 114,000 law jobs,* Financial Times, March 16th 2016. A recent Deloitte report is the latest to claim that a significant number of jobs will be lost to automation. It is not just low-skilled jobs that are under threat: "Around 114,000 jobs in the legal sector are likely to become automated in the next 20 years as technology transforms the profession."

34 See *Robots Seem to Be Improving Productivity, Not Costing Jobs*, Mark Munroe and Scott Andes, Harvard Business Review, June 16th 2015.

35 See *Are share buybacks jeopardizing future growth?*, Tim Koller, McKinsey & Company, October 2015. "Distributions to shareholders overall, including both buybacks and dividends, are currently around 85 percent of income, about the same as in the early 1990s. Instead, the trend in shareholder distributions reflects a decades-long evolution in the way companies think strategically about dividends and buybacks—and, more broadly, mirrors the growing dominance of sectors that generate high returns with relatively little capital investment."

Innovation will also create business opportunities. New goods and services may emerge: supply creates its own demand. When retailers started to offer online deliveries, the growth in e-commerce exploded. Many new jobs have been created. Critically, some of these include well-paid positions.[36] In the US, jobs growth has been particularly strong in industries which pay above-average wages (see charts 1f, 1g and 1h).[37]

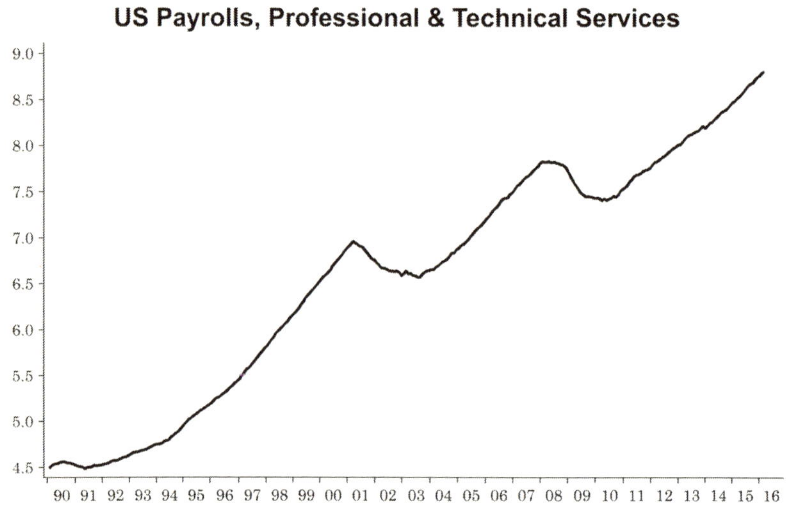

Source: GFC Economics

Chart 1f

The potential for automation to raise standards of living is self-evident. Nevertheless, it is absolutely correct to put in place policies that will facilitate the transition, so that displaced workers can move into new growth sectors. Equipping the workforce with the requisite skills is essential to complement the rise in productive investment. Otherwise,

---

36 See *Amazon to create 1,000 new jobs in Manchester*, BBC, March 9th 2016. Amazon recently announced the creation of 1,000 new, mostly high-skilled jobs in the UK. This could rise to 2,500, bringing the total number of permanent staff in the UK to 14,500. "The posts will include engineers, computing staff, human resources and operation managers."

37 Source: BLS, Earnings, Average Hourly Earnings, All Employees, Total Private. As of January 2016, average hourly earnings in computer systems design & related services equalled $45.08, $39.16 in professional & technical services and $38.96 in management & technical consulting services. This compared with an average of $25.35 in the private sector.

there is a danger that the benefits from innovation will not be maximised. Skill shortages will reduce the capacity for companies to create new services and products. The profitability of employing additional workers will diminish. In such a scenario, the cost-cutting innovations may dominate the complementarities, pushing down the median wage even more. Without the right focus on education and skills, the potential growth path of the economy will slow.[38]

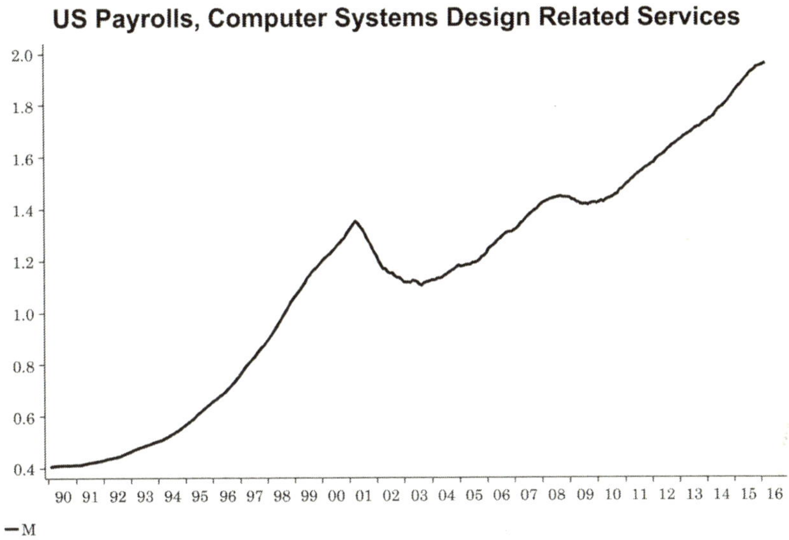

Source: GFC Economics

Chart 1g

Assessing the impact of technological change requires accurate data. Otherwise, this could lead to policy mistakes. At present, there are material concerns over the reliability of the statistics used to analyse and

38 Many new small businesses are technology-intensive. The advertising industry employs a large proportion of STEM (science, technology, engineering and mathematics) workers. Advertising technology platforms are creating their own start-ups (classified within a sub-category under the broader professional & business services category), or are within established companies. Indeed, some of the US's brightest minds are being lured into advertising. They are playing a pivotal role in enabling the commercialisation of new technologies, including 'machine learning'. See *Hats Off to Web Advertising. No, Really.* Wall Street Journal, July 6th 2015.

track the US economy.[39] Some of this reflects the very rapid changes brought about by technology itself.[40] A shift towards e-commerce is well under way.[41] Conventional methods may be less well-suited to tracking prices online.[42]

Investment is also changing, creating a particular challenge for statisticians. Companies are increasing spending on intangibles,

---

39 See *The U.S. Underestimates Growth*, Martin Feldstein, Wall Street Journal, May 20th 2015. "Calculating the growth of real GDP requires comparing the increase of nominal GDP to the increase in the price level. That is impossibly difficult [...] The measurement problem is particularly severe for new products."

40 It has been claimed that the impact of technology on the economy is overstated. See *The US tech sector is really small*, Matthew C Klein, Financial Times, January 8th 2016. "The share of Americans working in the tech industry, broadly construed, is significantly lower now than in the late 1990s and early 2000s [...] For comparison, America's manufacturing business, excluding the manufacturers of computers and electronics, employ about *four times* as many Americans as the software sector." The logic behind this argument is flawed. Technology transcends industries, and is not confined to a specific sector. Professional & business services invest heavily in intellectual property products. Furthermore, many technology-intensive firms are not classified as technology companies. For example, Amazon is classified as 'consumer discretionary', but its computer systems design, software programming, and cloud computing services are at the heart of the business. Tesla is a car company, but is leading the charge in driverless vehicles, which may eventually have applications beyond the automotive industry.

41 Source: United States, Domestic Trade, Retail Trade, Retail Sales, E-commerce (As Percent of Total Sales). 'E-commerce' has expanded steadily in the US, and accounted for 7.5% of total sales in Q4 last year. This was up from 6.6% a year earlier.

42 See *Introducing the Adobe Digital-Economy Project: Harnessing Big Data to Reveal New Economic Trends*, Luiz Maykot, March 16th 2016. A new Digital Price Index (DPI) from Adobe attempts to capture price trends from online sales more accurately. The DPI has some significant advantages over the CPI. The basket is updated on a daily basis, unlike the CPI which is updated every 3 years. On average, 80% of online spending on electronics is on 'new' products (defined as products that have been available for one year or less). The CPI will not capture significant deflation as the consumer shifts to newer products. The DPI also covers a greater range of products: 1.2m compared with 83k in the CPI. However, it does not include offline prices. This new series revealed that television deflation, for example, was significantly understated. Prices fell 19.4% y/y in January 2016, well below the official CPI estimate of -14.3% y/y. For computers, the DPI showed price declines of 13.1% y/y in the same month, whereas the CPI measure was only -7.1% y/y. 'Tablets' are not covered in the CPI. However, the y/y drop was 21.1% in the first month of 2016, according to Adobe.

including software and R&D, but also 'economic competencies' such as branding and advertising. Furthermore, the sophistication of recent inventions has made it difficult for the statisticians to disentangle the split between nominal and real values. Overestimating inflation will increase the risks of an unnecessary recession. In Dollar or nominal terms, it is sometimes easy to see the headline price of a new product or service. However, measuring the true (real) value is less straightforward. Frequently, companies will leave prices unchanged, but a product or service may incorporate enhanced performance characteristics. In this case, the real quantity purchased will be greater.

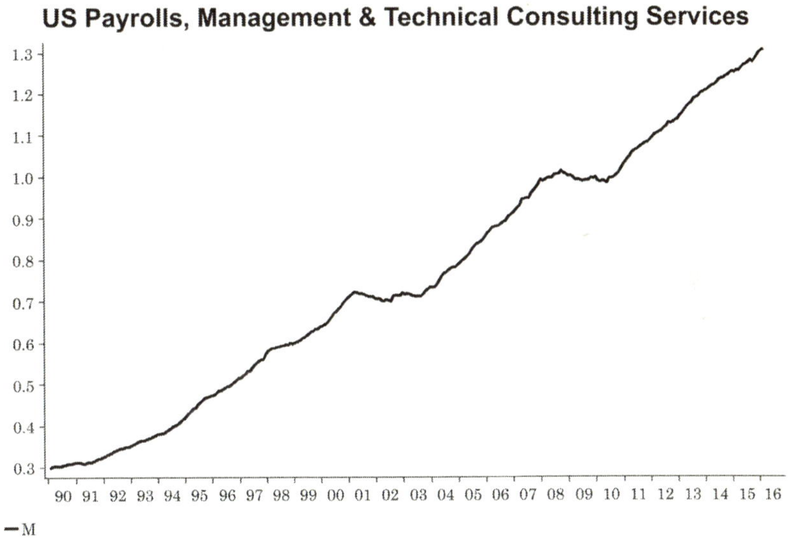

Source: GFC Economics

Chart 1h

It is sometimes argued that nominal GDP may be a better metric for assessing the ability of the economy (or governments) to service outstanding debt. The slow growth in nominal GDP witnessed since the financial crisis of 2008 has been seen as a particular problem: it is harder to reduce debt as a share of nominal GDP. This argument is wrong. Inflation has fallen, pushing government bond yields and nominal debt servicing costs lower. This should lead to smaller budget deficits. In the long run, the impact of lower inflation on nominal GDP growth will be cancelled out by the decline in bond yields. Real growth is more important for the long-term ability of governments to deal with their debt burdens.

Policy targets

If prices are falling because of quality improvements, the Federal Reserve's goal of 2% (core) inflation may be misplaced.[43] Deflation can be a sign of progress, reflecting underlying productivity enhancements. Much of the commentary over deflation has been unnecessarily pessimistic. Debt traps and debt deflation are usually presaged by a lack of financial stability and a build-up in private sector debt. Despite the recent rise in corporate sector borrowing, private sector debt in the US has declined as a share of GDP since the Credit Crunch (see chart 1i).[44] Debt servicing costs have dropped even more quickly, with default rates in the household sector at multi-decade lows (see charts 1j & 1k).[45]

---

43 See *Inflation Target Faces Scrutiny From All Sides*, Wall Street Journal, March 14th 2016.

44 Source: Federal Reserve and BEA. Private sector debt (credit market debt of non-financial business and financial liabilities of households and non-profit organisations) as a share of GDP was a record 189.03% in Q4 2008. It subsequently fell to a post-credit crunch low of 170.47% in Q3 2014, before rising to 171.98% in Q4 2015.

45 Source: MBA (Mortgage Bankers Association), National Delinquency Survey, All Loans, 30-59 Days Due Rate, Total and Federal Reserve, Delinquency Rates, All Banks, All Loans and Federal Reserve, Banking Ratios, Household Debt Service Ratios (DSR), Total. The delinquency rate on 30-59 days due loans dropped to 2.35% in Q4 2015, according to data from the MBA. This was the lowest on record. According to the Federal Reserve, delinquency rates on all loans fell to 2.19% in Q4 2015, the lowest since Q3 2007. Household debt payments as a share of disposable income edged up to 10.07% in Q3. This was marginally above the recent Q4 2012 low (9.86%), but well below the peak in Q4 2007 (13.21%). See also *J.P. Morgan, Wells Fargo Earnings Show Bad Loans on the Decline*, Wall Street Journal, July 16th 2015: "Banking giants J.P. Morgan Chase & Co. and Wells Fargo & Co. both said the percentage of loans they couldn't collect was close to zero in the second quarter. J.P. Morgan Chief Executive James Dimon even went so far as to call customers' credit quality 'pristine'."

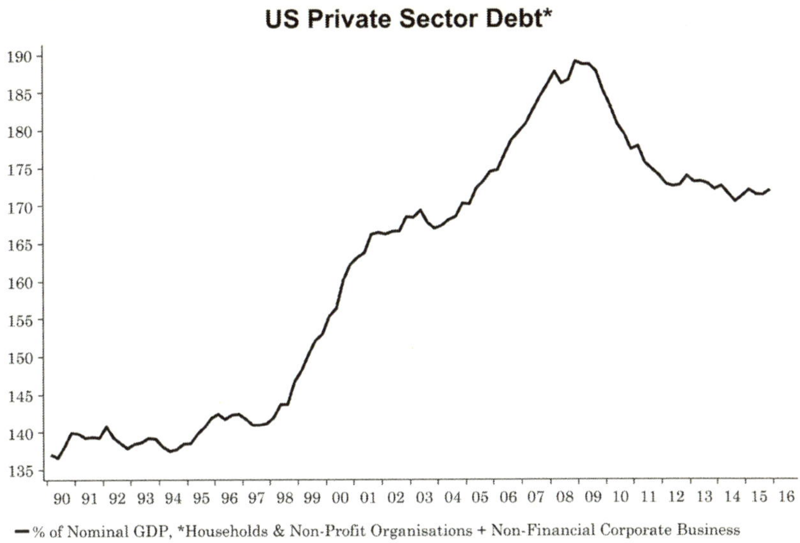

Source: GFC Economics

Chart 1i

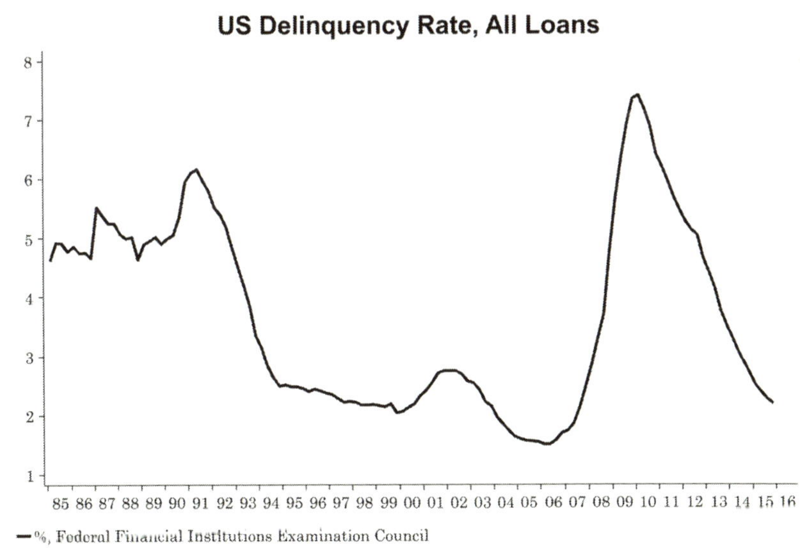

Source: GFC Economics

Chart 1j

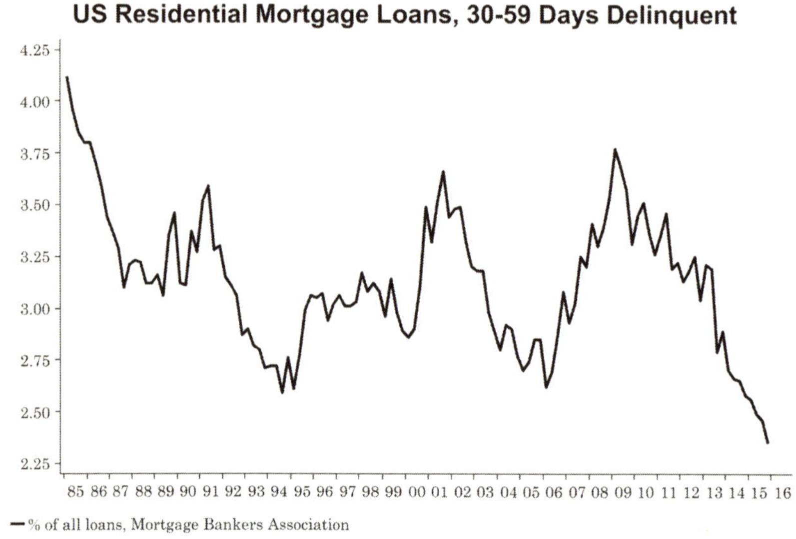

Source: GFC Economics

Chart 1k

At the beginning of 2016, core inflation was showing tentative signs of turning higher in the US, despite the steep fall in commodity prices recorded in the previous year.[46] Cyclical price pressures will emerge as the US approaches full employment. However, over the longer-run, structural disinflation from technology could well be an overriding influence. In this environment, the Fed's 2.0% inflation target may not be appropriate. The FOMC may need to widen its policy goals, targeting for example, the median wage. Technological changes will make inequality and labour market polarisation the more pressing issues.

46 Source: Personal Consumption Expenditures, Excluding Food & Energy Price Index and Commodity Indices, S&P GSCI, Index, Total Return, Close. The Goldman Sachs Commodity Index dropped 32.9% in 2015. The 'core' deflator (excluding food & energy) jumped to 1.67% y/y in the first month of 2016, up from a low of 1.26% y/y in July 2015.

Fiscal policy

It could be argued that the Federal Government should seize the opportunity afforded by rapid technological change to reduce its debt burden, aiming for a surplus on its budget. There is no guarantee that the current rapid rate of innovation and the growth of high tech jobs will endure. When an economy is approaching full employment, there is arguably no need for a government to be running a deficit.[47] A deficit might be justifiable if serious bottlenecks were starting to emerge that restrain the potential growth path of the US economy.[48] In this case, there may be an argument for running a deficit targeted at increasing public sector investment. If private sector spending on research and development started to drop – because companies lose their appetite to innovate – there may be a case for revisiting the decline in the public sector's contribution to research and development witnessed in recent years.[49]

---

47 Source: Congressional Budget Office. According to The Budget and Economic Outlook: 2016 to 2026 for January 2016, "In 2016, the federal budget deficit will increase in relation to the size of the economy for the first time since 2009". Indeed, "If current laws generally remained unchanged, the deficit would grow over the next 10 years, and by 2026 it would be considerably larger than its average over the past 50 years". The deficit for 2016 (fiscal year) is forecast to be $544 billion (2.9% of GDP), an increase of $105 billion over 2015 (fiscal year). Around $43 billion of this increase reflects timing effects (October 1st 2016, the first day of fiscal year 2017, falls on a weekend. These payments will be brought forward into fiscal year 2016). Nevertheless, the increase in the deficit for fiscal year 2016 is "largely attributable to legislation enacted since August 2015 – in particular the retrospective extension of a number of provisions that reduce corporate and individual income taxes".

48 Source: BEA, Government Consumption Expenditures & Gross Investment, Gross Investment, Constant Prices, Chained and Gross Domestic Product, Total, Constant Prices, Chained. As a share of real GDP, real gross government investment fell from a high of 4.55% in Q3 2009 to a low of 3.35% in Q1 2015. It had edged back up to 3.43% by Q4. Furthermore, the composition of government spending is changing, shifting away from discretionary spending (research, education, training, infrastructure) towards entitlement programmes. The former are important for raising the long-term economic growth path of the US. See *Budget Priorities Don't Bode Well for Future*, Greg Ip, Wall Street Journal, September 30th 2015.

49 Source: BEA, Government Consumption Expenditures & Gross Investment, Gross Investment, Intellectual Property, Research & Development, Constant

At this juncture, there appear to be few concerns vis-à-vis energy supply, with fracking and rising supply overseas conspiring to push oil prices down. Nevertheless, the challenge of combatting climate change suggests that the Federal Government should be taking a lead on investment in renewables. The Advanced Research Projects Agency-Energy (Arpa-E), a US government agency, has already made significant breakthroughs in energy storage technology.[50] Arpa-E was funded out of the Obama economic recovery plan of 2009. Several Arpa-E projects have since secured private funding, which may speed up the process of commercialisation. From this perspective, it is even more important that the Federal Reserve understands the potential for technology and rising productive investment to drive a long economic cycle: this will provide the space for the Federal Government to make important strategic investments to fight climate change.

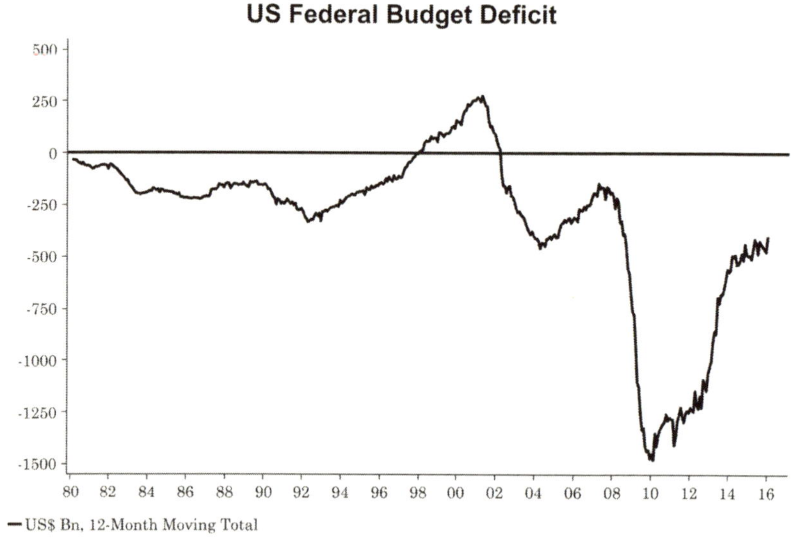

Source: GFC Economics

Chart 11

Prices, Chained. Real gross government investment in R&D declined 8.5% from the peak in Q3 2010, down from $148.2bn to $135.6bn in Q4 2015.

50 See *US agency reached 'holy grail' of battery storage sought by Elon Musk and Gates*, The Guardian, March 3rd 2016. "The most promising developments are in the realm of large-scale energy storage systems, which electricity companies need to put in place to bring more solar and wind power onto the grid."

Summary

The potential for an investment-led cycle in the US economy was outlined in detail in *The U.S. Economic Recovery.*[51] Over the past two years, the economic data have corroborated this optimistic outlook for the US. After a weather-related dip in Q1 2014, real GDP has expanded steadily. There have only been two quarterly contractions since Q2 2009. Non-farm employment is now 3.7% above the high reached prior to the sub-prime crisis.[52]

The key to job creation has been investment. Real non-residential investment tumbled by 20.0% between Q1 2008 and Q4 2009 in response to the Credit Crunch.[53] A steep rise in lending costs forced companies to slash capital spending.[54] Eventually, interest rate cuts and quantitative easing set the stage for a recovery. It was far from plain sailing. House prices had continued to slide as mortgage rates had not declined far enough. Arrears and default rates remained too high.[55] Nevertheless, when the FOMC shifted towards forward rate guidance in the summer of 2011, the case for a sustainable, enduring economic upswing became much clearer.[56]

---

51 See *The U.S. Economic Recovery*, Graham Turner, 2QT Publishing, 2014.

52 Source: BLS, Employment, CES, Nonfarm, Payroll, Total. Total non-farm employment was 143.560m in February 2016, compared with the pre-crisis peak of 138.432m in January 2008.

53 Source: BEA, Saving & Investment, Private Fixed Investment, Non-Residential, Total, Constant Prices. Non-residential private investment fell from $1.998tr in Q1 2008 to $1.598tr in Q4 2009.

54 Source: Fixed Income Indices, Merrill Lynch, U.S. High Yield Master II Index, All Maturities, All Ratings, Yield. Corporate bond yields (High Yield or non-investment grade) rose from 9.68% on January 2nd 2008 to a record 22.65% on December 12th 2008.

55 See *The U.S. Economic Recovery*, Graham Turner, 2014, 2QT Publishing, p. 29. "The authorities failed to recognise the importance of preventing defaults. The latter was a big contributor to the crisis of 2008, with the Federal Reserve too preoccupied with measures to ease liquidity shortages, when it should have been cutting interest rates more aggressively."

56 Ibid., p. 73. "A failure to understand the true significance of Keynes's work initially led to an incorrect application of monetary policy by the Federal Reserve. It was not until the summer of 2011 that the requisite policies were put in place. This involved relegating fiscal policy behind a primary focus on controlling interest

As long-term interest rates fell to new lows, the housing market stabilised and the economic recovery gained traction. Indeed, the US administration shifted to a much tighter fiscal policy, but this failed to tip the economy back into recession as many post-war Keynesians predicted (see chart 1l). When the first edition of this book was written, real non-residential investment had rebounded by 27.0% between the low of Q4 2009 and Q4 2013 (see chart 1m).[57] As a share of real GDP, it had climbed from the cyclical low of 10.99% in Q4 2009 to 12.74%.[58]

Source: GFC Economics

Chart 1m

The rise in capital spending has since accelerated. By Q3 2015, real non-residential investment had increased to 13.55% of real GDP, surpassing the previous high of 13.42% reached in Q1 2008.[59] It is hard

rate expectations and thus bond yields. The introduction of *forward rate guidance* on August 2011 was closer to the prescription to be drawn from Keynes's analysis. It proved much more successful than many economists expected."

57 At the time of writing, the latest available data were for Q4 2013 (2nd estimate). Historical vintages of data are available at the Federal Reserve Bank of Philadelphia Real-Time Data Research Center: https://www.philadelphiafed.org/research-and-data/real-time-center/real-time-data

58 See *The U.S. Economic Recovery*, Graham Turner, 2014, 2QT Publishing, p. 61.

59 Source: BEA, United States, Real Private Fixed Investment, Non-residential,

to reconcile these numbers with the claims from a number of influential commentators that investment in the US has been weak and is holding back the economy.[60]

Chained and Real Gross Domestic Product, Total, Chained. Private fixed non-residential investment as a share of GDP rose to a high of 13.55% in Q3 2015, before slipping to 13.46% in Q4. It has been argued that it is wrong to consider real investment as a ratio or a share of real GDP. This question is considered in more detail in chapter 3.

60 See, for example, *The Fed Has Hurt Business Investment*, Michael Spence & Kevin Warsh, Wall Street Journal, October 26th 2015.

Chapter 2
Cheap, but tight is working

A test of financial stability in the US

Source: GFC Economics

Chart 2a

The US stock market fell heavily during the early weeks of 2016 (see chart 2a).[1] Part of this correction in US equities was triggered by a rise in corporate bond yields, which had gathered momentum in the final months of 2015 (see chart 2b).[2] This was not the first time that higher corporate borrowing costs had signalled a turning point in US equities. The economic downturns of 2000/01 and 2008/09 both followed a sizeable increase in corporate bond yields. During the run-up to the sub-prime housing crisis, non-investment grade corporate (or junk) bond yields climbed steadily from the low of 7.58% witnessed on February

1 Source: Equity Indices, S&P 500, Index. The S&P 500 fell 10.5% between December 31st 2015 and February 11th 2016.

2 There were also mounting concerns over the slowdown in China, falling commodity prices, emerging markets and the strength of the Dollar.

26th 2007, eventually hitting a peak of 22.65% on December 12th 2008.[3] Junk bond yields also rose during the final months of the dotcom boom.[4]

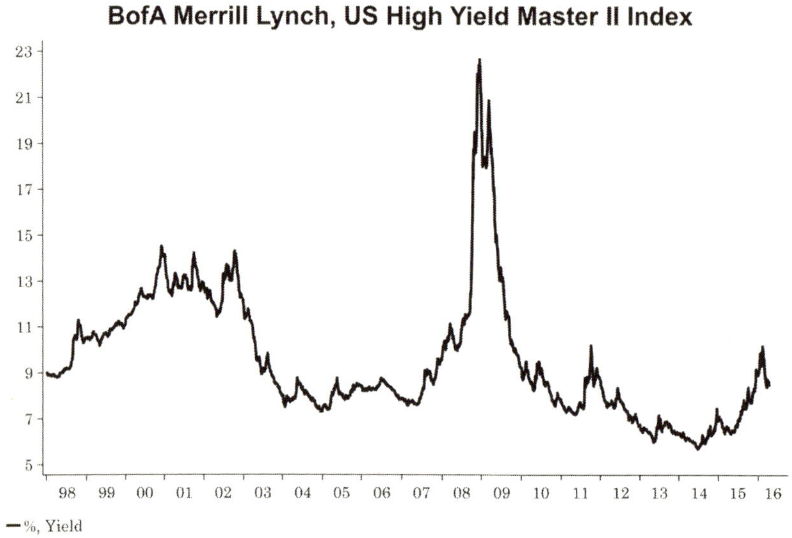

Source: GFC Economics

Chart 2b

In recent decades, economic growth has routinely stalled because lending has been allowed to rise too quickly. The increase in US corporate bond yields during the final weeks of 2015 reflected a build-up in debt concentrated in the energy sector, both globally and in the US.[5] In the

3 Source: Fixed Income Indices, Bank of America (BofA) Merrill Lynch, U.S. High Yield Master II Index, All Maturities, All Ratings, Yield. The rise in yields accelerated following the collapse of Lehman Brothers on September 15th 2008. By Friday September 12th, yields had risen to 11.65%.

4 Source: Fixed Income Indices, BofA Merrill Lynch, U.S. High Yield Master II Index, All Maturities, All Ratings, Yield. The average yield troughed at 8.80% on April 3rd 1998 and began to rise thereafter. By March 10th 2000 (the peak of the NASDAQ), yields had climbed to 11.68%. The sell-off intensified in Q4 2000: yields surged from 12.24% on September 15th 2000 to a peak of 14.51% on December 4th 2000.

5 See *Oil and debt*, Dietrich Domanski, Jonathan Kearns, Marco Lombardi & Hyun Song Shin, BIS Quarterly Review, March 2015, pp. 57-58. "Issuance of debt securities by oil and other energy companies [globally] has far outpaced the substantial overall issuance by other sectors. Oil and gas companies' bonds outstanding increased from $455 billion in 2006 to $1.4 trillion in 2014, a growth rate of 15% per annum. Energy companies have also borrowed heavily from banks. Syndicated loans to the oil and gas sector in 2014 amounted to an estimated $1.6 trillion, an annual increase of 13% from $600 billion in 2006 … US oil companies

US, corporate bonds outstanding had climbed from an average of 19.5% of GDP in 2007 to 26.5% of GDP in Q4 2015, a record high (see chart 2c).[6] Junk bond yields in the US had tumbled to a low of 5.69% on June 23rd 2014, despite this increase in issuance. Towards the end of 2015 they rose steadily, hitting a high of 10.17% on February 11th 2016.[7]

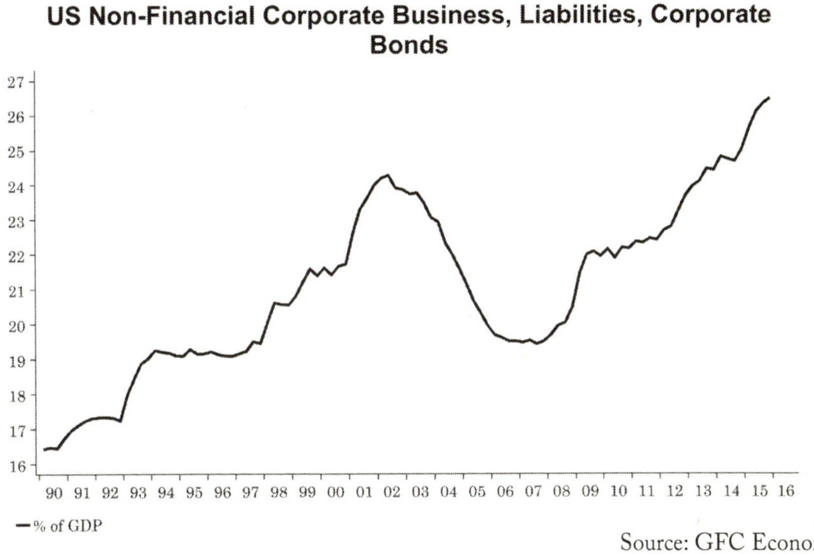

Source: GFC Economics

Chart 2c

However, the Dodd-Frank Act of 2010 had been highly effective in bringing down household debt as a share of GDP. New regulations targeted mortgage lending, which fell as a share of GDP from a high of 73.5% in Q1 2009 to 52.3% in Q4 2015 (See chart 2d).[8] The decline in household leverage was crucial to preventing a broader, deeper sell-off in corporate bonds. The stronger balance sheets of households and the low

---

have also borrowed heavily. They account for around 40% of both syndicated loans and debt securities outstanding. Much of this debt has been issued by smaller companies, in particular those engaged in shale oil exploration and production."

6 Source: Federal Reserve, Flow of Funds, Balance Sheet, Nonfarm Non-Financial Corporate Business, Liabilities, Debt Securities, Corporate Bonds & Bureau of Economic Analysis (BEA), Gross Domestic Product, Total, Current Prices.

7 Source: Fixed Income Indices, BofA Merrill Lynch, U.S. High Yield Master II Index, All Maturities, All Ratings, Yield.

8 Source: Federal Reserve, Flow of Funds, Balance Sheet, Households & Nonprofit Organizations, Liabilities, Loans, Home Mortgages and BEA, Gross Domestic Product, Total, Current Prices.

debt servicing costs ensured that consumer spending did not turn down: unemployment continued to fall.[9] Investors were forced to acknowledge that the economy was not heading into recession. By March 21st 2016, non-investment grade corporate bond yields had dropped back to 8.39%, before edging up to 8.65% one week later.[10] Contrary to widespread perceptions, the rise in yields of late-2015 was not signalling a repeat of 2007/08. Instead, this was a modest correction reflecting overinvestment in commodity-related sectors.

Furthermore, bank lending to companies had dropped significantly as a share of GDP, despite a rise in borrowing by the oil industry. Loans to non-financial corporates totalled 14.2% of GDP in Q4 2015, down from 21.0% in Q4 2008 (see chart 2f). Notably, banks had a much lower exposure to commercial mortgages (2.9% of GDP, compared with a peak of 6.5% in Q1 2008).[11]

Capital ratios for banks had also risen.[12] US banks were better placed to withstand the fallout from energy sector defaults. Common equity ratios of the largest US banks had more than doubled since the 2008 crisis. Furthermore, banks were now subject to a numerical liquidity requirement, to ensure they have "buffers of high-quality liquidity assets sufficient to meet cash outflows during a 30-day episode of systemic and idiosyncratic liquidity stress".[13] In addition, the Financial Stability

---

9 Source: BEA, Real Personal Consumption Expenditures, Total, Chained and U.S. Department of Labor, Unemployment, Jobless Claims, Initial, Total. The y/y rate for real personal consumption expenditures rose to 2.77% in February 2016, up from 2.60% y/y in January. Excluding gas & electricity services, consumption even stronger, climbing from 2.72% y/y to 3.03% y/y. For the week ending March 12th, the 4-week moving average for initial claims had dropped to 259,500. This was the lowest since December 15th 1973, and suggests the economy actually strengthened in the first quarter of 2016 (see chart 2e).

10 Source: Fixed Income Indices, BofA Merrill Lynch, U.S. High Yield Master II Index, All Maturities, All Ratings, Yield.

11 Source: Federal Reserve, Flow of Funds, Balance Sheet, Nonfarm Non-Financial Corporate Business, Liabilities, Loans, Mortgages & BEA, Gross Domestic Product, Total, Current Prices.

12 See *Federal Reserve Board approves final rule to help ensure banks maintain strong capital positions,* Federal Reserve, July 2nd 2013.

13 See *The Lender of Last Resort Function in the United States*, Stanley Fischer, February 10th 2016, p. 2.

Oversight Council had "designated four key non-banking institutions as 'systematically important financial institutions,' and these firms are also subject to supervision and regulation by the Federal Reserve".[14]

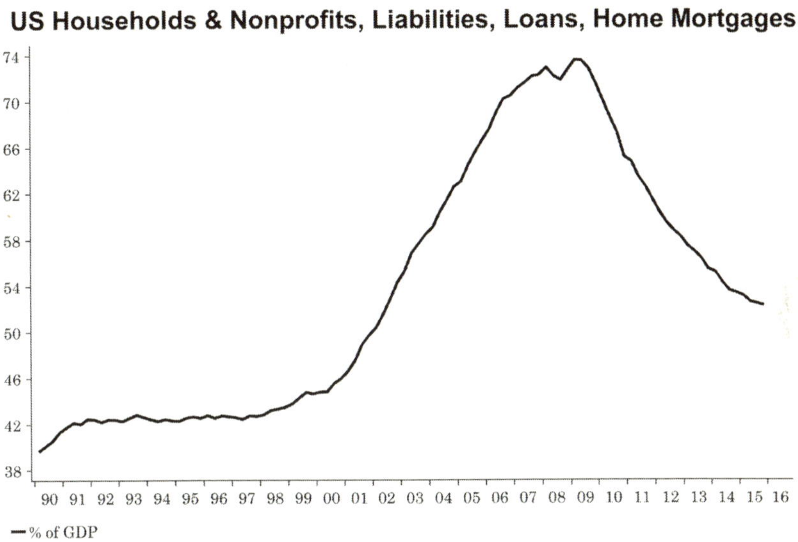

Source: GFC Economics

Chart 2d

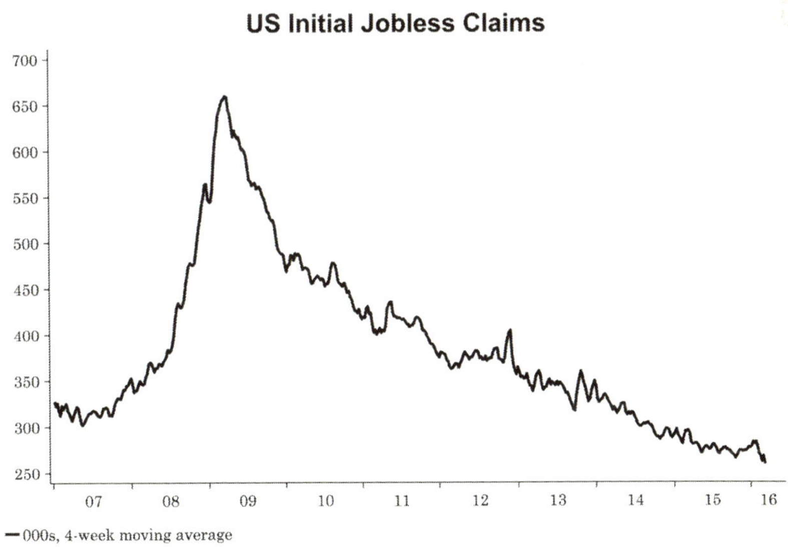

Source: GFC Economics

Chart 2e

14 Ibid.

Dodd-Frank

The Dodd-Frank Wall Street Reform and Consumer Protection Act of 2010 has been described as "one of the most comprehensive financial reform laws in U.S. history".[15] The Dodd-Frank Act contains "multiple provisions related to mortgage finance".[16] The Act introduced a number of criteria that needed to be satisfied for a qualified residential mortgage (QRM). These included documentation of a borrower's financial resources, debt-to-income caps, limits on payment shocks for adjustable rate mortgages (so-called 'balloon' mortgages), and restrictions on loan terms for mortgages that have been shown to exhibit a higher risk of default.[17] Mortgages should now have regular periodic payments that do not result in an increase in the principal balance, or result in a deferral of the repayment of the principal (i.e. the mortgage cannot have a negative amortisation feature). Total points and fees payable in connection with a loan must not be greater than three percent of the total loan amount. Loan terms should not exceed 30 years, except in high-cost locales.[18]

An initial QRM proposed rule was issued by regulators on April 29th 2011. This also included a controversial minimum 20 per cent down payment on mortgages.[19] Representative Barney Frank, who chaired the House Financial Services Committee between 2007 and 2011, argued that "Substantially diminishing

---

15 See *Effects of the Ability to Repay and Qualified Mortgage Rules on the Mortgage Market*, Neil Bhutta & Daniel Ringo, FEDS Notes, December 29th 2015.

16 See *Mortgage Reform Under The Dodd-Frank Act*, Mark A. Calabria, Cato Working Paper, January 2014, p. 2.

17 Ibid.

18 See *Effects of the Ability to Repay and Qualified Mortgage Rules on the Mortgage Market*, Neil Bhutta & Daniel Ringo, FEDS Notes, December 29th 2015.

19 See *Mortgage Reform Under The Dodd-Frank Act*, Mark A. Calabria, Cato Working Paper, January 2014.

the number of loans that are made for residential mortgages that should not have been made was the single biggest thing we did."[20]

Critics claim that stricter regulations have disproportionately reduced mortgage availability to low income and minority households and contributed to the sharp fall in home ownership. The void has been filled by the emergence of large-scale buy-to-rent investors. The "large inventory of homes on the market in the aftermath of the housing crisis made it easier for buy-to-rent investors to create geographically-concentrated pools of similar properties."[21] Furthermore, "technological developments that occurred in the 2000s such as cloud computing, the widespread use of personal mobile devices, and mobile internet connectivity have allowed for scattered-site property renovation, maintenance and management to occur in a much more flexible, efficient manner".[22]

The Dodd-Frank Act has endured its share of critics.[23] An overregulated banking sector, it has been argued, has held back the recovery. The opponents to regulation have failed to recognise the purpose of Dodd-Frank. In a cheap, but tight monetary framework, effective control of bank lending will allow productive investment to drive a non-inflationary and sustainable economic recovery.[24]

---

20 See *Five Years Later, Dodd Frank Creators Say the American Banking System Is Better Off*, Wall Street Journal, July 19th 2015.

21 See *Large-Scale Buy to Rent Investors in the Single-Family Housing Market: The Emergence of a New Asset Class*, James Mills, Raven S. Molloy & Rebecca E. Zarutskie, Finance and Economics Discussion Series 2015-084, Federal Reserve Board, September 2015.

22 Ibid.

23 See *Dodd-Frank's Nasty Double Whammy*, Phil Gramm, Wall Street Journal, July 23rd 2015.

24 For a more detailed exposition of this framework see *The U.S. Economic Recovery*, Graham Turner, 2QT Publishing, 2014.

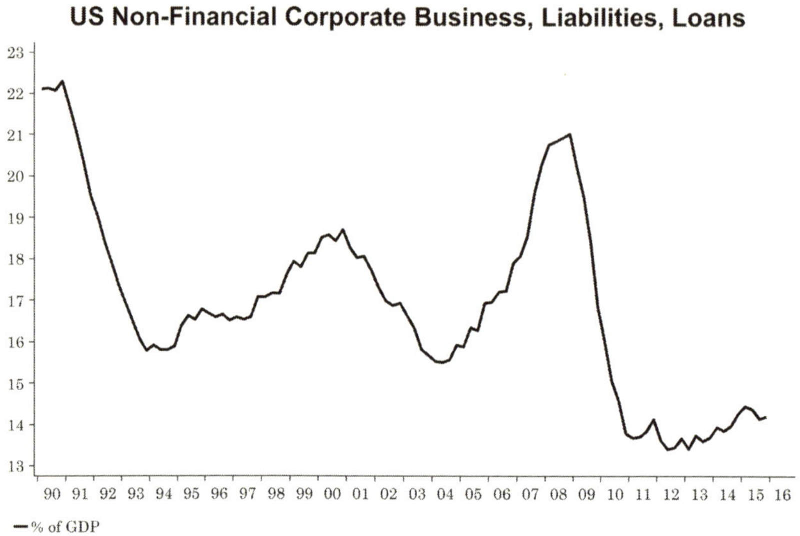

Source: GFC Economics

Chart 2f

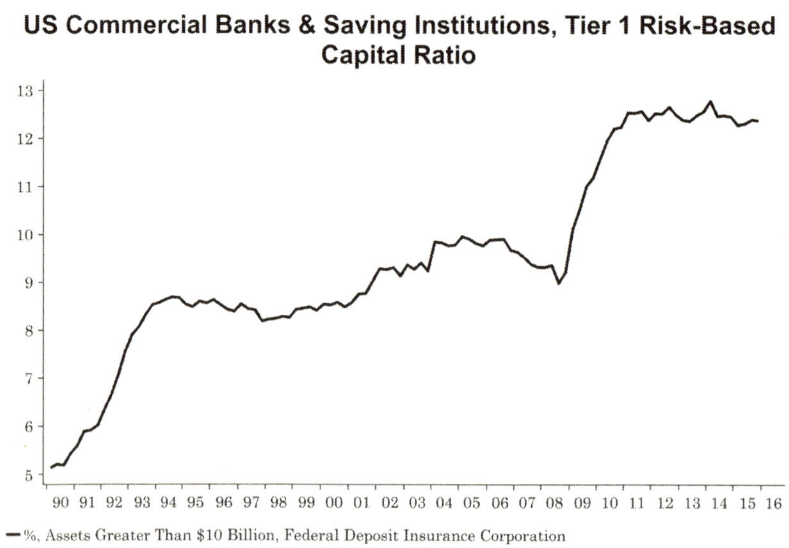

Source: GFC Economics

Chart 2g

Financial stability

Significant progress has been made to shore up the financial system since 2008. There is no guarantee that the new regulations will prevent the next crisis. Nevertheless, they have made the system more robust.

These regulations were summarised in a speech by Federal Reserve Vice Chairman Stanley Fisher. They include: "*(1) requirements for more and higher-quality capital and other loss-absorbing capacity at banks; (2) new requirements for liquidity buffers at banks; (3) more stringent capital and liquidity requirements at the largest, most systemically important firms; (4) stress-testing of the largest banks; (5) the shift of the clearing of some derivatives to central counterparties (CCPs); (6) new margin requirements for uncleared derivatives transactions; (7) the designation of systemically important nonbank financial institutions by the Financial Stability Oversight Council; and (8) enhanced sharing of information among regulators and monitoring of risks to financial stability*". [25]

Increased capital requirements are an integral part of this framework. Quality of capital refers to the ability to absorb unexpected losses. One form of 'high loss absorbing capital' is known as Tier 1 capital, which includes common stock, preferred stock, and retained earnings.[26] The Tier 1 risk-based capital ratio is then defined as the ratio of Tier 1 capital to risk-weighted assets.

According to the Federal Deposit Insurance Corporation (FDIC), the Tier 1 risk-based capital ratio for all insured institutions climbed from an average of 10.3% in 2007 to

25 See *Financial Stability and Shadow Banks: What We Don't Know Could Hurt Us*, Stanley Fischer, December 3rd 2015, p. 2.

26 See *Financial Stability Report*, Office of Financial Research, 2015.

12.8% in Q3 2015.[27] For the largest institutions (assets in excess of $10bn), this share increased from 9.5% to 12.4% over the same period (see chart 2g).[28]

There has also been a greater emphasis on liquidity. The liquidity coverage ratio forces institutions with assets over a certain threshold to hold high-quality liquid assets.[29]

Attempts have also been made to tackle "Too Big To Fail". Globally Systemically Important Banks (G-SIBs) identified by the Financial Stability Board (an international organisation), are required to hold an additional capital "surcharge".[30] This surcharge ranges from 1.0% to 4.5% of risk-weighted assets.[31]

---

27 Source: Federal Deposit Insurance Corporation (FDIC). Insured Institutions, Commercial Banks & Saving Institutions, Asset Size Group Ratios, All Insured Institutions, Tier 1 Risk-Based Capital Ratio (PCA).

28 Source: FDIC. Insured Institutions, Commercial Banks & Saving Institutions, Asset Size Group Ratios, More Than $10 Billion, Tier 1 Risk-Based Capital Ratio (PCA).

29 See *Federal banking regulators finalize liquidity coverage ratio,* Federal Reserve, September 3rd 2014. "The rule will for the first time create a standardized minimum liquidity requirement for large and internationally active banking organizations. Each institution will be required to hold high quality, liquid assets (HQLA) such as central bank reserves and government and corporate debt that can be converted easily and quickly into cash in an amount equal to or greater than its projected cash outflows minus its projected cash inflows during a 30-day stress period. The ratio of the firm's liquid assets to its projected net cash outflow is its 'liquidity coverage ratio', or LCR. The LCR will apply to all banking organizations with $250 billion or more in total consolidated assets or $10 billion or more in on-balance sheet foreign exposure and to these banking organizations' subsidiary depository institutions that have assets of $10 billion or more. The rule also will apply a less stringent, modified LCR to bank holding companies and savings and loan holding companies that do not meet these thresholds, but have $50 billion or more in total assets. Bank holding companies and savings and loan holding companies with substantial insurance or commercial operations are not covered by the final rule."

30 See *Federal Reserve Board approves final rule requiring the largest, most systemically important U.S. bank holding companies to further strengthen their capital positions*, Federal Reserve, July 20th 2015.

31 See *2015 update of list of global systemically important banks (G-SIBs)*, Financial Stability Board, November 3rd 2015. The highest capital surcharge currently

Another proposed rule would require that G-SIBs also maintain "a mix of long-term debt and equity, together referred to as total loss absorbing capacity, to cover potential losses in the event of bank failure."[32]

Further regulations are due in the future: "An important new element of the post-crisis capital regime is the Countercyclical Capital Buffer (CCyB), which the Federal Reserve put out for comment on December 21st 2015. The CCyB is designed to be activated when there is an elevated risk of above-normal losses in the future and released when the risk of above-normal losses recedes. The higher levels of capital would increase the resilience of the largest banks because they would be better positioned to absorb the losses."[33]

In its annual Financial Stability Report, the Office of Financial Research also identified key areas where regulation may be missing. It is possible that "Financial risks have migrated outside the regulatory perimeter". Furthermore, "Run and fire-sale risks persist in securities financing markets."[34] This point was echoed in a speech by Federal Reserve Governor Daniel Tarullo in November 2015, who noted the "risks of short-term wholesale funding by nonbank intermediaries. Indeed, constraints imposed on banking organizations may prompt more short-term wholesale funding to migrate outside the regulated sector."[35]

---

imposed is 2.5% on HSBC and JP Morgan Chase. A 2.0% capital surcharge has been levied on four institutions and 1.5% on five institutions. The remaining 19 have been given a 1.0% additional capital requirement.

32 See *Financial Stability Report,* Office of Financial Research, 2015, p. 42. See also *Federal Reserve Board proposes new rule to strengthen the ability of largest domestic and foreign banks operating in the United States to be resolved without extraordinary government support or taxpayer assistance*, Federal Reserve, October 30th 2015.

33 See *Monetary Policy, Financial Stability, and the Zero Lower Bound*, Stanley Fischer, January 3rd 2016.

34 See *Financial Stability Report,* Office of Financial Research, 2015, p. 8.

35 See *Thinking Critically about Nonbank Financial Intermediation*, Governor Daniel K. Tarullo, November 17th 2015.

The resilience of the financial system and the US economy was underlined by the dispersion in corporate bond market performance. Table 1 shows the change in yields between June 23rd 2014 and February 11th 2016 for the different sectors of the Bank of America (BofA) Merrill Lynch high-yield corporate bond index. The rise in yields was concentrated in a few select industries related to the commodities cycle (see chart 2h). The energy, metals & mining and steel sectors contributed 292.2 basis points to the 448.1 basis point increase in average yields.[36]

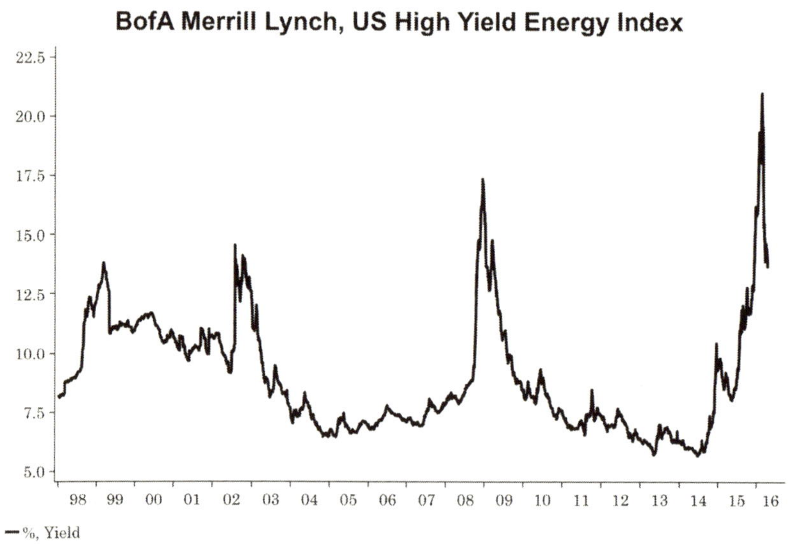

Source: GFC Economics

Chart 2h

36 Source: Fixed Income Indices, BofA Merrill Lynch, U.S. High Yield Index, All Maturities, All Ratings, Yield and author's calculations. These sectors experienced the sharpest rise in yields over this period: 1530 basis points for energy, 1180 basis points for metals & mining and 780 basis points for steel. Note: this exercise used 2016 weights.

Merrill Lynch, US High-Yield Corporate Bond Index, by sector

	Yield, 23/06 2014	Yield, 11/02 2016	Change over period (23/06/2014 - 11/02/2016)	Weight (face value as a % of total)	Contribution to change in yield (basis point)
Total	5.69	10.17	4.48	100.0%	448.1
Energy	5.68	21.00	15.32	15.1%	231.8
Metals/Mining	6.95	18.76	11.81	4.0%	46.8
Telecommunications	5.70	9.62	3.92	9.8%	38.4
Div. Financial Services	4.09	9.48	5.39	4.1%	22.2
Services	6.22	10.66	4.44	4.3%	19.3
Healthcare	5.33	7.35	2.02	9.3%	18.7
Utilities	5.33	10.05	4.72	3.1%	14.6
Technology	6.27	9.38	3.11	4.6%	14.4
Steel	5.64	13.46	7.82	1.7%	13.6
Cable/Satellite TV	4.93	7.28	2.36	5.5%	12.9
Chemicals	5.83	11.41	5.58	2.1%	12.0
Broadcasting	6.74	10.79	4.05	2.6%	10.4
Super Retail	6.60	9.68	3.08	3.2%	9.9
Aerospace	5.50	11.51	6.01	1.5%	9.2
Capital Goods	5.18	8.90	3.71	1.7%	6.4
Homebuilders/Real Estate	4.61	6.80	2.19	2.8%	6.1
Automotive & Auto Parts	5.06	7.74	2.68	2.2%	6.0
Building Materials	5.38	7.99	2.62	1.8%	4.8
Banks & Thrifts	4.79	5.88	1.10	4.3%	4.8
Transportation Ex Air/ Rail	7.29	13.15	5.87	0.8%	4.5
Publishing/Printing	6.79	12.24	5.44	0.8%	4.2
Containers	5.70	7.47	1.77	2.4%	4.2
Insurance	5.36	9.98	4.62	0.8%	3.9
Diversified Media	5.81	8.05	2.24	1.4%	3.2
Consumer Products	6.17	8.41	2.24	1.3%	2.9
Food & Drug Retail	6.38	8.37	1.98	0.9%	1.9
Food/Beverage/Tobacco	5.50	6.46	0.97	1.7%	1.7
Environmental	6.16	9.80	3.63	0.4%	1.3
Paper	6.67	8.78	2.12	0.6%	1.2
Leisure	5.27	7.42	2.15	0.5%	1.2
Entertainment/Film	5.48	6.84	1.36	0.6%	0.8
Air Transportation	5.22	7.36	2.14	0.3%	0.7
Railroad	6.25	10.63	4.38	0.1%	0.5
Hotels	4.95	5.48	0.53	0.3%	0.2
Restaurants	7.90	7.26	-0.64	0.6%	-0.4
Gaming	8.96	8.77	-0.20	2.5%	-0.5

Source: United States, Fixed Income Indices, Merrill Lynch, All Maturities, All Ratings

Table 1

Junk bond yields climbed by a similar magnitude between February 26th 2007 and September 12th 2008, prior to the collapse of Lehman Brothers. However, the three sectors that sold off the most accounted for just 148.7 basis points of the total 406.5 basis point rise in junk bond yields (automotive & auto parts, diversified financial services and gaming). Eleven sectors each contributed 15 basis points or more to the overall increase in yields; in the more recent correction that began in 2014, there were only six. Yields climbed by six percentage points or more in eight industries just before the sub-prime housing crisis, double the number of sectors witnessed in the more recent sell-off. The wider breadth of the sell-off in corporate bonds during 2007 and 2008 reflected the deeper underlying problems within the US financial system. Banks were running into trouble: record household debt and falling house prices were pushing mortgage arrears up sharply. This culminated in the collapse of Lehman Brothers on September 15th 2008. The rise in corporate bond yields then accelerated, and nearly all sectors were hit hard.[37]

Furthermore, the commodity-related sectors where non-investment grade corporate bond yields rose from June 2014 onwards accounted for only a small fraction of total employment. According to the Bureau of Labor Statistics, employment in mining, primary metals, fabricated metal products and petroleum & coal products represented 1.8% of total non-farm payrolls in February.[38] By contrast, 70.9% of payrolls were in private services.[39] Many service sectors proved resilient to the

---

37 Source: Fixed Income Indices, BofA Merrill Lynch, U.S. High Yield Index, All Maturities, All Ratings, Yield and author's calculations. Yields eventually peaked at 22.65% on December 12th 2008. Between February 26th 2007 and December 12th 2008, 27 out of 36 sub-sectors experienced double-digit percentage point increases in yields. All sub-sectors saw yields rise by more than six percentage points during this period.

38 Source: Bureau of Labor Statistics (BLS), Employment, CES, Mining, Primary Metals, Fabricated Metal Products, Petroleum & Coal Products.

39 Source: BLS, Employment, CES, Nonfarm, Private Service-Providing, Payroll, Total.

correction in junk bonds.[40] Accordingly, employment gains within services remained strong.[41]

Outstanding non-investment grade corporate sector debt has more than doubled since the crisis of 2008. According to BofA Merrill Lynch, the face value of high-yield corporate bonds averaged $682.6bn in 2007. By January 2016, the value of these bonds outstanding had risen 100.9% to $1.371tr. The energy sector accounted for 9.7% of non-investment grade corporate bonds in 2007 (average).[42] This had risen to 15.1% by January 2016.

BofA Merrill Lynch, US High Yield Index, Face Value

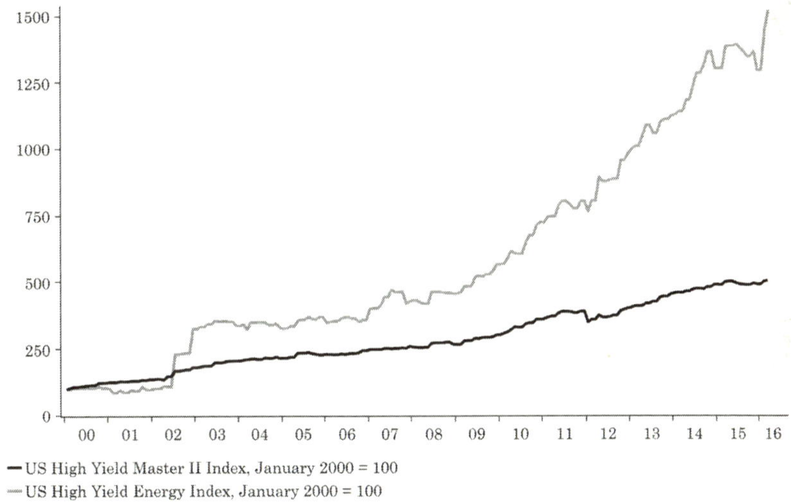

Source: GFC Economics

Chart 2i

40 Merrill Lynch provides a detailed breakdown of services, including retail, leisure, technology, etc. In addition, there is a 'services' sub-category, which experienced a more notable rise in yields. However, this is a narrow measure corresponding to support services (more closely linked to the BLS's administrative & support services classification), and therefore excludes more productive 'professional & technical services'.

41 Source: BLS, Employment, CES, Nonfarm, Private Service-Providing, Payroll, Total. Private services payrolls climbed 2.5% y/y to 101.4m in December 2015, outpacing the rise in total employment (2.0% y/y to 143.1m) over this period. Services payrolls also grew at a quicker rate in 2014 (2.4% y/y compared with 2.2% y/y for overall employment).

42 Source: Fixed Income Indices, BofA Merrill Lynch, U.S. High Yield Energy Index, All Maturities, All Ratings, Yield.

Energy was by far the most heavily indebted sector in the non-investment grade corporate bond market. The sell-off in energy bonds clearly reflected the overextension of this sector, the rapid expansion of capacity and the subsequent collapse in oil prices (see chart 2i). Telecommunications and healthcare were the next biggest sectors, accounting for 9.8% and 9.3% of total non-investment grade corporate bonds, respectively.[43] These were up from 6.9% and 6.0% in 2007. However, telecommunications and healthcare saw only a modest rise in yields during the correction (see chart 2j).[44] The increase in yields for leisure and retail was limited too (see chart 2k).[45] Consumer-related sectors were relatively immune to the sell-off in corporate bonds, reflecting the drop in leverage for the household sector.

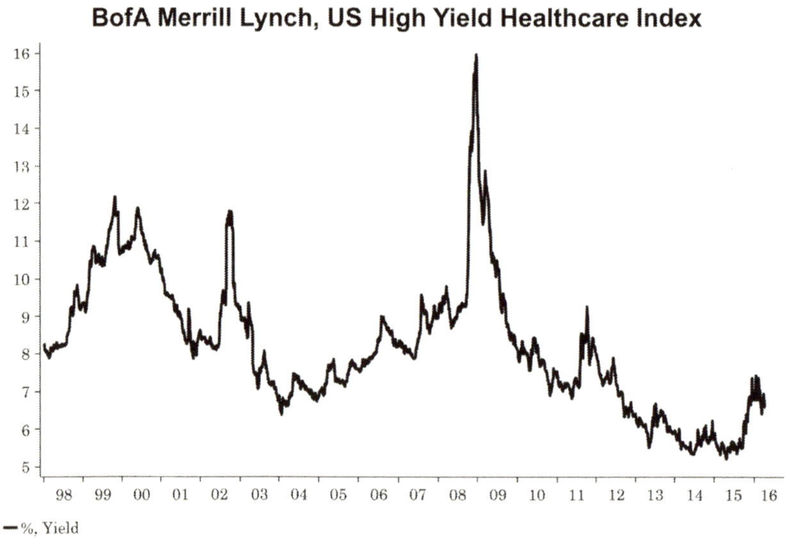

Source: GFC Economics

Chart 2j

43 Source: Fixed Income Indices, BofA Merrill Lynch, U.S. High Yield Healthcare Index, All Maturities, All Ratings, Yield and High Yield Telecommunications Index, All Maturities, All Ratings, Yield.

44 Between June 23rd 2014 and February 11th 2016, yields rose only 392 basis points for telecommunications and 202 basis points for healthcare. By contrast, the yield on energy sector debt climbed 1532 basis points over this period.

45 Yields on 'leisure' and 'super retail' rose 215 basis points and 308 basis points between June 23rd 2014 and February 11th 2016, respectively.

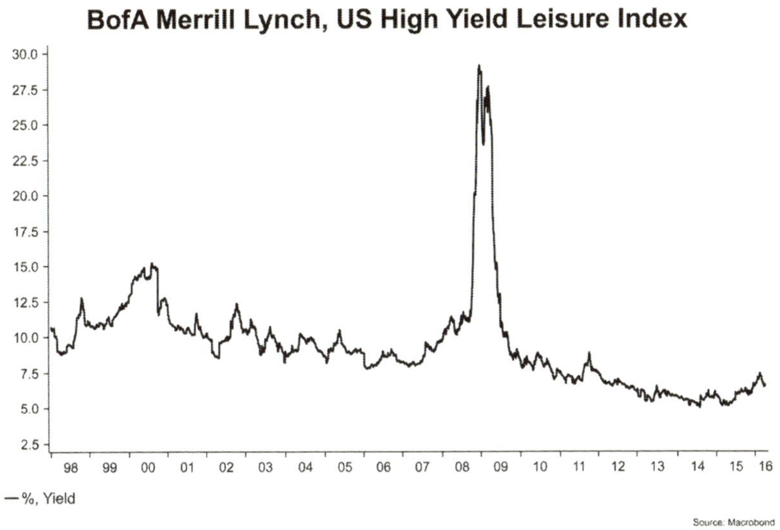

Source: GFC Economics

Chart 2k

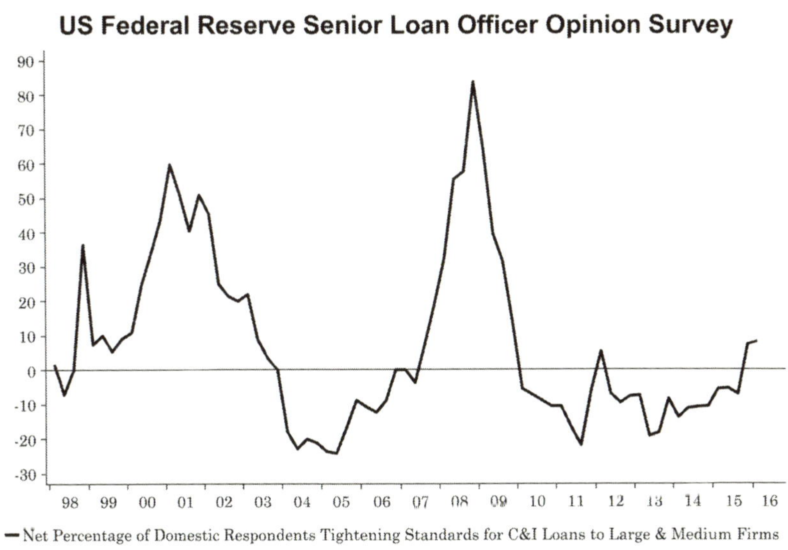

Source: GFC Economics

Chart 2l

Other areas of the economy that have accumulated greater leverage could pose a risk. Consumer credit growth accelerated following the crisis of 2008 and hit a record 19.3% of GDP in Q4 2015 (see chart 2m).[46] This was largely due to a sharp rise in auto and student loans. Auto loans were exempted from the Dodd-Frank regulations, which were aimed at Wall Street, not 'Main Street'.[47] It was a false dichotomy to distinguish between the two. The Federal Reserve Bank of New York subsequently warned of an increase in sub-prime auto lending, drawing comparisons with mortgage lending prior to 2008.[48] Delinquencies were rising for some sub-prime auto loans.[49] Auto loans outstanding climbed from a low of 4.6% of GDP (Q3 2010) to 5.7% in Q4 2015.[50] This was still below the all-time high of 6.4% set in Q2 2003.[51] Nonetheless, student loans also grew, from 3.5% of GDP in Q1 2006 to an all-time high of 7.3% in Q4 2015.[52] The increase in student loans had made it harder for first-time buyers to secure a foot on the housing ladder.[53]

The rise in auto lending and student loans will have to be addressed by the authorities. The cheap, but tight monetary framework advocated in

---

46 Source: United States, Flow of Funds, Balance Sheet, Households & Nonprofit Organizations, Liabilities, Total and BEA, Gross Domestic Product, Total, Current Prices. This compares to a cyclical trough of 16.6% of GDP (Q3 2010) and the previous peak of 18.1% (Q1 2009).

47 See *Ally seeks to quell fears of a car loans bubble*, Financial Times, February 2nd 2016.

48 See *Surge in Subprime Auto Lending Draws Attention*, Wall Street Journal, November 19th 2015.

49 See *Subprime Flashback: Early Defaults Are a Warning Sign for Auto Sales*, Wall Street Journal, March 13th 2016.

50 Source: Federal Reserve, Flow of Funds, Level, Consumer Credit, Households & Nonprofit Organizations, Auto Loans, Liabilities and BEA, Gross Domestic Product, Total, Current Prices.

51 Ibid.

52 Source: Federal Reserve, Flow of Funds, Level, Consumer Credit, Households & Nonprofit Organizations, Student Loans and BEA, Gross Domestic Product, Total, Current Prices.

53 See *Congratulations to Class of 2014, Most Indebted Ever*, Wall Street Journal, May 16th 2014. See also *Larry Summers: Student Debt Is Slowing the U.S. Housing Recovery*, Wall Street Journal, May 21st 2014.

The U.S. Economic Recovery remains far from complete. Nevertheless, it should be reiterated: household debt as a share of GDP has fallen sharply from the highs of 2007 due to the decline in mortgage lending.

Critics will argue that low interest rates lead to wasteful investment. However, the write-offs in the energy sector will need to be set against the broader benefits of lower borrowing costs, pushing investment higher in other productive sectors of the economy. Real investment in information technology has risen sharply and has played a critical role in driving the seven-year economic expansion in the US. Even as oil prices fell and energy companies cut their capital spending plans, productive investment remained close to record highs as a share of real GDP.

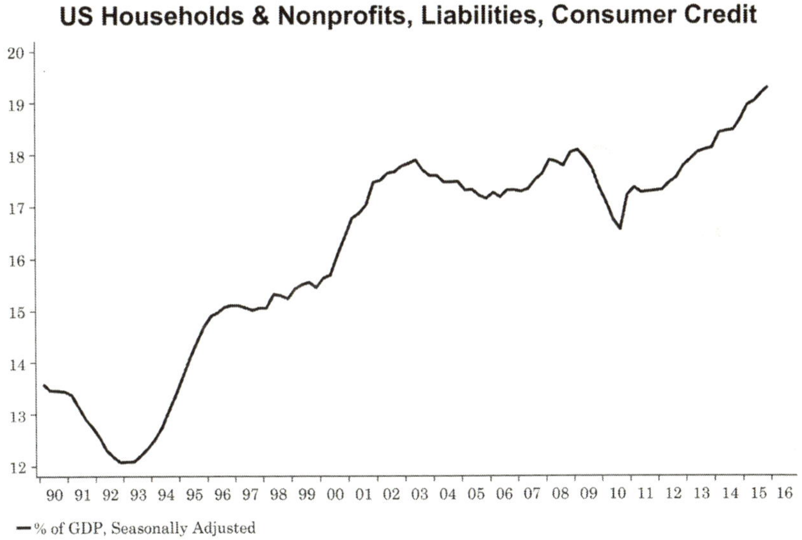

Source: GFC Economics

Chart 2m

A test of cheap, but tight

The rise in corporate bond yields from the summer of 2014 onwards led to only a modest tightening of lending standards in the US, again underlining the resilience of the financial system. According to the Federal Loan Officer Survey, banks did start to increase lending standards (see chart 21).[54] For large & medium firms, the net percentage of domestic banks tightening standards for commercial & industrial (C&I) loans climbed from 7.4 to 8.2 in Q4 2015.[55] This is relatively low: in the run-up to the housing crisis, the net percentage of banks tightening standards jumped from 7.5 in Q3 2007 to 19.2 in Q4 2007.[56] The tightening of credit conditions bore greater resemblance to the Euro crisis, when this indicator peaked at 5.4 in Q1 2012. The net percentage of domestic banks increasing spreads (loan rates over bank's cost of funds) climbed from -20.6 to -16.7 in Q4 2015 for large & medium firms.[57] Again, this was a comparatively small rise: this measure was up from -32.1 in Q3 2007 to 34.6 in Q4 2007.

Furthermore, there was no appreciable tightening of lending standards for mortgages, despite the rise in corporate bond yields. The responses to the Federal Reserve's Senior Loan Officer Survey have been broken down into seven categories of mortgage loans from 2015 onwards. Lending standards eased for all but two categories in Q4 2015.[58] By contrast, prior to the

---

54 Source: Federal Reserve. Business Surveys Senior Loan Officer Opinion Survey on Bank Lending Practices, January 2016.

55 Source: Federal Reserve, Business Surveys, Senior Loan Officer Opinion Survey, Tightening Standards for Commercial & Industrial Loans, Large & Medium Firms.

56 Ibid.

57 Source: Federal Reserve. Business Surveys, Senior Loan Officer Opinion Survey, Increasing Spreads of Loan Rates over Banks' Cost of Funds, Large & Medium Firms.

58 Source: Federal Reserve, Business Surveys, Senior Loan Officer Opinion Survey, Tightening Standards for Mortgage Loans: 1) GSE-eligible, 2) government, 3) QM non-jumbo, non-GSE-eligible, 4) QM jumbo, 5) non-QM jumbo, 6) non-QM non-jumbo, 7) subprime.

financial crisis of 2008, banks were raising lending standards from Q3 2006 onwards. By the end of 2015, the modest decline in banks' willingness to lend to companies had not spilled over into mortgages.

China: risk or opportunity?

The strong jobs data in the US for 2014 and 2015 reflect the array of business opportunities that have been generated by technological progress.[59] Of course, investment-led growth could go wrong for any number of reasons. Inequality is still rising in the US.[60] In an election year, the risks of a political backlash leading to protectionism are self-evident. The popularity of less conventional candidates in the US presidential campaign – Donald Trump and Bernie Sanders – is partly a manifestation of the decline in the real median wage.[61] Mortgage lending may be under control, but the sharp rise in student debt could be a constraint on the potential growth path of the US economy, given the importance of education in equipping

---

59 Source: BLS, Job Openings & Labor Turnover Survey (JOLTS), Job Openings, Professional & Business Services. Job openings in professional & business services climbed to 1.089m in January 2016. This was up 76.5% since January 2014, and 214.7% above the low of August 2009. This sector had outperformed the rest of the economy: total private openings had climbed 44.6% and 155.2%, respectively.

60 See *America's Middle-class Meltdown: Core shrinks to half of US homes,* Financial Times, December 9th 2015. See also *America's Middle Class Is No Longer the Majority*, Wall Street Journal, December 9th 2015. The impact of technology on inequality can become self-reinforcing. See *The New U.S. Digital Divide: Between the Haves and the Have-Mores*, Wall Street Journal, December 17th 2015, "The rich are different from you and me. They have more technology. That's the conclusion of a new report from the McKinsey Global Institute, Digital America: A Tale of the Haves and Have-Mores".

61 See *Voters' Dour Mood Is Clear, Consequences Much Less So*, Wall Street Journal, January 4th 2016. One pollster finds half the US is "angry at politicians beyond anything we have ever seen before". See also *The Bleak Reality Driving Trump's Rise*, Wall Street Journal, December 15th 2015. "In a world of mobile capital and global labor markets, we have not figured out how to maintain jobs and incomes for workers with modest education and skills." See also *U.S. Election Debate Complicates Passage of Pacific Trade Pact*, Wall Street Journal, December 28th 2015. See also *Surge in Protectionist Measures Blamed for Sapping Trade*, Wall Street Journal, November 12th 2015.

workers with the necessary skills.[62] US technology companies are battling a hostile European Commission, which may stymie their expansion in Europe.[63] Apple, Google, Microsoft, Amazon and others are also being targeted for backdated tax payments.[64] European governments are in turn fighting back, offering a more competitive tax regime.[65]

The ability of US firms to access the Chinese market may be hindered by heavy-handed regulation and the determination of the Communist Party

---

62 See *U.S. Helps Shaky Colleges Cope With Bad Student Loans*, Wall Street Journal, December 21st 2015. See also *A Smaller Share of High-School Grads Are Heading to College – Especially Poorer Ones*, Wall Street Journal, November 25th 2015.
See also *Should Anyone Be Eligible for Student Loans?*, Wall Street Journal, December 6th 2015. See also *Federal Aid's Role in Driving Up Tuitions Gains Credence,* Wall Street Journal, August 2nd 2015.

63 See *EU Data-Privacy Law Raises Daunting Prospects for U.S. Companies*, Wall Street Journal, December 16th 2015. Several law suits over the past year have highlighted the European Commission's (EC) view that US technology companies are abusing their market power. The EC argues that it is trying to "restore a level playing field" for established businesses that provide competing services (see *European Union to Scrutinize Usage of Big Data by Large Internet Companies*, Wall Street Journal, January 17th 2016). However, there is a danger that this will encourage domestic companies to "remonopolise" their home markets. For example, Dutch telecom operator KPN has been accused of abusing its former dominant market position by not offering access to its networks on fair terms (see *Vodafone sues KPN alleging anti-competitive behaviour*, Financial Times, December 10th 2015). Although most of the legal action is related to US technology giants such as Google, Facebook and Amazon, free online services (Uber, Airbnb, Bookings.com, etc) also face resistance from local service providers. Google already settled charges related to its comparison-shopping service and is also facing competition charges on multiple other fronts, ranging from its contracts with advertisers to its Android mobile-operating system (see *EU to Pursue Google Parent Alphabet on Multiple Fronts, Vestager Says*, Wall Street Journal, October 26th 2015). The EC will also examine whether Google News should pay newspapers for displaying snippets of their articles. The EC also launched two antitrust cases against the US company Qualcomm for distorting competition in the market for chips used in smartphones and other mobile devices (see *EU accuses Qualcomm of impeding rivals*, Financial Times, December 8th 2015). In Germany, anti-trust authorities are investigating Amazon and Apple for an agreement on selling audiobooks. The Uber car service has been banned in Germany and France. German data-protection authorities also ordered Facebook to allow users to utilise pseudonyms as opposed to real names. European privacy cases against Facebook and other major tech firms accumulated across several member states, such as the Netherlands, France and Spain.

64 See *7 Corporate Giants Accused of Evading Billions in Taxes,* Fortune, March 11th 2016.

65 See *The Latest Lure From Abroad for U.S. Firms*, Wall Street Journal, November 9th 2015.

to ring-fence the Internet in China.[66] The recent disclosure of large-scale theft of US Government files by Chinese hackers underlines the ongoing threat posed by cybercrime.[67] The political risks are also high. President Xi's clampdown on dissent could be a deterrent to tech entrepreneurs in China. The Communist Party's grip on power is threatened by the difficult task of reducing the dependency of easy credit to drive economic growth. According to the Bank for International Settlements, total debt in China is now higher than in the US.[68]

Nevertheless, it is important to recognise the parallels between the US and China. Technology is key to job creation in both countries. China is in the midst of a rapid transition away from low-value manufacturing. Technology and services are being targeted to raise standards of living.[69]

---

66 See *China Touts Its Great Firewall in Push for Internet Control*, Wall Street Journal, December 16th 2015. China is pursuing a highly regulated path of "cyber development". The Chinese President Xi Jinping believes that tight controls over online standards and the flow of information are a matter of national 'internet sovereignty', free for respective governments to decide upon. This model may impinge on the ability of US companies to reap the full rewards from Chinese technological advances. See *In Beijing, Internet Inspires Fear and Hope*, Wall Street Journal, January 5th 2016. "Chinese leaders' boundless optimism for the Internet is running up against their anxiety about its destabilising potential". See also *Will China's Censorship Spread?*, Wall Street Journal, December 16th 2015. "Since the inaugural World Internet Conference last year, China has been promoting its notion of 'Internet sovereignty' for global Internet governance – each country should have the ultimate power to determine what online traffic flows in and out of its territory."

67 See *Obama's Cyber Meltdown*, Wall Street Journal, June 23rd 2015. See also *Report Warns of Chinese Hacking*, Wall Street Journal, October 19th 2015, "A US cybersecurity company says it has evidence hackers linked to the Chinese government may have tried to violate a recent agreement not to hack private firms in each other's country for economic gain". See also *Cyber security: Attack of the health hackers*, Financial Times, December 21st 2015. The cyber-attack on US health insurer Anthem - believed to originate in China - set off a wave of panic across the healthcare industry, which saw the hackers penetrate over 100m medical records in 2015". See also *Banks Battle Staffers' Vulnerability to Hacks*, Wall Street Journal, December 20th 2015. See also *Why Terrorists Love Silicon Valley*, Wall Street Journal, July 5th 2015.

68 Source: Bank for International Settlements, Statistical Bulletin, March 2016. Total credit in China (to households, non-financial corporations, and government) was 248.6% of GDP in Q3 2015. The comparable measure for the US was 244.0%.

69 See *China seeks quantum leap to a new economic model*, Charles Oliver, Financial Times, November 5th 2015. See also *Xi's Dream for a High-Tech China Is Becoming a Reality*

The sharp increase in spending on research and development reflects the growing importance of intellectual property in China (see chart 2n).[70]

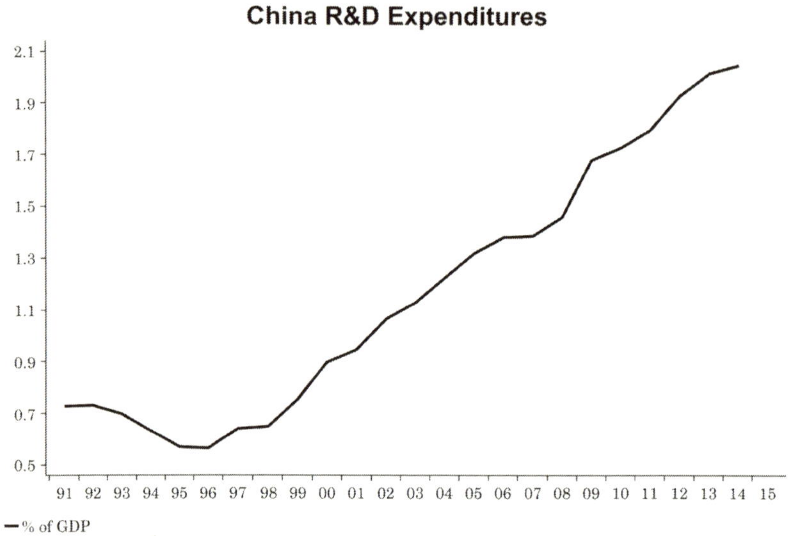

Source: GFC Economics

Chart 2n

As China's economy evolves it will provide growth opportunities for US companies, but also pose a competitive threat (see chart 2o).[71] Chinese companies are developing their technical expertise.[72] Alibaba, Baidu and

---

in Stocks, Bloomberg Business, October 29th 2015. See also *Want to See Technology Taking Over Finance? Look at China,* Wall Street Journal, December 28th 2015.

70 See *The 2015 Global Innovation 1000: Innovation's New World Order*, PricewaterhouseCoopers (PwC), Winter 2015, Issue 81. According to PwC, R&D spending in China jumped 31% in the year to March 2015. In a separate publication, the OECD estimated that Chinese R&D spending hit 2.05% of GDP in 2014, a record high.

71 Source: BEA, International Transactions, By Area & Country, China, Exports of Services. US services exports to China climbed 166.3% from $17.061bn in 2009 to $45.431bn in 2015. This compares with a 38.5% increase for services exports to all countries over this period. As of 2015, China accounted for 21.8% of services exports to the Asia and Pacific region, compared with just 13.0% in 2009.

72 Source: U.S. Census Bureau, Foreign Trade, Commodities, Trade Balance, Advanced Technology Products. In the 12 months to January 2016, China accounted for 34.9% of advanced technology imports into the US. By comparison, the EU share of advanced technology imports was just 18.6%.

Tencent are competing head-to-head with Apple, Google and Facebook. Xiaomi and Huawei are undercutting Apple.[73] Huawei reported a 44% surge in smartphone sales in 2015, compared with a rise of 10% for the overall market.[74] Chinese companies are highly innovative in a number of fields, including driverless cars, artificial intelligence, big data and renewables.

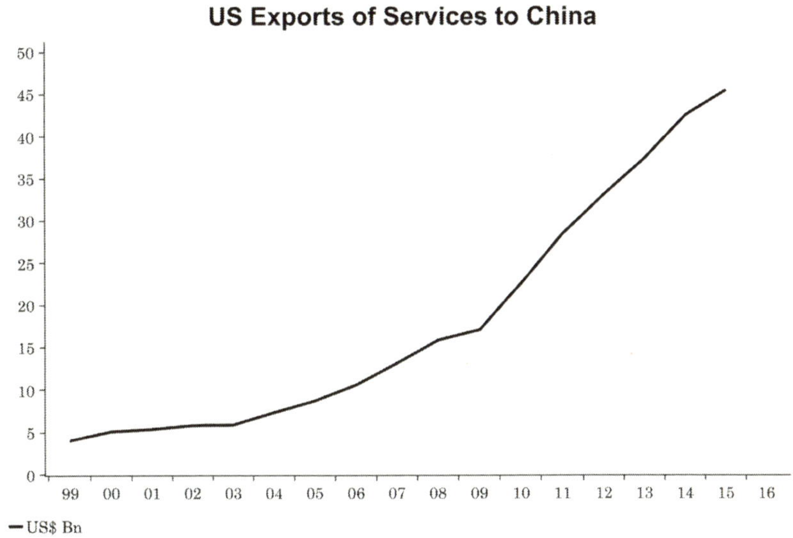

Source: GFC Economics

Chart 2o

Online spending accounted for 10.8% of total sales in China in 2015.[75] This compares with a share of 7.5% in the US.[76] The growth in e-commerce in China has fuelled a logistics network and has accelerated the development of fintech.[77] Seven of the world's 50 most successful

73 See *China's Huawei Hopes to Connect With U.S. Smartphone Market,* Wall Street Journal, December 16th 2015. See also *China Aims to Build Its Own Secure Smartphones*, Wall Street Journal, November 20th 2015.

74 See *Huawei boosts global market share*, Nikkei Asian Review, February 1st 2016.

75 See *Retail Sales of China Consumer Goods Exceeded $4,573B in 2015*, China Internet Watch, February 2nd 2016.

76 Source: U.S. Census Bureau, Retail Sales, E-commerce.

77 See *China migration: Delivering the Jack Ma economy,* Financial Times, September 16th 2015.

fintech companies are Chinese.[78] The expansion in mobile payment services has also been impressive, boosted by the entry of tech companies Alibaba and Tencent into the private banking sector. According to Euromonitor International, mobile payments in China totalled $213bn in 2015, compared with $164bn in the US.[79]

The success of *online-to-offline* commerce in China (i.e. the collaboration between online services and traditional retailers) is being closely watched by US tech companies. Facebook is trying to emulate WeChat, as it attempts to widen the number of services available directly on its Messenger and WhatsApp applications. WeChat already allows users to pay for meals, buy movie tickets and hail taxis. The delivery of services via smartphone is becoming a battleground for tech companies as 'e-customers' switch from PCs to smartphones.

Recent profit numbers released in the US have highlighted the importance of smartphone advertising revenues.[80] Apple's shareholders fret that the company has been too slow in shifting its core business away from hardware.[81] China is ahead of the curve on this score. Indeed, more than a third of online spending in China was conducted via smartphones and tablets last year.[82] The corresponding rates are much lower for the US (21%), the UK (18%) and Japan (14%). Chinese high-tech companies are consolidating online-to-offline commerce by buying stakes in physical retailers.[83] They are also entering into more partnerships with foreign technology firms; the cooperation between Uber and Alibaba is one notable example.[84]

---

78 See *China overtakes UK in global fintech race*, Financial Times, December 14th 2015.

79 See *Want to See Technology Taking Over Finance? Look at China*, Wall Street Journal, December 28th 2015.

80 See *Alphabet drive to the top fuelled by core internet business*, Financial Times, February 2nd 2016.

81 See *Apple seeks app to change perceptions about its core business*, Financial Times, January 27th 2016.

82 See Paypal cross-border consumer research 2015, November 17th 2015.

83 See, for example, *Alibaba places big bet on bricks and mortar*, Financial Times, August 11th 2015.

84 See *Uber expands cooperation with Alibaba's Alipay*, Wall Street Journal, February 1st 2015.

The fast expansion of China's digital economy has fuelled a rise in the number of entrepreneurs, particularly in Shenzhen and Beijing. The cost of starting a new business has tumbled: according to World Bank data, this dropped from 17.8% of GNI per capita in 2003 to 0.7% in 2015. The cost of setting up a company is now lower than in the US. In a bid to develop a tech hub, Shanghai is offering compensation of between 30-60% to venture tech firms that suffer losses due to start-up failures.[85] Technology is also flourishing away from the coast. Chengdu is now home to 110 internet start-ups and is attracting interest from high-tech manufacturers such as Foxconn and Intel.[86]

---

85 See *Shanghai lures tech investors with bailout offers*, Wall Street Journal, January 29th 2015.

86 See *Chengdu pushes to become China's Silicon Valley*, Financial Times, January 3rd 2016.

Chapter 3
US investment & productivity
(first published September 24th 2014)

Productivity is a critical variable that influences the potential growth path of an economy. It determines how quickly inflation will accelerate in response to GDP growth.[1] FOMC member Daniel Tarullo detailed some of the "Structural Challenges for the American Economy" in April 2014.[2] There was, he noted, a strong divergence of opinions on productivity. Pessimists argue that the information technology (IT) revolution is not delivering the gains generated by earlier innovations, such as electrification and mass production.[3] A more optimistic interpretation suggests technological change has not slowed and will yield substantial productivity gains.[4] Indeed, the true contribution of IT to the current economic cycle may be underestimated. For the purpose of this book, IT is defined as information processing equipment and software.

---

1 Conventionally, the potential growth path of an economy is defined as the sum of the underlying trend for productivity and the growth in the labour force.

2 See *Longer-Term Challenges for the American Economy,* Daniel K. Tarullo, April 9th 2014.

3 See, for example, *The Great Stagnation: How America Ate All the Low-Hanging Fruit of Modern History, Got Sick, and Will (Eventually) Feel Better,* Tyler Cowen, Dutton, 2011. See also *Revisiting U.S. Productivity Growth over the Past Century with a View of the Future*, Robert J. Gordon, National Bureau of Economic Research, Working Paper 15834, March 2010. See also *Is U.S. Economic Growth Over? Faltering Innovation Confronts the Six Headwinds,* Robert J. Gordon, National Bureau of Economic Research, Working Paper 18315, August 2012.

4 See, for example, *Race Against the Machine: How the Digital Revolution Is Accelerating Innovation, Driving Productivity, and Irreversibly Transforming Employment and the Economy,* Erik Brynjolfsson and Andrew McAfee, Lexington, Digital Frontier Press, 2011. See also *The Second Machine Age: Work, Progress, and Prosperity in a Time of Brilliant Technologies*, Erik Brynjolfsson and Andrew McAfee, W.W. Norton & Co, 2014. See also *U.S. Productivity Growth: An Optimistic Perspective*, Martin N. Baily, James Manyika, and Shalabh Gupta, International Productivity Monitor, 25, Spring 2013. See also *Economic Prospects for the Long Run*, Ben Bernanke, May 18th 2013. See also *Is the Information Technology Revolution Over?*, David M. Byrne, Stephen D. Oliner, & Daniel E. Sichel, Finance and Economics Discussion Series, Federal Reserve Board, March 2013.

The pessimistic view is largely predicated on a historical narrative of the productivity data provided by the Bureau of Economic Analysis (BEA). Robert J. Gordon notes that American productivity growth in the eight decades prior to 1972 (2.36% y/y, total economy) far outpaced the rate thereafter (1.59% y/y).[5] Productivity has also shown a marked deceleration since 2010.[6] Slower productivity growth implies profit margins are likely to be squeezed earlier into any given economic expansion. Inflation will accelerate sooner and interest rates will have to rise more quickly, offering a less constructive backdrop for equity markets. Other critics argue that whilst investment in technology could generate significant improvements in productivity, this will mostly benefit skilled workers. Profit margins may expand, at the same time embedding the secular downtrend in wages & salaries as a share of GDP, amplifying inequality.[7] In the absence of stronger real wage growth, consumption will stall. Rising consumer debt provided an offset to lacklustre wages during the last housing boom.[8] This may not have been a deliberate policy. Nevertheless, with households still

5 See *The Demise of U.S. Economic Growth: Restatement, Rebuttal, and Reflections,* Robert J. Gordon, National Bureau of Economic Research, Working Paper 19895, February 2014.

6 Source: Bureau of Labor Statistics (BLS), Output Per Hour of All Persons, Non-Farm Business. Productivity growth accelerated to 3.2% y/y and 3.3% y/y in 2009 and 2010 respectively. This has subsequently slowed, averaging 0.7% y/y between 2011 and 2013.

7 Source: Bureau of Economic Analysis (BEA), Personal Income & Its Disposition, Compensation Of Employees, Wages & Salaries and GDP, Total, Current Prices and U.S. Census Bureau, Income, Median, Total, Households, All Races, Total, Constant Prices. There was a 9.0% drop in the real median household income between the peak in 1999 and 2012. For 2013, the real median income rose 0.3% y/y. The share of GDP captured by wages & salaries fell to a post-war low of 42.1% in Q4 2011 in the aftermath of the *Great Recession*, and has since risen to 43.0% in Q2 2014. However, this is significantly below the peak of 51.7% reached in Q1 1970.

8 See *Aspects of Inequality in the Recent Business Cycle,* Sarah Bloom Raskin, April 18th 2013. The FOMC member Sarah Bloom Raskin was one of the first to admit that the deep recession of 2008 was not the sole consequence of an overly liberalised financial sector, but was also symptomatic of an underlying downward trend in the share of wages taken as a proportion of GDP and rising inequality. See also *The U.S. Economic Recovery,* Graham Turner, GFC Economics, 2QT Publishing, 2014.

deleveraging, it is even more important that real wages improve for an economic recovery to endure.[9]

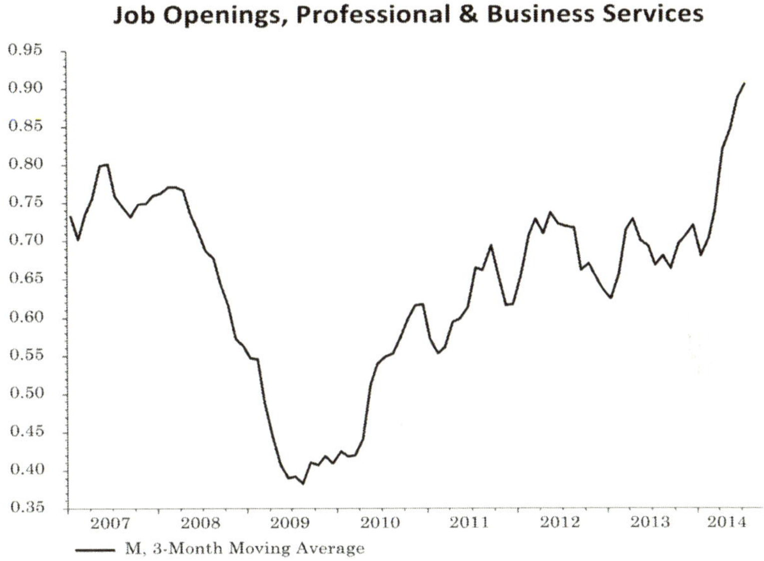

Source: GFC Economics

Chart 3a

Rapid technological change may displace workers and 'destroy' jobs, but it can also create new business opportunities. Job openings in professional & business services have reached new highs, for example (see chart 3a).[10] Alternatively, if technology eliminated more employment opportunities than it generated, this would suggest that productivity is rising more quickly. The onus would then be on central banks to adjust policy to accommodate this higher potential growth path for the economy, generating a quicker increase in real GDP.

---

9 Source: Federal Reserve, Flow of Funds, Level, Households & Nonprofit Organizations, Liabilities and GDP, Current Prices, Total. The ratio of financial liabilities for households and non-profit institutions (personal sector) to GDP has fallen from a high of 99.0% in Q1 2008 to 80.6% in Q2 2014, the lowest since Q1 2003.

10 Source: BLS, Job Openings & Labor Turnover Survey (JOLTS), Job Openings, Professional & Business Services, Level. Job openings in professional & business services reached a new cyclical high of 913k in July 2014. The previous cyclical high was 879k in June 2005.

Source: GFC Economics

Chart 3b

From the more optimistic perspective, high profit margins and a low share of labour income are not inconsistent with a robust recovery (see chart 3b). Rising profits can fund greater levels of investment, underpinning productivity gains *and* higher employment. As the economy approaches full employment, the rise in productivity can be used to pay for real wage increases: this could lead to a long, non-inflationary cycle.[11] Furthermore, by using retained earnings and not leverage to fund investment, the risks of contagion from a rise in bank lending to companies can be reduced.

Past experience has shown that "productivity growth has largely occurred hand in hand with employment growth."[12] There may well be a trade-off

11 How this interacts with the Non-Accelerating Inflation Rate of Unemployment [NAIRU] is open to debate. Logically, faster productivity growth does not change the NAIRU. It simply means that it takes longer to get to full employment. Nevertheless, a successful investment-led cycle, one buttressed by cheap, but tight money may allow wages to rise more quickly without squeezing profit margins. This would imply that the NAIRU remains low, or might fall. Equally, strong investment-led growth could fund higher wages, but without putting upward pressure on the ratio of wages to GDP.

12 See *U.S. Productivity Growth: An Optimistic Perspective*, Martin N. Baily, James Manykia, Shalabh Gupta, *International Productivity Monitor*, no. 25, Spring 2013, p. 5.

between employment and productivity in the short run, but this tends to disappear over ten-year time spans.[13] Innovations can "create new jobs, new lines of business and new profit opportunities."[14] Indeed, "long-run productivity growth is still the most important way to improve living standards".[15]

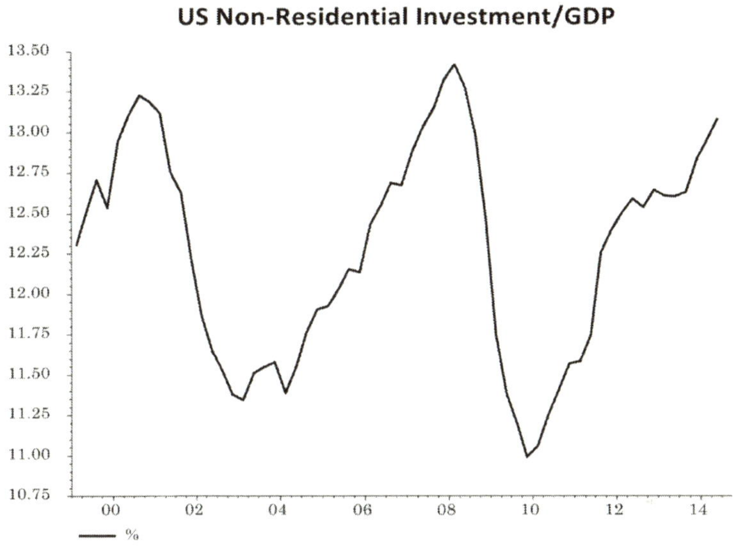

Source: GFC Economics

Chart 3c

The key to ensuring that technology – or any other innovation – does not merely boost 'capital' at the expense of 'labour income' lies in a *cheap, but tight* monetary policy. Successful control over debt will provide central banks with the latitude to keep interest rates on hold and aim for full employment. Once that has been achieved, real wages can start to rise more quickly. However, so long as investment remains high as a share of GDP, real wage gains need not be inflationary.

---

13 See *Growth and renewal in the United State: restoring America's economic engine*, McKinsey Global Institute, February 2011.

14 See *U.S. Productivity Growth: An Optimistic Perspective*, Martin N. Baily, James Manykia, Shalabh Gupta, International Productivity Monitor, no. 25, Spring, 2013, pp. 4-5.

15 Ibid., p. 5.

Dissecting Investment

As a share of GDP, real non-residential investment fell from a high of 13.42% of GDP in Q1 2008 to 11.00% in Q4 2009, in response to the collapse of the housing market (all investment numbers are in real terms unless otherwise stated).[16] By Q2 2014, it had risen again to 13.09% (see chart 3c). The latest GDP report also included significant upward revisions.[17] Only a slower recovery in structures is preventing the non-residential investment to GDP ratio from exceeding its peak reached in Q1 2008 (13.42%). Nevertheless, there is every chance that this could be surpassed during the current economic cycle.

Source: GFC Economics

Chart 3d

Indeed, the latest report for durable goods orders suggests firms are accelerating their capital spending plans. Non-defence capital goods orders, excluding aircraft, hit an all-time high in the three months to

---

16 Source: BEA, Real Private Fixed Investment, Non-residential and GDP, Total, Constant Prices, Chained.

17 For example, this was 12.62% in Q1 2014 according to the first estimate released on April 30th 2014. This has subsequently been revised up to 12.96%.

July 2014, climbing by a 3-month/3-month annualised rate of 11.1% (see chart 3d).[18] This suggests that non-residential investment could hit a new cyclical high as a share of GDP in Q3 2014.

Nevertheless, this may understate the increase in 'productive' investment. It is important to disaggregate non-residential investment into three components: intellectual property products, equipment and structures. The first two have been expanding more rapidly. Although the more recent productivity numbers (from the Bureau of Labor Statistics) may have been 'disappointing', the strong rise in 'productive' investment suggests that the *underlying trend* for productivity is likely to accelerate.

Intellectual Property Products

According to the BEA, intellectual property products investment as a share of GDP rose to a secular high of 4.03% in Q2 2014 (see chart 3e).[19] In real terms, investment in intellectual property products has climbed 14.3% since the high of Q2 2008 (3.76% of GDP), prior to the collapse of Lehman Brothers. Indeed, the decline that followed the financial crisis was remarkably shallow – just 3.5% from peak to trough – and only lasted three quarters.[20] It challenges the conventional view that the 2008 financial crisis has cast a long shadow over the potential growth path of the economy.

---

18 Source: U.S. Census Bureau, Manufacturing New Orders, Non-Defence Capital Goods, Excluding Aircraft. The 3-month moving average for July 2014 was 5.3% above the previous cyclical high (3-months to June 2008).

19 Source: BEA, Real Private Fixed Investment, Non-Residential, Intellectual Property Products.

20 Source: BEA, Real Private Fixed Investment, Non-Residential, Intellectual Property Products. Real investment in intellectual property products fell between Q2 2008 and Q1 2009. The comparatively short-lived decline shows that many technology companies were far less dependent on financial markets for funding. It is also possible that the high level of spending on research & development in this sector had sown the seeds for a quick rebound in investment for software.

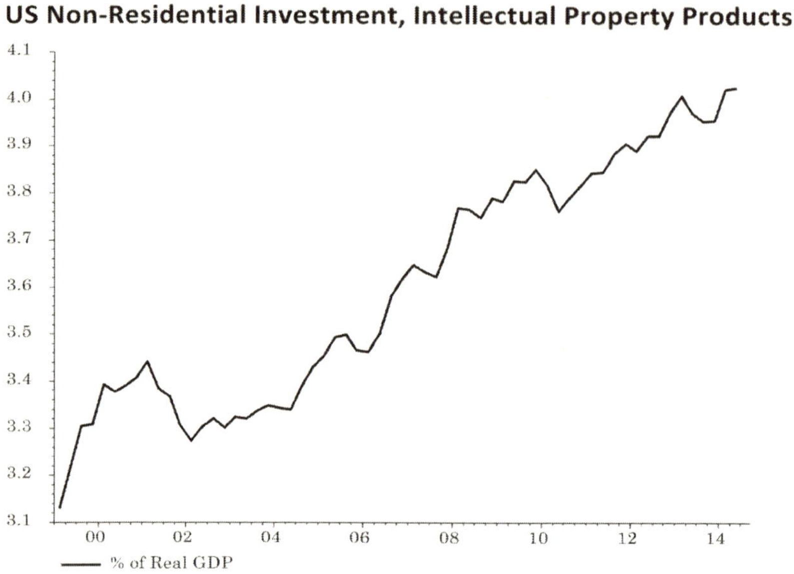

Source: GFC Economics

Chart 3e

Within intellectual property products, the biggest driver has been software. Investment in software carried on rising immediately after the 2008 financial crisis, dipping during the first half of 2010, before climbing again (see chart 3f). Software expenditures had expanded to an all-time high of 1.91% of GDP by Q1 2013.[21] This has since slipped to 1.89%, but remains substantively higher than at any point during the last economic cycle. There has also been a small rise in investment for 'entertainment, literary & artistic originals', from 0.45% of GDP in Q2 2008 to 0.50% by Q2 2014.[22] Spending on research & development has climbed too, from 1.59% of GDP to 1.64% over the same period (see chart 3g).[23]

---

21 Source: BEA, Real Private Fixed Investment, Non-Residential, Software. Note, software development expenditures are included in software investment. However, it excludes software embedded or bundled in computers and other equipment.

22 Source: BEA, Real Private Fixed Investment, Non-Residential, Entertainment, Literary & Artistic Originals.

23 Source: BEA, Real Private Fixed Investment, Non-Residential, Intellectual Property Products, Research & Development.

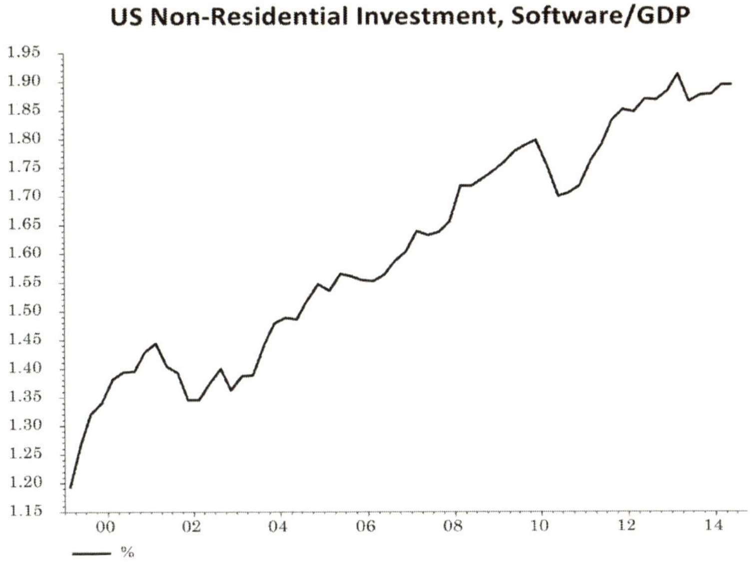

Source: GFC Economics

Chart 3f

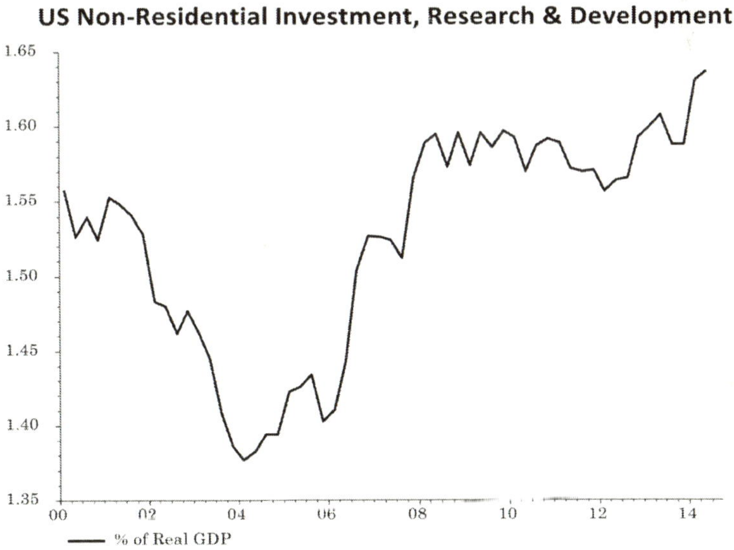

Source: GFC Economics

Chart 3g

The Bureau of Economic Analysis does not provide a quarterly breakdown of research & development. Nonetheless, the annual data show that between 2007 and 2013, research & development spending has risen 7.2% in manufacturing and 11.4% in non-manufacturing.[24] Within manufacturing, the biggest increase has been in semiconductor & other electronic component manufacturing, with R&D up 48.7% over this six-year period.[25]

Equipment

Investment in equipment has also been running at secular highs, after climbing to 6.25% of GDP in Q2 this year.[26] This compares with a high of 6.07% during the housing boom (Q4 2007) and 5.83% following the dotcom bubble (Q3 2000). There are four components to investment in equipment. Information processing equipment is the largest and hit a new high of 1.98% of GDP in Q2 (see chart 3h).[27] Transportation equipment is the second largest: investment in transport equipment was 1.55% of GDP in Q2, up from a low of 0.47% in Q2 2009.[28] Industrial investment has risen sharply as a share of GDP in the last two quarters, up from 1.27% in Q4 2013 to 1.39%.[29] Lastly, investment in 'other' equipment was 1.36% as a share of GDP in Q2 2014, up from a low of 1.09% in Q4 2009.[30]

---

24 Source: BEA, Real Private Fixed Investment, Non-Residential, Intellectual Property Products, Research & Development, Business, Manufacturing and Non-manufacturing.

25 Source: BEA, Real Private Fixed Investment, Non-Residential, Intellectual Property Products, Research and Development, Semiconductor & Other Electronic Component Manufacturing.

26 Source: BEA, Real Private Fixed Investment, Non-Residential, Equipment.

27 Source: BEA, Real Private Fixed Investment, Non-Residential, Equipment, Information Processing.

28 Source: BEA, Real Private Fixed Investment, Non-Residential, Equipment, Transportation.

29 Source: BEA, Real Private Fixed Investment, Non-Residential, Equipment, Industrial. This is close to the high of 1.42% reached in the housing boom (Q2/Q3 2007), but still below the peak of 1.61% reached in Q3 2000 following the dotcom boom.

30 Source: BEA, Real Private Fixed Investment, Non-Residential, Equipment, Other. Other equipment consists primarily of furniture and fixtures, agricultural

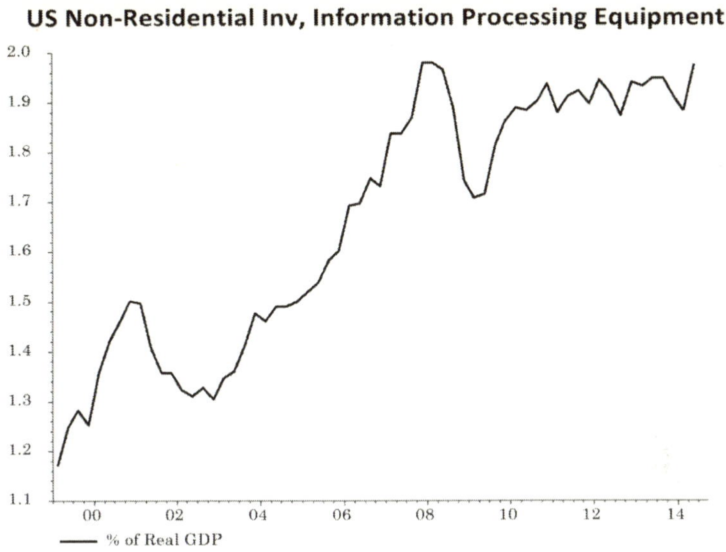

Source: GFC Economics

Chart 3h

Structures

By contrast, investment in structures has been weak (see chart 3i). As a share of GDP, it had fallen from a peak of 4.34% in Q3 2000 to a low of 2.30% in Q1 2011. The contribution of investment in structures to GDP has since risen to 2.83% in Q2 2014, but it remains below the peak of the sub-prime housing boom (3.66% in Q2 2008).[31] This decline in spending on structures is key to understanding the drop in non-residential investment spending (as a share of GDP) since the high of Q1 2008.

---

machinery, construction machinery, mining and oilfield machinery, service industry machinery, and electrical equipment not elsewhere classified.

31 Source: BEA, Real Private Fixed Investment, Non-Residential, Structures. Note, real investment in structures for Q1 2014 has subsequently been revised up from 2.74% of GDP (advanced estimate) to 2.79% of GDP.

US Non-Residential Investment, Structures/GDP

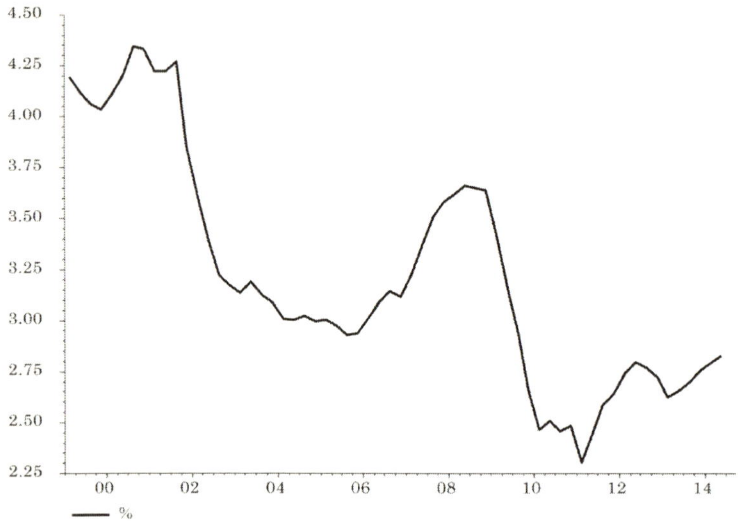

Source: GFC Economics

Chart 3i

Nevertheless, some of the biggest declines within this category have been in areas that may be less decisive for the 'productive' potential of the US economy. For example, compared to 2007, real investment in multi-merchandise shopping had dropped 58.8% by 2013.[32] Real investment in offices had dipped 50.1%.[33] This includes structures or buildings in the financial sector. Real investment has shrunk 51.4% for religious structures and 52.3% for lodging.[34] Other notable falls include educational & vocational, amusement & recreation and food & beverage establishments.[35]

32 Source: BEA, Real Private Fixed Investment, Non-Residential, Structures, Multi-Merchandise shopping.

33 Source: BEA, Real Private Fixed Investment, Non-Residential, Structures, Offices.

34 Source: BEA, Real Private Fixed Investment, Non-Residential, Structures, Religious Facilities and Lodging.

35 Source: BEA, Real Private Fixed Investment, Non-Residential, Structures, Educational & Vocational and Amusement & Recreation and Food & beverage establishments.

Source: GFC Economics

Chart 3j

Conversely, investment in structures has risen 10.6% for transportation, 17.2% in the power sector and 27.9% for mining exploration, shafts & wells (which includes petroleum & natural gas).[36] These sectors might contribute more to the potential growth path, easing possible bottlenecks (transportation) and driving energy costs lower (in the case of the latter two). Given these increases, the overall decline in investment for structures as a share of GDP is unlikely to be detrimental to long-term growth prospects. It is worth adding that some areas of investment in structures have increased strongly in the past as a result of easy money. More effective control over lending may be playing a part in shifting the composition of investment towards the more 'productive' components.

Indeed, investment in equipment *and* intellectual property products (combined) has reached an all-time high as a share of GDP, climbing to 10.28% in Q2 2014 (see chart 3j).[37] This is well above the peaks of 9.81%

36 Source: BEA, Real Private Fixed Investment, Non-Residential, Structures, Transportation and Power and Mining Exploration and Shafts & Wells.

37 Source: BEA, Real Private Fixed Investment, Non-Residential, Equipment and

reached in Q1 2008 (housing bubble) and 9.22% in Q3 2000 (dotcom bubble). The rise in investment in equipment and intellectual property products suggests that the 'productive' potential of the US economy may be expanding more quickly than assumed.

Information Technology Deflation

As a share of GDP, IT investment rose to a record 3.87% of GDP in Q2 2014.[38] Furthermore, the contribution of IT to potential productivity gains may be underestimated. Prices may not be adjusted correctly for quality improvements. In national account terms, the deflators or prices may be too high. As a result, the recovery in IT and 'productive' investment may have been stronger than recorded in the official statistics, in real terms and as a share of GDP. Indeed, for the last four quarters, the deflator for information processing equipment has fallen by an average of 0.5% y/y. This compares with an average decline of 5.1% y/y from 2001 to 2010.[39]

The importance of IT in driving economic growth cannot be gauged unless prices accurately reflect the improvements in the semiconductor chips embedded in information processing equipment. A research paper from the Federal Reserve published in March 2013 suggested that the decline in prices for semiconductors or microprocessor units reported by the Bureau of Labor Statistics may have been "substantially understated".[40]

Intellectual Property Products. For Q1 2014, real equipment investment has been revised up from the advanced estimate of 5.90% of GDP to 6.16%. Investment in intellectual property products has also been revised upwards, from 3.99% of GDP to 4.02%.

38 Source: BEA, Real Private Fixed Investment, Non-Residential, Information Processing Equipment and Software.

39 Source: BEA, Real Private Fixed Investment, Non-Residential, Information Processing. The deflator is calculated as the ratio of the nominal value of a series to its corresponding real value.

40 See *Is the Information Technology Revolution Over?*, David M. Byrne, Stephen D. Oliner, & Daniel E. Sichel, Finance and Economics Discussion Series, Federal Reserve Board, March 2013.

The debate over how fast prices are falling centres on the 'technology cycle'. This is "the amount of time required to achieve a 30 percent reduction in the width of the smallest feature on a chip."[41] Across the semiconductor sector, the technology cycle averaged three years until 1993, but then accelerated to approximately two years from 1993 to 2012.[42] According to Byrne, Oliner & Sichel, the semiconductor industry has achieved "massive reductions in scaling over time, leaving the width of a chip component in 2012 about 450 times smaller than in 1969."[43] These reductions follow the introduction of new semiconductor technology. The authors of this paper concluded:

> "The scaling advances were especially rapid from 1993 to 2003 and a bit a slower after 2003. Even so, the average cycle since 2003 has remained substantially shorter [i.e. quicker] than the three-year cycle in effect before the 1990s. For Intel's MPUs, there has been no pullback at all from the two-year cycle."[44]

Technology companies had successfully navigated their way past a number of obstacles. This included dealing with the heat generated from an improvement in the speed of chips.[45] As a result, the authors of the Federal Reserve paper estimated that the "end-user performance of Intel's MPU chips improved roughly 30 percent per year on average from 2001 to 2012. End users have continued to see substantial gains in performance".[46]

---

41 Ibid., p. 15. "Because chips are rectangular, a 30 percent reduction in the both the horizontal and vertical directions implies about a 50 percent reduction (0.7*0.7) in the area required for the smallest chip component".

42 Ibid., p. 25-26.

43 Ibid., p. 15.

44 Ibid., p. 15-16, 26. The semiconductor technology cycle averaged 3.0 years between 1969 and 1993. From 1993 to 2012 it averaged 2.1 years. The latter can be further subdivided: the average cycle fell to 1.9 years between 1993 and 2003 and then 2.3 years between 2003 and 2012.

45 Ibid., p. 16. Intel responded in 2006 by raising the 'clock-speed' more slowly: the target of raising performance centred on "placing multiple copies of the core architecture on each chip" and by "improving the design of those cores".

46 Ibid., p. 16.

The producer price index (PPI) released by the Bureau of Labour Statistics (BLS) paints a very different perspective. According to the BLS, microprocessor prices in the PPI fell by an average of 50% y/y between the late 1990s and 2007.[47] However, since 2007 the rate of decline has slowed abruptly, with the PPI barely dropping in 2012. For August 2014, prices for semiconductor and related devices dipped by just 4.9% y/y.[48]

An alternative index adopted by the Federal Reserve has attempted to correct for potential measurement problems with the BLS data. A new hedonic price index has adopted a range of "product characteristics data to estimate the product price holding quality constant."[49] Prices for specific microprocessor units were collected from industry leader Intel.[50] This new index incorporated performance scores for microprocessors, but also accounted for changes in the "mix of computing end-use markets over time".[51] In addition, the index used prices on the first introduction of each microprocessor model to avoid a potential bias in estimating quality improvements.[52]

---

47 Ibid., p. 17.

48 See BLS, Producer Price Index, Industry Data, Industry: Semiconductors & Related Device, 33441312, Microprocessors (Including Microcontrollers).

49 See *Federal Reserve Microprocessor Price Index*, Federal Reserve, March 11th 2013.

50 Ibid., "MPU scores on "benchmarks" – programs designed to test performance on common computing tasks – were used from System Performance Evaluation Corporation (SPEC). For an overall performance score, a geometric mean of composite scores for integer and floating point benchmark tests from SPEC® CPU2006 was used."

51 Ibid., "To account for changes in the mix of computing end-use markets over time, the hedonic regression includes MPU product class (e.g. mainstream, performance, extreme) as reported by IDC Corp. To account for the impact on performance from other features of the computer used to test the MPU, the hedonic regression includes system memory; system vendor (e.g.Dell, IBM); and, for server systems, number of processors. The log-price of each MPU model was regressed on the performance score, control variables and quarterly dummy variables. Coefficients on the dummy variables were used to construct a price index."
Furthermore, "Separate indexes were created for MPUs used in desktop PCs and servers. Mobile system MPUs were not included because of the limited data availability and relatively small share of domestic production for this class of chips. Desktop and server indexes were weighted by global revenue shares reported by IDC Corp. to create a composite price index."

52 Ibid., "Only prices reported on the first introduction of each model were employed

The new hedonic price index is consistent with the performance data suggesting that the technology cycle has remained around two years. It estimates that prices for semiconductor chips fell by an average of 36.4% y/y between 2007 and 2011. These numbers were updated and extended in a press release update on March 28th 2014.[53] Microprocessor or semiconductor prices were estimated to have dropped 30% y/y in 2012.[54]

The potential mismeasurement of prices is not confined to semiconductors. The price declines for microprocessor units are not reflected in a broad array of electronic goods, including navigation equipment, electro-medical

---

to mitigate concern that transaction prices reflect discounts that evolve over the life of the model. (Many list prices were unchanged when closely-related models with better performance were introduced)."

See also *Is the Information Technology Revolution Over?*, David M. Byrne, Stephen D. Oliner, & Daniel E. Sichel, Finance and Economics Discussion Series, Federal Reserve Board, March 2013, p. 17-18. The authors "compiled wholesale price lists for Intel MPUs and matched these prices to benchmark performance scores and other chip characteristics." They then "estimated a hedonic regression back to 2006 using only the list price at the time of introduction." They "omitted the list prices for subsequent periods because in many cases those prices were not adjusted down when a more powerful, closely-related chip entered the market, contrary to the pattern in earlier years. The absence of price adjustment raises concern that existing chips are being sold at a discount relative to the constant list price that widens when new models are introduced. Thus, to the extent that significant chip sales are taking place at transaction prices that fall ever further below the list prices, a standard procedure that relied on those list prices or other similar prices reported by manufacturers would be biased." Their "hedonic index, which only uses prices at the time of each new chip's introduction, provides a very rough way of avoiding this potential bias."

53 See *Federal Reserve Statistical Release*, March 28th 2014, p. 6. This was revised to show a decline of 37% y/y for 2007 to 2011. The hedonic price index was updated in a number of ways. "First, this revision incorporated additional observations in the sample used in the 2013 analysis. Second, the increased sample size enabled a more flexible specification of the hedonic model used in the analysis. Third, the updated methods controlled for heat management properties of different MPUs. Finally, some controls were eliminated from the specification and the sample was adjusted to improve consistency over time." It should be noted that this revision applied to these updated methods to just the 2012 data. Nevertheless, it is expected that "the new methods will be introduced to the 2007-11 period in a future annual revision."

54 Ibid., p. 6. "Previously, the price deflator for MPUs in 2012 was estimated to have declined about 4 percent".

equipment and a "variety of types of industrial process equipment."[55] The rising producer prices reported by the BLS for many of these sectors may indicate that quality adjustments need to be reassessed.

Resource constraints have limited the adoption of hedonic techniques. Indeed, quality adjustments have proved difficult for software. The BEA is still using proxies for a significant fraction of software prices. As a result, "the BEA's prices for own-account and custom software have increased in recent years".[56] However, for pre-packaged software, scanner data suggest there have been sizeable declines in quality-adjusted prices. Furthermore, these "declines are faster than those in the PPI for prepackaged software and contrast sharply with the price increases for custom and own-account software, suggesting that further work on software prices would be valuable."[57] For the record, the deflator used by the BEA for investment in software was 0.12% y/y in Q1 2014. During the ten years to Q4 2010, it averaged -0.55% y/y.[58]

Robotics

The Boston Consulting Group (BCG) has forecast that spending on robots will jump from just over \$15bn in 2010 to around \$67bn by 2025.[59] The BCG argues that "robotics and automation are crossing price, performance and adoption thresholds … a tipping point may be

55 See *Is the Information Technology Revolution Over?*, David M. Byrne, Stephen D. Oliner and Daniel E. Sichel, Finance and Economic Discussion Series, Federal Reserve, March 2013, p. 20. See also *Faster, Smaller, Cheaper: an Hedonic Price Analysis of PDAs*, Paul D. Chwelos, Ernst R. Berndt & Iain M. Cockburn, Applied Economics, 40, 2008. The authors develop hedonic price indexes for personal digital assistants from 1994 to 2004, and they find average price declines ranging from 19 to 26 percent per year.

56 See *Is the Information Technology Revolution Over?*, David M. Byrne, Stephen D. Oliner and Daniel E. Sichel, Finance and Economic Discussion Series, Federal Reserve, March 2013, p. 19.

57 Ibid.,

58 Source: BEA, United States, Price Indexes for Private Fixed Investment, Nonresidential, Intellectual Property Products, Software, Index.

59 See *The Rise of Robotics*, Alison Sander & Mel Wolfgang, BCG Perspectives, August 14th 2014, p. 1.

near." The application of programming is getting easier and the cost of high-quality robots is dropping rapidly. Robots are becoming smaller, "increasing the breadth of potential applications."[60]

Industrial robots have already played a significant role in "industries requiring heavy lifting and repetitive, precise movements".[61] According to the BCG, "Approximately 40 percent of the industrial robots used today are in the automotive sector".[62] However, low-cost robots now "have the potential to fundamentally change manufacturing by increasing precision and productivity without incurring high costs".[63] This could sharply reduce labour costs for manufacturers where larger industrial robotics have previously not been applicable: "robots are making small-batch production economically more feasible, because line changeovers are much faster", reinforcing the trend towards shorter product life cycles.[64]

Warehouse robots are transforming retailing and increasing the competitive advantage for 'first movers'.[65] Robots are also moving into personal services. In Japan, engineers are exploring how robots can provide nursing and care for the elderly. The Google car – which currently has a "virtually unblemished safety record of 700,000 accident-free miles" – has

---

60 Ibid., p. 2.

61 See *U.S. Productivity Growth: An Optimistic Perspective*, Martin N. Baily, James Manykia, Shalabh Gupta, International Productivity Monitor, no. 25, Spring 2013, p. 8.

62 See *The Rise of Robotics*, Alison Sander & Mel Wolfgang, BCG Perspectives, August 14th 2014, p. 2.

63 See *U.S. Productivity Growth: An Optimistic Perspective*, Martin Neil Baily, James Manykia, Shalabh Gupta, International Productivity Monitor, no. 25, Spring 2013, p. 8. Baxter, a low-cost robot, has been developed by Boston Robotics "with the capability to work safely alongside humans. Baxter's arms can sense a human in their path and stop movement. It can be 'reprogrammed' for new tasks by a human operator who physically manipulates its arms to move, bend, lift or drop in the desired way. At a sticker price of $20,000, the company claims its costs are equivalent to a human worker earning $4 per hour".

64 See *The Rise of Robotics*, Alison Sander & Mel Wolfgang, BCG Perspectives, August 14th 2014, p. 3.

65 Ibid., p. 3. "Amazon.com, the world's largest online retailer, paid $775 million in cash in 2012 to buy Kiva Systems, which makes warehouse robots. Small, fast, and flexible, these robots are constantly in action, moving large merchandise lots from shelves to the packing and shipping areas."

already been authorised in four US states. [66] Driverless vehicles will slash costs across a raft of sectors. Agricultural robots (or 'agbots') – designed to pick fruit and vegetables – will reduce labour costs too.[67]

Until recently, 3D printing has largely been used to create prototypes or objects that would be difficult to machine. However, this new technology could "usher in a new eco-system of smaller value chains and new companies providing printable designs on the web, instead of products on the shelf."[68] Products will become "endlessly customisable", creating an opportunity for small businesses to compete head-on with traditional, large manufacturers. It will accelerate the shift towards 'just-in-time' manufacturing. Profit margins will be squeezed for larger companies. Simultaneously, there will be growth opportunities in new markets.

Connecting machines through common networks on the internet will facilitate remote monitoring and raise productivity: instructions can be provided to one set of machines based on the activity of other machines or equipment. This may lead to manufacturing facilities that "can be fully shut down and started up by the owner sitting at home with the help of an internet connection." Extending this principle could lead to "closed-loop systems which would automatically make decisions based on optimization algorithms and stimuli from various equipment in the network."[69] In addition, new materials, including breakthroughs in nanotechnology and biologics, promise to "fundamentally change manufacturing."[70]

---

66 Ibid., p. 4. See also *Polanyi's Paradox and the Shape of Employment Growth*, David H. Autor, MIT, National Bureau of Economic Research and JPAL, August 2014, p. 33-34. This paper contains an intriguing discussion on the limitations to technology imposed by the external environment. The author notes that the Google Car "lacks the capability to process, interpret and respond to an environment that has not been pre-processed by its human engineers." This means that "if the car's software determines that the environment in which it is operating differs from the key static features of its pre-specified map ... then the car signals for its human operator to take command." Nevertheless, these obstacles may soon be surmounted by advances in *machine learning*.

67 Ibid., p. 4.

68 See *U.S. Productivity Growth: An Optimistic Perspective*, Martin N. Baily, James Manykia, Shalabh Gupta, International Productivity Monitor, no. 25, Spring 2013, p. 8.

69 Ibid., p. 9.

70 Ibid.,

All of these examples centre on manufacturing. Robots have largely displaced workers employed in routine tasks. Explicit, codifiable procedures have been replicated by computer programmers. Abstract tasks, requiring problem-solving capabilities, intuition and creativity have in the past not been automated. However, machine learning algorithms are allowing non-routine tasks to be computerised. Information technology now has the potential to raise productivity in the much larger services sector.

Machine learning uses "statistics and inductive reasoning to supply best guess answers in cases where formal procedural rules are unknown".[71] Exposure, training and reinforcement allow machine learning algorithms to accomplish tasks that have proved challenging to codify with explicit procedures. Indeed, "Machines and their learning-based algorithms have leapt forward in pattern-matching ability and in the nuances of interpreting and communicating complex information." As a result, "jobs that had once seemed the sole province of humans – including those of pathologists, petroleum geologists, and law clerks – are now being performed by computers."[72]

In some cases, "particularly when it comes to finding answers to problems, software already surpasses even the best managers. Knowing whether to assert your own expertise or to step out of the way is fast becoming a critical executive skill."[73] Furthermore, "the results of previous machine-learning exercises can be fed back into the algorithms."[74] Effectively, "each layer becomes a foundation for the next layer of machine learning, and the whole thing scales in a multiplicative way every year."[75] With the foundations in place, a prior innovation can be used to create another innovation. "This is very different from the common idea that innovations get used up like low-hanging fruit. Now each innovation actually adds to

---

71 See *Polanyi's Paradox and the Shape of Employment Growth*, David H. Autor, MIT, National Bureau of Economic Research and JPAL, August 2014, p. 34.

72 See *Artificial intelligence meets the C-suite,* McKinsey Quarterly, September 2014, p. 1.

73 Ibid., p. 2.

74 Ibid., p. 5.

75 Ibid.

our stock of building blocks and allows us to do new things."[76] Daniela Rus – chair of the Computer Science and Artificial Intelligence Lab at MIT – believes that current projections understate how rapidly machine learning will become mainstream.[77]

Substitution Versus Complementarities

There are many countervailing forces to the cost cutting implied by some 'productive' investment. Notably, "abstract task-intensive activities benefit from strong complementarities with computerization".[78] Higher productivity or technological progress does not lead to a straight substitution of capital for labour. It may also increase demand for skilled labour. Computers amplify the comparative advantage of workers with solving skills, adaptability and creativity.

Indeed, "senior managers are far from obsolete. As machine learning progresses at a rapid pace, top executives will be called on to create the innovative new organizational forms … [they] will have to emphasize their creative abilities, their leadership skills, and their strategic thinking."[79]

Productivity Trends

Robert J. Gordon is one widely cited source of estimates suggesting that the growth in productivity has slowed. Mr Gordon notes that "The growth rate of American productivity in the eight decades before 1972 was 2.36 percent per year, compared to 1.59 percent per year since 1972. That permanent decline of 0.8 percent per year represents a new way to measure the extent to which the single-dimension digital Third Industrial Revolution (from 1972) has fallen short of the multi-

---

76 Ibid.

77 Ibid., p. 4.

78 See *Polanyi's Paradox and the Shape of Employment Growth*, David H. Autor, MIT, NBER and JPAL, August 2014, p. 20.

79 See *Artificial intelligence meets the C-Suite*, McKinsey Quarterly, September 2014, p. 2.

dimensional Second Industrial Revolution (1875 – 1972)".[80] He adds "There is no need to forecast any slowdown in the pace of future innovation for this gloomy forecast to come true, because the slowdown already occurred four decades ago." The digital revolution is a "mere shadow" of the second industrial revolution, he claims.

Low educational achievement, record student debt and inequality are just three reasons cited by Mr Gordon for a slowdown in innovation. Others point to a "decline in the dynamism of the US labour market", and less "creative destruction", as potential obstacles.[81] The precise impact of these trends remains open to debate.

It is clear, however, that any analysis which relies upon official productivity statistics may be wrong, because of the potential for revisions and reinterpretation. The 1999 conversion of the U.S. National Accounts to chain-weighted price and quantity indexes resulted in a major upward revision to US GDP growth during 1929-48. Mr Gordon concluded that this added further support to the previous "big wave" hypothesis that productivity growth during the middle of the twentieth century was historically unique.[82]

In truth, these revisions demonstrate the pragmatism required when interpreting historical productivity data. Furthermore, when investment is rising strongly, the onus is on sceptics to argue why this will not translate into stronger productivity growth in the future. After all, a surge in information technology investment was key to a revival in productivity growth between 1995 and 2000.[83] Those who simply extrapolate historical productivity data to make substantive claims

---

80 See *The Demise of U.S. Economic Growth: Restatement, Rebuttal, and Reflections,* Robert J. Gordon, National Bureau of Economic Research, Working Paper 19895, February 2014, p. 1.

81 See *Longer-Term Challenges for the American Economy,* Daniel K. Tarullo, April 9th 2014, p. 4.

82 See *Revisiting U.S. Productivity Growth Over The Past Century With A View of The Future,* Robert J. Gordon, National Bureau of Economic Research, Working Paper 15834, March 2010, p. 1.

83 Source: BLS, Output Per Hour of All Persons, Non-Farm Business. Productivity growth accelerated to an average of 2.69% y/y between 1996 and 2000 respectively.

regarding the potential growth path of the US economy will need to provide a more compelling argument to support their case.

Investment & Productivity *update*

The U.S. Economic Recovery outlined a policy framework (*cheap, but tight*) that would facilitate a rise in productive investment.[84] In support of this thesis, a detailed breakdown of the investment figures was provided in the original GFC Economics Article *US Investment & Productivity*. The subsequent data confirm that investment has been strong in areas that should boost the potential growth path of the US economy. The following section reviews in detail how the investment numbers have changed since the publication of the original article, comparing the *second estimate of Q2 2014* with the *third estimate of Q4 2015*.

Revisions to US Investment and Key Sub-Components

	Q2 2014 (2nd estimate)	**Q2 2014** (latest revised estimate)	**Q4 2015** (3rd estimate)
Non-residential private fixed investment	13.09%	13.39%	13.44%
Equipment	6.25%	6.37%	6.47%
Structures	2.96%	2.92%	2.74%
Intellectual property products	4.03%	4.11%	4.25%
Software	1.89%	1.96%	2.04%
R&D	1.64%	1.66%	1.72%
'Productive investment' (equipment + intellectual property products)	10.28%	10.48%	10.72%

Source: Bureau of Economic Analysis

Table 2

As a share of real GDP, real non-residential investment was 13.09% in Q2 2014 (subsequently revised to 13.39%). It hit a new high of 13.55% in Q3 2015, before falling back to 13.44% in the following quarter (see chart 3k).[85] Intellectual property products investment climbed from

84 See *The U.S. Economic Recovery*, Graham Turner, 2QT Publishing, 2014.

85 Source: Bureau of Economic Analysis (BEA), Real Private Fixed Investment, Nonresidential and Gross Domestic Product, Total, Constant Prices, Chained. The first edition of the article had forecast that non-residential private fixed investment as a share of GDP would surpass the previous cyclical peak of 2008 during the current economic expansion. There was also a suggestion that this

4.03% of GDP in Q2 2014 to a secular high of 4.29% in Q2 2015, before edging down to 4.25% in Q4 (see chart 3l).[86] In real terms, investment in this category is up 24.2% vis-à-vis the previous cyclical high of Q2 2008.[87] As a share of real GDP, real investment in software has risen from 1.89% to 2.04% in Q4 2015 (see chart 3m).[88] This was just shy of the all-time high set in Q2 2015 (2.05%). Similarly, real R&D spending rose from 1.64% of GDP in Q2 2014 to a record 1.75% one year later, but had slipped to 1.72% by Q4 2015 (see chart 3n).[89]

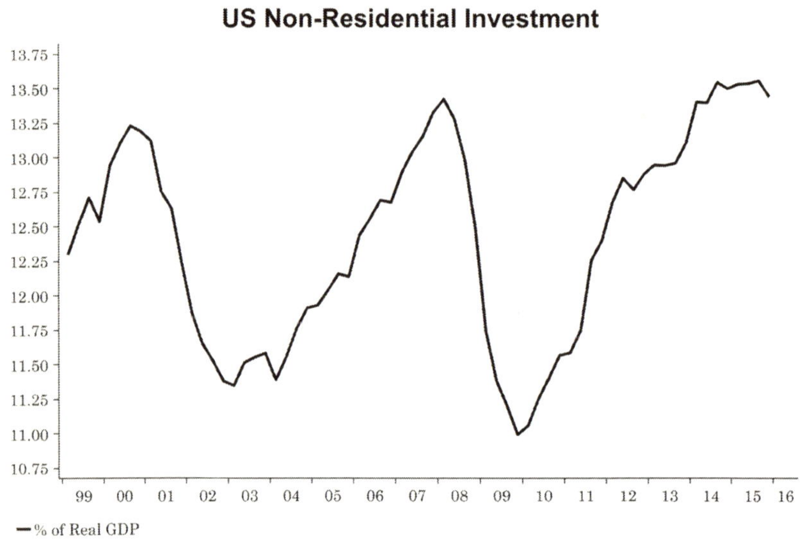

Source: GFC Economics

Chart 3k

would occur by Q3 2014. Subsequent revisions have shown this to be correct.

86 Source: BEA, Real Private Fixed Investment, Nonresidential, Intellectual Property Products and Gross Domestic Product, Total, Constant Prices, Chained. As noted before, there are three components of intellectual property products: software, research & development (R&D), and entertainment, artistic & literary originals.

87 Source: BEA, Real Private Fixed Investment, Nonresidential, Intellectual Property Products, Chained.

88 Source: BEA, Real Private Fixed Investment, Nonresidential, Intellectual Property Products, Software and Gross Domestic Product, Total, Constant Prices, Chained.

89 Source: BEA, Real Private Fixed Investment, Nonresidential, Intellectual Property Products, Research & Development and Gross Domestic Product, Total, Constant Prices, Chained.

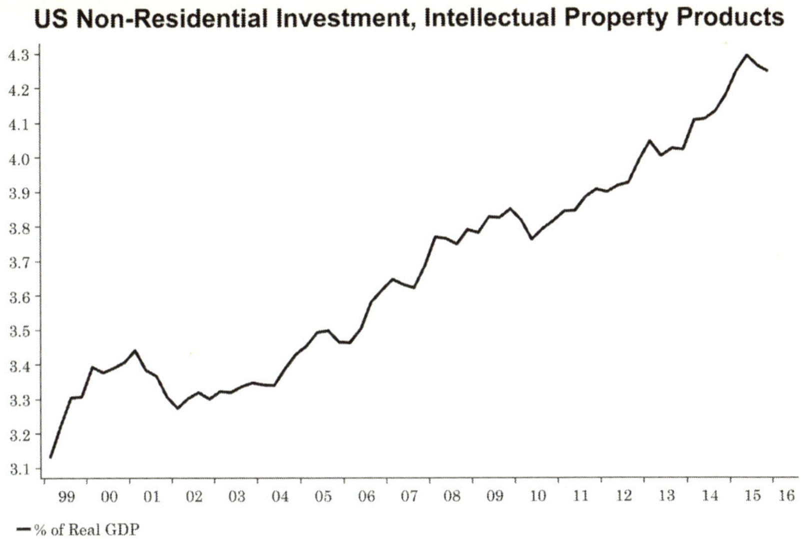

Source: GFC Economics

Chart 3l

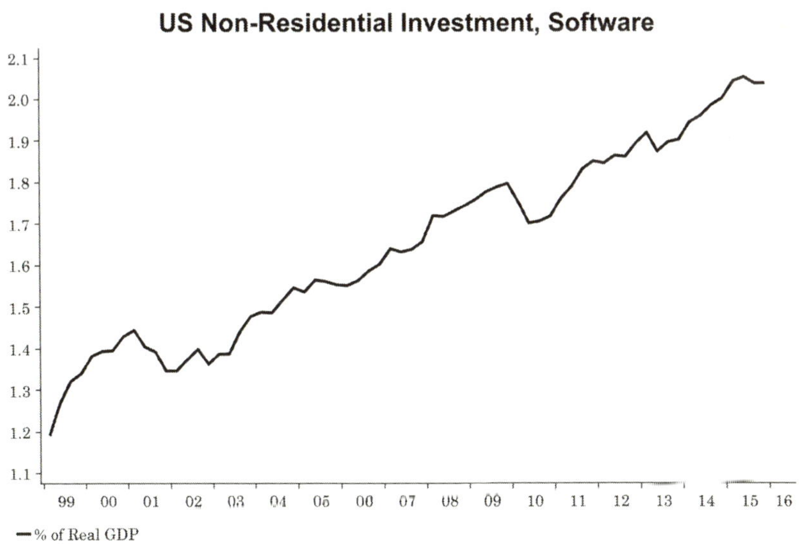

Source: GFC Economics

Chart 3m

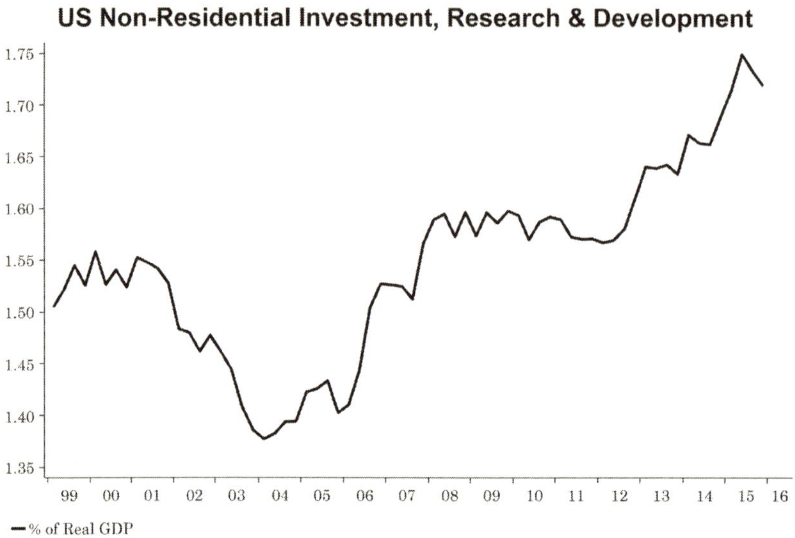

Source: GFC Economics

Chart 3n

More detailed research & development (R&D) data is available on an annual basis. Manufacturing R&D expenditures have now registered a real increase of 14.9% between 2007 and 2014.[90] Real non-manufacturing investment has risen 19.9% over this seven-year period.[91] Within manufacturing R&D, semiconductor & other electronic component manufacturing climbed 54.9%.[92]

Real equipment investment has risen from 6.25% of real GDP in Q2 2014 (revised to 6.37%) to 6.47% in Q4 2015 (see chart 3o). This is marginally below the all-time high of 6.55% recorded in Q3 2014.[93]

90 Source: BEA, Real Private Fixed Investment in Intellectual Property Products, Research & Development, Business, Manufacturing, Chained.

91 Source: BEA, Real Private Fixed Investment in Intellectual Property Products, Research & Development, Business, Nonmanufacturing, Chained.

92 Source: BEA, Real Private Fixed Investment in Intellectual Property Products, Research & Development, Business, Manufacturing, Semiconductor & Other Electronic Component Manufacturing, Chained.

93 Source: BEA, Expenditure Approach, Gross Private Domestic Investment, Fixed Investment, Nonresidential, Equipment, Total and Gross Domestic Product, Total, Constant Prices, Chained.

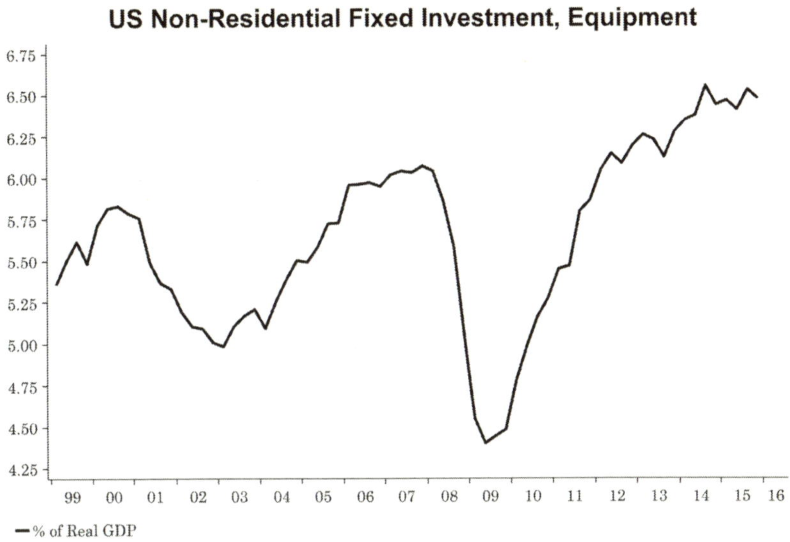

Source: GFC Economics

Chart 3o

The data can be broken down into four subcomponents.[94] Information processing equipment climbed to record high of 2.14% in Q3 2015, and was unchanged in the following quarter.[95] Investment in transportation equipment was also up strongly, rising from 1.55% to 1.76%.[96] By contrast, industrial equipment investment slipped from 1.39% to 1.37% of real GDP, reflecting the impact of the drop in oil prices and cutbacks in the energy sector.[97] Investment in 'other equipment' has also been soft (down from 1.36% to 1.25% of real GDP).[98]

---

94 Information processing equipment, industrial equipment, transportation equipment, and other equipment.

95 Source: BEA, Expenditure Approach, Gross Private Domestic Investment, Fixed Investment, Nonresidential, Equipment, Information Processing Equipment and Gross Domestic Product, Total, Constant Prices, Chained.

96 Source: BEA, Expenditure Approach, Gross Private Domestic Investment, Fixed Investment, Nonresidential, Equipment, Transportation and Gross Domestic Product, Total, Constant Prices, Chained.

97 Source: BEA. Expenditure Approach, Gross Private Domestic Investment, Fixed Investment, Nonresidential, Equipment, Industrial and Gross Domestic Product, Total, Constant Prices, Chained.

98 Source: BEA. Expenditure Approach, Gross Private Domestic Investment, Fixed

Investment in structures has recovered much more slowly since the financial crisis of 2008. Indeed, as a share of real GDP, real investment in structures dropped from 2.96% in Q2 2014 to 2.74% in Q4 2015. This compares with a cyclical high of 3.66% in Q2 2008, and a peak of 4.34% in Q3 2000.[99] Detailed data for 2014 are now available. Between 2007 and 2014, multi-merchandise shopping contracted 50.1% in real terms.[100] Real investment in offices dropped 37.4% on a comparable basis.[101] The decline intensified for religious structures (to -59.5%), but eased for lodging (-45.9%).[102]

Certain areas of investment in structures have remained strong. Real investment in transportation structures is now up 16.0% since 2007.[103] Real investment has risen 31.4% in the power sector and 37.9% in mining exploration, shafts and wells.[104]

In some cases, the decline in investment for structures is clearly structural and related to technology: the drop in spending on shopping malls, for example, is a reverse of the rise in e-commerce. The contraction in office construction again may be driven by technology, with smaller companies and changing work arrangements leading to lower demand.

Combining expenditures on intellectual property products and equipment arguably provides a better measure of 'productive investment'. In Q4 2015, these two categories combined equalled 10.72% of real GDP, up from 10.28% in Q2 2014.[105]

Investment, Nonresidential, Equipment, Other and Gross Domestic Product, Total, Constant Prices, Chained.

99 Source: BEA. Expenditure Approach, Gross Private Domestic Investment, Fixed Investment, Nonresidential, Structures, Total and Gross Domestic Product, Total, Constant Prices, Chained.

100 Source: BEA. Real Private Fixed Investment in Structures, Nonresidential, Commercial & Health Care, Multimerchandise Shopping, Chained.

101 Source: BEA. Real Private Fixed Investment in Structures, Nonresidential, Commercial & Health Care, Office, Chained.

102 Source: BEA. Real Private Fixed Investment in Structures, Nonresidential, Other Structures, Religious and Lodging, Chained.

103 Source: BEA. Real Private Fixed Investment in Structures, Nonresidential, Other Structures, Transportation, Chained.

104 Source: BEA. Real Private Fixed Investment in Structures, Nonresidential, Power & Communication, Power and Mining Exploration, Shafts & Wells, Chained.

105 Source: BEA, Real Private Fixed Investment, Nonresidential, Equipment and

Further notes

Alternative ways to analyse the official investment data

The ratio of real investment to real GDP has been used to judge the strength of capital spending in an economy. However, economists from the BEA have cautioned against using this ratio when dealing with real 'chain-type' data.[106] Specifically, they warn that the components of real GDP will not sum to the whole. Furthermore, the comparison becomes less reliable further away from the 'base' year. From this perspective, it is argued that nominal shares, or real contributions to growth, are more reliable when it comes to assessing the underlying trend for investment.

In truth, there are issues with all three methods. Nominal figures ignore the role of deflators (or prices). High-tech investment goods have consistently experienced relative price declines. This is true even with the upward bias to the technology deflators, as discussed in the original article. Nominal shares understate the importance of real investment in driving the economy. If nominal investment is low, firms may be criticised for not spending enough on investment. Nevertheless, if firms can purchase the same quantity of capital equipment for a lower price, they can devote surplus resources to other uses, without impinging on real investment.

In nominal terms, non-residential private fixed investment as a share of GDP remains well below the previous two cyclical highs. It peaked at 14.63% during the dotcom boom (Q3 2000), 13.51% during the housing bubble (Q1 2008), but was only 12.94% in Q3 2014 (the peak of the current cycle). It has since fallen back to 12.71% in Q4 2015.[107]

Intellectual Property Products, Chained, and Gross Domestic Product, Total, Constant Prices, Chained.

106 See *A Guide to the Use of Chain Aggregated NIPA Data*, Karl Whelan, Federal Reserve Board, June 2000.

107 Source: BEA, Private Fixed Investment, Nonresidential and Gross Domestic Product, Total, Current Prices.

Source: GFC Economics

Chart 3p

However, nominal investment in intellectual property products hit an all-time high of 4.07% of nominal GDP in Q1 2015, and again in Q2 that year, surpassing the previous peak of 4.01% in Q1 2001.[108] This measure fell to 4.04% in Q4 2015. Productive investment (intellectual property products & equipment) climbed to 10.10% in Q3 2015, before slipping back to 10.02% in Q4 (see chart 3p). The former was the highest since Q4 2001. By comparison, the mean since records began (Q1 1947) stands at 8.53%.[109] Even in nominal terms, it is difficult to support the view that investment has stagnated in the post-crisis period. On the contrary, productive investment has been rising strongly.

108 Source: BEA, Private Fixed Investment, Nonresidential, Intellectual Property Products and Gross Domestic Product, Total, Current Prices.

109 Source: BEA, Private Fixed Investment, Nonresidential, Equipment and Private Fixed Investment, Nonresidential, Intellectual Property Products and Gross Domestic Product, Total, Current Prices.

More on hedonics

Variation in prices may be attributed to either differences in quality or 'pure' price changes. The difficulty lies in accurately capturing quality change. Technology has improved the processing speed, storage capacity and screen resolution of modern computers. For a given nominal price, these quality improvements will lower the 'true' cost. Hedonic methods seek to *control* for these different characteristics by relating variation in prices to differences in goods' attributes. The remainder can then be attributed to a 'pure' price change.[110]

Under certain conditions, matched-model indices yield similar price measures to hedonic methods.[111] More specifically, the dataset must be "a panel of *prices* on models whose characteristics are constant over time – to allow the matching of most observations in the data – and that the observations be high frequency – to minimize the numerical influence of observations that cannot be matched (i.e., turnover observations)."[112] In some cases, matched-model methods are unsuitable: housing is one such area, due to the "unique" characteristics of houses.[113]

Table 3 shows the extent of hedonic adjustment in the Consumer Price Index (CPI), as of November 2014.[114]

Many of the price indices used by the Bureau of Economic Analysis (BEA) in constructing the national accounts data are derived from the CPI. In 2008, 19.5% of GDP was hedonically adjusted (the latest estimate from the BEA).[115] Since then, the BEA's classification scheme

---

110 For an in-depth treatment, see *A Practical Guide to Price Index and Hedonic Techniques*, Ana M. Aizcorbe, Oxford University Press, 2014.

111 Chain-type price indices are an example of matched model price indices.

112 See *When Do Matched-Model and Hedonic Techniques Yield Similar Price Measures?*, Ana Aizcorbe, Carol Corrado, & Mark Doms, Federal Reserve Bank of San Francisco Working Paper, June 16th 2003, p. 2.

113 See *A Practical Guide to Price Index and Hedonic Techniques*, Ana M. Aizcorbe, Oxford Univesity, 2014, p. 44.

114 See *Hedonic Quality Adjustment in the CPI*, http://www.bls.gov/cpi/cpihqaitem.htm.

115 See *Appendix A: Components of GDP that are deflated with hedonic-type price indexes*, Bureau of Economic Analysis (BEA), http://www.bea.gov/national/pdf/hedonic_09.pdf.

has changed for several consumer products. It is therefore difficult to calculate the exact proportion for the most recent annual data (2014).[116] However, table 4 provides a good approximation of hedonically-adjusted components in the GDP report.

Hedonic Price Adjustments in the Consumer Price Index

Item	Relative Importance December 2013
Men's Suits, Sport Coats and Outerwear	0.113
Men's Shirts and Sweaters	0.207
Men's Pants and Shorts	0.160
Boys' Apparel	0.188
Women's Outerwear	0.114
Women's Dresses	0.154
Women's Suits and Separates	0.604
Girls' Apparel	0.204
Men's Footwear	0.216
Boys' and Girls' Footwear	0.169
Women's Footwear	0.326
Educational Books and Supplies	0.195
Major Appliances	0.159
Televisions	0.161
Other Video Equipment	0.030
Rent of Primary Residence	6.977
Owners' Equivalent Rent of Primary Residence	22.505
Total	32.482

Table 3

116 GFC Economics contacted the BEA for an updated version table with hedonically-adjusted GDP components. The response was as follows: "Since this table was last produced, our classification scheme for several consumer products has changed and some of the specific line items aren't published anymore. Some categories have been grouped into other categories and not reported separately, and so on, and we are unable to release unpublished data."

Hedonic Price Adjustments in the National Income and Product Accounts

GDP
Computers and peripheral equipment
PES
Exports
Imports
Software
Private
Government
Structures
Private residential
Private nonresidential
State and local government
Telecom
PES (communications equipment)
Photocopiers
PES
Audio and video
PCE
Apparel
Household appliances
Rent PCE

Table 4

The use of hedonic methods has become more widespread over time.[117] However, measurement issues are far from resolved. The problem may be particularly acute in prices for high-tech goods and services. Matched-model indices may not suitably capture quality improvements in products

117 See *The role of hedonic methods in measuring real GDP in the United States*, Dave Wasshausen & Brett R. Moulton, Bureau of Economic Analysis, October 2006.

that are changing rapidly. Furthermore, such price indices may struggle to capture quality in *new* goods or services. The proliferation of new goods & services has been well-documented in the press, facilitated by technological innovation. Conventional price indices may not be able to match the goods: hedonic methods would be more appropriate. However, hedonic methods can be time consuming and expensive, which could limit their implementation. This is an important point in light of recent cuts to US Government statistical departments.[118]

Software

The mismeasurement of quality may extend to software as well, an area where little research has been conducted. Software can be broken down into three subcomponents: own-account, custom and pre-packaged.[119] Real investment in pre-packaged software has risen 175.8% from 1999 to 2014.[120] Custom and own-account were up 77.6% and 80.7% over the same period, respectively (see chart 3q).[121]

The deflator for pre-packaged software is based on the producer price index for application software publishing. This is adjusted for quality change based on studies comparing both hedonic and matched-model indices. By contrast, own-account and custom software are deflated using a weighted average of the pre-packaged software price and an input-cost index.

---

118 See *Economists say cuts could cloud US jobs data*, Financial Times, November 18th 2015.

119 Prepackaged software is sold or licensed in standardised form. Custom software is developed specifically for a business or enterprise. Own-account software consists of expenditures that are used directly for developing software "in-house" for the business or government's own use. For more details, see *Recognition of Business and Government Expenditures for Software as Investment: Methodology and Quantitative Impacts, 1959-98*, Bureau of Economic Analysis, May 5th 2000.

120 Source: BEA, Real Private Fixed Investment in Intellectual Property Products, Software, Prepackaged, Chained.

121 Source: BEA, Real Private Fixed Investment in Intellectual Property Products, Software, Custom and Own Account, Chained.

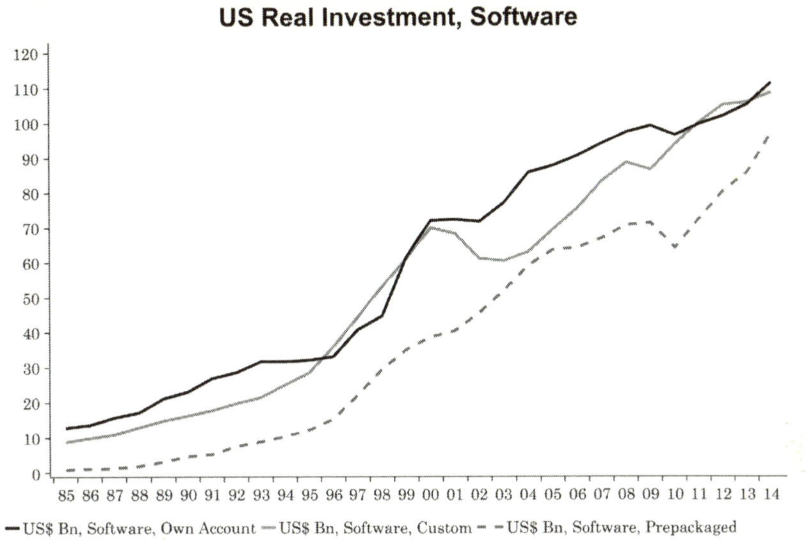

Source: GFC Economics

Chart 3q

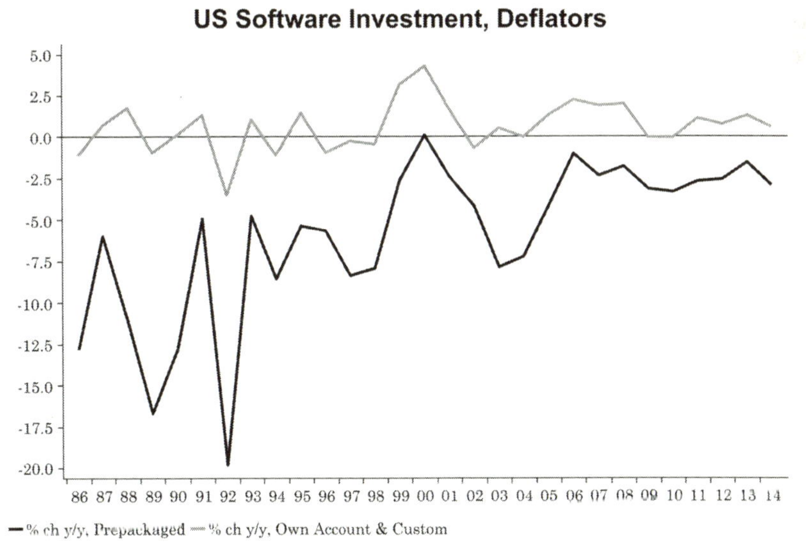

Source: GFC Economics

Chart 3r

The pre-packaged software deflator has shown greater price declines than the deflator for own-account and custom software. Between 1985 and 2014, the average annual fall for the former was 6.00%, whilst the latter averaged +0.63% y/y during this period (see chart 3r).[122] A weighted average of the two may therefore understate the extent of the drop in prices.

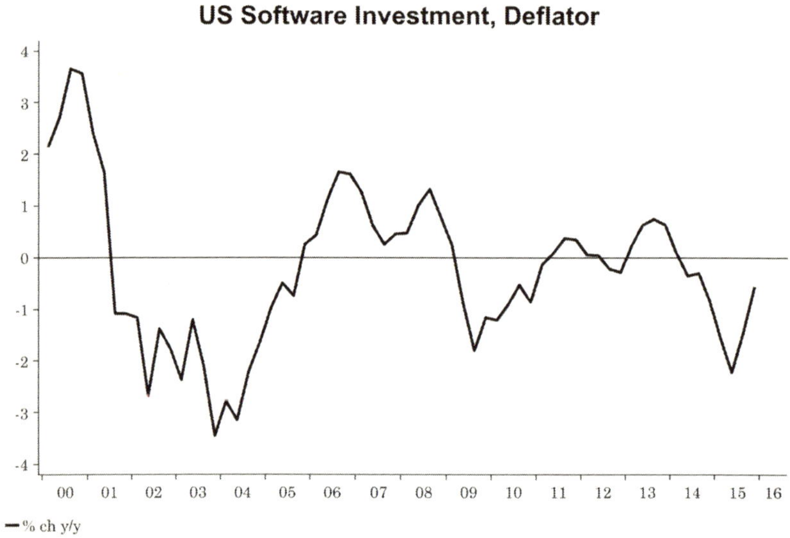

Source: GFC Economics

Chart 3s

The deflator for overall software fell 0.56% y/y in Q4 2015 (see chart 3s).[123] Properly adjusting for quality improvements may reveal that the true rate of deflation has been much quicker. Indeed, anecdotal evidence would suggest that the pace of innovation is accelerating.[124]

122 Source: BEA, Real Private Fixed Investment in Intellectual Property Products, Software, Prepackaged and Own Account, Chained. Note: the deflators for custom software and own-account software are the same.

123 Source: BEA, Price Indexes for Private Fixed Investment, Nonresidential, Intellectual Property Products, Software, Index.

124 See chapter 8 for examples of recent technological advances with a wide range of applications.

Chapter 4
Underestimating technology deflation and productivity
(first published June 1st 2015)

More thoughts on productivity

The slowdown in productivity has turned into a "problem of global proportions", it would appear. According to the Conference Board, "Something is going wrong with the way firms are equipping their workforces to produce more".[1] An alternative and more optimistic perspective needs to be considered. Technology deflation in the US could be underestimated: real GDP could be higher as a result. This article revisits some of these arguments in detail, closely scrutinising two important pieces of research co-authored by David Byrne.[2] The first of these papers highlights the rise in imports, which has created a sizeable upward bias to the deflators. The second paper focusses on the potential mismeasurement of price declines in semiconductors. Instead of suggesting that productivity growth has slowed, statisticians and economists need to consider the possibility that a significant proportion of the economic data is failing to fully capture technological innovation.

Revisiting the old, pessimistic argument

In June 2014, the San Francisco Federal Reserve published a working paper, claiming that the slowdown in productivity growth witnessed

1 See *Weak productivity turns into a problem of global proportions*, Financial Times, May 25th 2015.

2 See *The recent slowdown in high-tech equipment price declines and some implications for business investment and labor productivity*, David N. Byrne & Eugenio Pinto, FEDS Notes, March 26th 2015 and *How Fast are Semiconductor Prices Falling?*, David N. Byrne, Stephen D. Oliner and Daniel E. Sichel, AEI Economic Policy Working Paper Series, March 2015.

in recent years cannot be traced to the recent *Great Recession per se.*[3] Productivity growth was stalling even before the financial crisis of 2008 (see chart 4a). Furthermore, there is little evidence to suggest that recessions damage productivity over the long-run: *The Great Depression* was, the paper noted, an "extraordinarily innovative period".[4] There was no reason to believe that productivity should slow because of the sub-prime crisis in 2008. Sectors of the economy that were euphoric during the boom, such as housing and finance, were not the source of this deceleration in productivity growth. Productivity had slowed towards its 1973-1995 pace before the "exceptional, but temporary, information-technology (IT)-fueled" gains witnessed during the dotcom boom (late-1990s).[5]

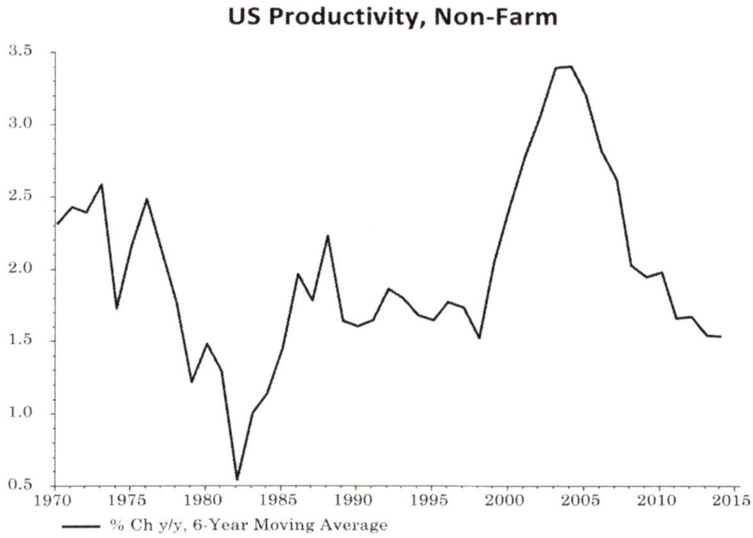

Source: GFC Economics

Chart 4a

The San Francisco Fed argued that the dip in productivity growth can be traced to a post-2000 slowdown in the pace of technological progress in semiconductors. The industry moved to a shorter product cycle in the mid-1990s. This led to "faster gains in performance and quicker prices

3 See *Productivity and Potential Output Before, During, and After the Great Recession,* John Fernald, Federal Reserve Bank of San Francisco Working Paper, June 2014.

4 Ibid., p. 10.

5 Ibid., p. 2.

declines".[6] However, the 'scaling advances' in semiconductors and the reductions in officially recorded prices have subsequently slowed.

The paper also cites the importance of "intangible organizational capital".[7] A drop in IT capital accumulation would, by implication, have reduced some of the indirect benefits of the late-1990s boom. Industry and state data show that the pre-Great Recession slowdown in productivity was concentrated in sectors that either produce or use IT intensively. As a result, the San Francisco Fed paper argues that the pace of innovation has dropped. It concludes, "Cyclically weak investment has (in turn) contributed to slow potential growth".[8]

The possibility that "the IT revolution might return after a pause" was considered.[9] Machine learning and robots could lead to faster productivity growth in the coming decades. Regardless, a slowdown in productivity growth would imply there is less economic slack, which could potentially shorten the life-span of the current recovery.

Hedonics and bias to imports and deflators

Extrapolating the recent tepid declines in prices is an important factor underpinning forecasts of a drop in high-tech innovation and a dip in potential output growth. A more recent *FEDS Note* argues that the deflators used by the Bureau of Economic Analysis (BEA) in the National Income and Product Accounts are wrong.[10] Business investment is understated in real terms. Indeed, the authors of this FEDS Note argue that real spending on high-tech equipment would have been 17% higher at the end of 2014, *if* prices had continued to fall in the last five years at the same pace as the previous five years.[11]

---

6 Ibid., p. 11.

7 Ibid.

8 Ibid., p. 4.

9 Ibid., p. 23.

10 See *The recent slowdown in high-tech equipment price declines and some implications for business investment and labor productivity*, David N. Byrne & Eugenio Pinto, FEDS Notes, March 26th 2015.

11 Ibid., p. 2.

The BEA constructs investment deflators by aggregating producer and import price indices. The deflator for computer equipment has fallen much more slowly in recent years, primarily reflecting the greater influence of the import price index. Indeed, the approach used by the BEA has a subtle albeit important shortcoming: "because the domestic production price and the import price are collected by distinct BLS [Bureau of Labour Statistics] price programs, identical items that are merely sourced differently are treated as distinct products, and the aggregation of PPIs and IPIs treats the entire discount associated with switching to a lower cost-imported computer as a reflection of inferior quality."[12] This matters because the closure of a large number of production plants in the US has led to a sharp rise in imports.[13] The substitution from domestically-produced to imported goods has resulted in an overstatement of prices. Incomplete quality control in these price deflators has compounded the flaw in this methodology. There are four areas of concern:

1) *Inadequate information on product characteristics.* "When sufficient product feature information is available, hedonic regressions of model prices on technical features of the computers can be used to apportion a price change into contributions from quality changes versus price inflation."[14] However, observations collected from importers may contain insufficient information to employ the necessary hedonic adjustment. In these cases, "BLS price analysts judgementally split the price premium for the entering product into a quality component and a pure price difference component." In some cases where "supporting evidence on characteristics is not available, BLS price analysts may tend to attribute the difference between the prices of entering and exiting items to inflation, rather than quality."[15]

---

12 Ibid., p. 5. See also *Offshoring Bias in U.S. Manufacturing*, Susan Houseman, Christopher Kurz, Paul Lengermann & Benjamin Mandel, Journal of Economic Perspectives, 25(2), Spring 2011.

13 Ibid., p. 6. "After a wave of offshoring by other companies in the wake of the 2001 downturn, Dell Inc. accounted for the lion's share of U.S. domestic PC production. The company closed plants in Austin, Texas (2008), Lebanon, Tennessee (2009), and Winston-Salem, North Carolina (2010), and shifted production from the U.S. market to Mexico and other offshore locations."

14 Ibid.

15 Ibid.

2) *Delayed introduction of new products to the indices.* New products may rapidly gain market share by offering the end-user better performance at lower prices. Any delay in the inclusion of these products into a price index could lead to an overstatement of deflators. The authors suggest that "This appears to have been a significant problem for the BLS import price index in recent years."[16] For example, tablet PCs, which penetrated the market rapidly from 2010 onwards, were not introduced into the import price index until 2012, when they had already gained a market share of 31%.[17]

3) *More detailed application of hedonics.* A number of products may require more "effort to control for quality."[18] For example, the BLS does not estimate a hedonic model for tablet PCs.[19] Products other than laptop PCs, desktop PCs and servers may also require more detailed analysis, to capture underlying improvements.

4) *Indirect control for performance in BLS hedonic models.* The hedonic models used by the BLS employ a set of variables that correspond to technical features of IT equipment, such as memory and speed of the processor. They do not focus on performance measures, which are of direct interest to the user. It has been shown that directly controlling for performance, as opposed to an input-based hedonic specification, produces significantly faster price declines for semiconductor chips.[20]

Measuring semiconductor deflation

The FEDS note discussed in the previous section built on more detailed research by one of the authors (David Byrne at the Federal Reserve) outlining potential flaws in the official prices for semiconductors and related technology goods.[21] The producer price index in the US suggests

---

16 Ibid.

17 Ibid.

18 Ibid.

19 Ibid.

20 See *How Fast are Semiconductor Prices Falling?*, David N. Byrne, Stephen D. Oliner & Daniel E. Sichel, AEI Economic Policy Working Paper Series, March 2015.

21 Ibid.

semiconductor prices have "barely been falling in recent years... in sharp contrast to the rapid declines in MPU [microprocessor unit] prices reported from the mid-1980s up to the early 2000s and the exceptionally rapid declines in the latter half of the 1990s."[22] However, the performance of MPUs has continued to advance at a rapid pace. This paper focussed on MPUs rather than a broader set of semiconductor products.[23]

Around the time of this divergence between prices and performance (i.e. second half 1990s onwards), Intel – the leading producer of MPUs – altered its pricing strategy. As a result, the matched-model methodology used by the BLS to calculate the PPI for MPUs underestimated the extent of deflation. Alternative hedonic price indexes may offer a more accurate insight into the true price declines. The authors' preferred hedonic index fell by an average of 43% y/y between 2008 and 2013.[24] By contrast, the official PPI declined at an average annual rate of 8% over this period.[25] This paper included new hedonic regressions and utilised measures of performance based on typical tasks for computer users, rather than technical variables capturing physical characteristics (such as feature size) and engineering specifications (such as clock speed).

The pace of technical advance in the semiconductor industry accelerated in the mid-1990s. The so-called technology cycle – the average time required for manufacturers to double the capacity of a semiconductor chip – was three years until 1993. It then dropped to around two years from 1993 to 2012. Those improvements were particularly fast between 1993 and 2003, and somewhat slower thereafter. Nevertheless, since 2003,

---

22 Ibid., p. 1.

23 Ibid., pp. 3-4. This is done for several reasons: "First, MPUs are a large segment of the semiconductor sector; in 2014, they represented about half of U.S. shipments (the scope of the PPI). Second, price series for MPUs extend back to the mid-1980s, allowing for comparisons of price trends over time. Given that price trends in this sector often are used to infer rates of technical progress, this historical comparability is important. Finally, we believe that developments in MPU technology likely provide a rough guide to developments in other parts of the semiconductor sector, such as the chips that are used in smartphones and tablets."

24 Ibid.

25 Source: BLS, Producer Price Index, Industry Data, Industry: Semiconductors & Related Device, 33441312, Microprocessors (Including Microcontrollers)

the average cycle has "remained substantially shorter than the three-year cycle in effect before the 1990s." Indeed, for Intel, "there has been no pullback at all from the two year-cycle."[26] The pace of miniaturisation has been sustained.

A number of important changes in the MPU architecture in recent years complicated the task of identifying the correct set of technical characteristics needed to measure performance. Clock speeds stopped rising in response to problems with heat generation. However, Intel continued to increase performance in other ways. The US company "boosted performance instead by placing multiple copies of the core architecture on each chip – a change enabled by smaller feature size – and by improving the design of these cores."[27]

It is possible to evaluate performance scores based on data from the Standard Performance Evaluation Corporation (SPEC). These scores provide information on standard tasks, reflecting the needs of computer users. The numbers are supplemented by a second performance measure (the "rate" score) that reflects more accurately the performance gains from adopting multiple cores.

The SPEC data show that performance of MPUs rose on average 32% y/y from 2000 to 2013. This compares with an average improvement of 60% y/y from 1990 to 2000 and 36% y/y over 1971 to 1990. In short, "performance continued to improve even as clock speed stalled out in the early to mid-2000s."[28]

However, Intel also substantially changed its pricing strategy in response to a changing competitive environment vis-à-vis Advanced Micro Devices (AMD) – the primary challenger in the MPU market. Prior to 2003, the listed prices for Intel's MPUs "tended to drop fairly rapidly in the year or two following its introduction, especially once a

---

26 See *How Fast are Semiconductor Prices Falling?*, David N. Byrne, Stephen D. Oliner & Daniel E. Sichel, AEI Economic Policy Working Paper Series, p. 6, March 2015.

27 Ibid., p. 7.

28 Ibid., p. 8.

new, higher performance model became available [at a similar price]."[29] By 2006, the listed price largely remained constant, even when a new high performance model became available at a similar price. Between 2002 and 2006, AMD "consistently released products whose price/performance characteristics were similar to or beat Intel's."[30] In 2006, "Intel began to turn the corner by offering new MPUs that dominated those sold by AMD."[31] With less competition from AMD, Intel enjoyed greater scope to manage its price structure.

Posted listed prices by Intel "do not represent true transaction prices because Intel offers 'age-related discounts' to selected purchasers as models age."[32] Hence, listed prices for older models might not be actual transaction prices. The matched-model index used by the BLS essentially failed to capture the true price trends under the new pricing regime.[33] When a new, higher-quality model was introduced, the price of the old model would tend to fall under the old pricing regime: the price per unit of quality would be broadly equalised across models. In this case, the differential between prices would represent an improvement in quality: the matched-model index would accurately reflect the increase in performance. Under the new pricing regime, a matched-model index would conclude that quality-adjusted prices were unchanged, because the price of the first model stayed the same.

A hedonic index would, using appropriate measures of quality or performance, correctly capture price trends.[34] Nevertheless, a 'full-

29 Ibid., p. 9.

30 Ibid., p. 10. See also *Competition and Quality Choice in the CPU Market*, Chris Nosko, The University of Chicago, May 2014.

31 Ibid.,

32 Ibid., p. 13.

33 Ibid., p. 11. "Matched-model indexes control for quality change between two periods, say period 0 and period 1, by averaging price changes for models that were in the market in both periods. The underlying idea is to measure "pure" (or quality-adjusted) price change for products whose quality did not change because they were in the market in both periods 0 and 1."

34 See *How Fast are Semiconductor Prices Falling?*, David N. Byrne, Stephen D. Oliner & Daniel E. Sichel, AEI Economic Policy Working Paper Series, p. 12, March 2015. "Hedonic price indexes identify 'pure' price change by explicitly controlling

sample' hedonic index based on observable posted prices could still "go astray because the posted prices are measured with error."[35] Indeed, "an unweighted full-sample hedonic index would put too much weight on price observations for which there were few transactions. In contrast, an unweighted introduction-period hedonic index likely would do a better job of capturing the trend in quality-adjusted prices."[36] If sales of the older model fell, an unweighted index full-sample would be biased "because model-level quantity data are not readily available."[37]

By contrast, an introduction-period hedonic index would accurately reflect price trends in quality-adjusted discounts. Indeed, the authors report that the full-sample hedonic index based on SPEC performance declined less rapidly than the introduction-period index in each period, with the largest difference occurring after 2008. This would be expected as a result of 'age-related discounting' and a fall or drop-off in volumes with older models.[38]

These mismeasurements pose an important question for statisticians of the BEA, extending far beyond semiconductors (see chart 4b). The issues around correct adjustments for quality apply to a large range of technology goods: "In recent years, the price index for computing equipment in the National Income and Product Accounts has fallen quite slowly by historical standards. If MPU prices have, in fact, continued to decline rapidly, why have prices for computers - which rely on MPUs for their performance - not followed suit? We believe there is a reasonable chance that the official price indexes for computers have been measured with error, reflecting in part the challenge of identifying the relevant and likely changing set of physical characteristics used to measure quality."[39] In addition, "The end-user performance measure employed in this

for quality change with measures of product characteristics or performance. The hedonic approach regresses prices on these measures, with the price change left after controlling for quality taken to be the quality-adjusted price change."

35 Ibid., p. 14.

36 Ibid., p. 15.

37 Ibid., p. 14.

38 Ibid., p. 23.

39 Ibid., p. 27.

paper could help break this knot for computer prices". The authors are "investigating this possibility in further work."[40]

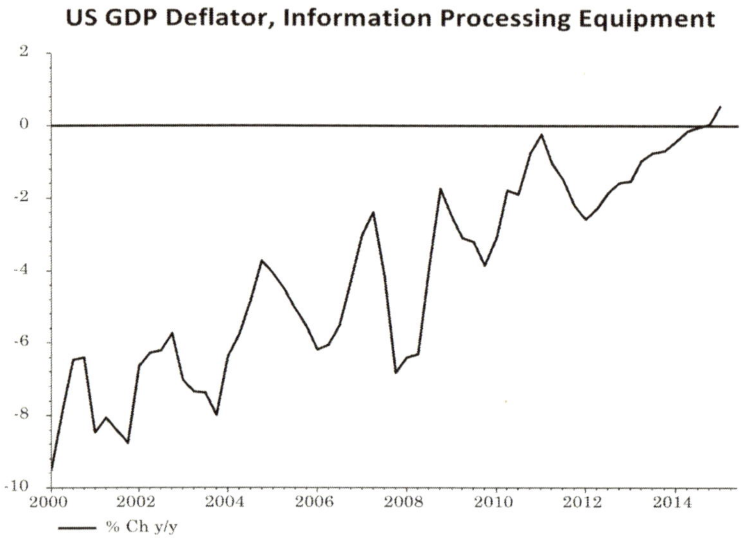

Source: GFC Economics

Chart 4b

Furthermore, there is a strong case for suggesting that the deflator bias may extend to a number of components of services consumption. Technology is playing an increasingly important role in the 'delivery' of services: if the statisticians are behind the curve in measuring deflation in more established technology goods, the deflators for services need to be examined more closely too.[41]

40 Ibid.

41 See chapter 6.

Underestimating technology deflation *update*

An ongoing research series at the Federal Reserve has attempted to assess whether the deflators are accurate. This has been headed by David Byrne, Principal Economist at the Federal Reserve.[42] This research utilises both hedonic and 'matched-model' techniques. In some cases, hedonics are not required: it has been shown that 'matched-model' methods and hedonics yield similar estimates of price indices under certain circumstances. For matched models, the data have to be sufficiently "granular" (very detailed, collected at high frequencies).[43] Innovations in technology have facilitated the collection and storage of ever more detailed data. This has improved the prospect of capturing quality change with matched-models. The following section presents three additional examples of technology deflation mismeasurement, based on up-to-date research.

Communications equipment prices[44]

Recent work by David Byrne and Carol Corrado has looked into mismeasurement in communications equipment prices. While communication technology has advanced at a rapid pace, this has not been fully reflected in the official statistics (see chart 4c).[45] The authors construct price indices for 12 types of communication equipment by collecting data from high-tech consultancies. Overall, their aggregate deflator for domestic production falls 9.8% per year since 1985, nearly 10 percentage points faster than the official US producer price index

---

42 Co-authors include Eugenio Pinto, Caro Carrado, Stephen Oliner and Daniel Sichel.

43 See *A Practical Guide to Price Index and Hedonic Techniques*, Ana M. Aizcorbe, Oxford University Press, 2014. See also *The recent slowdown in high-tech equipment price declines and some implications for business investment and labor productivity*, David Byrne and Eugenio Pinto, FEDS Notes, March 26th 2015.

44 See *Recent Trends in Communications Equipment Prices*, David Byrne & Carol Corrado, FEDS Notes, September 29th 2015. See also *Prices for Communications Equipment: Rewriting the Record*, David Byrne and Carol Corrado, Finance and Economics Discussion Series, 2015.

45 The official investment price index is based on the BLS PPI, the IPI, BEA research, and outside sources, including a price index published by Federal Reserve.

(PPI). Furthermore, this divergence has widened in recent years: price declines have not slowed (see chart 4d). This would imply that any given amount of nominal investment had a greater contribution to the real capital stock. While output would need to be revised higher, communications equipment investment accounts for a comparatively small share of GDP. Future revisions are not expected to have a major impact on growth. Nevertheless, IT capital services have historically "made outsized contributions to labor productivity".[46] This is significant in light of the concerns regarding weak productivity growth in the US.

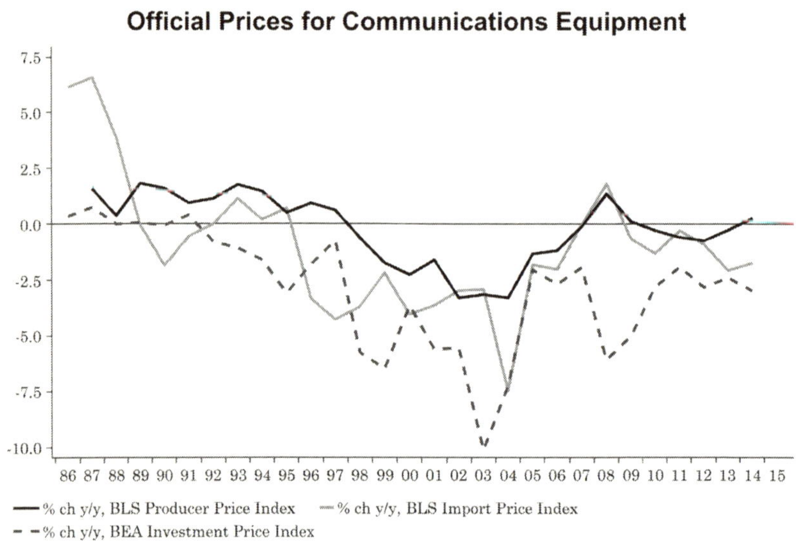

Source: *Recent Trends in Communications Equipment Prices*, David Byrne & Carol Corrado, FEDS Notes, September 29th 2015

Chart 4c

46 See *Recent Trends in Communications Equipment Prices*, David Byrne & Carol Corrado, FEDS Notes, September 29th 2015.

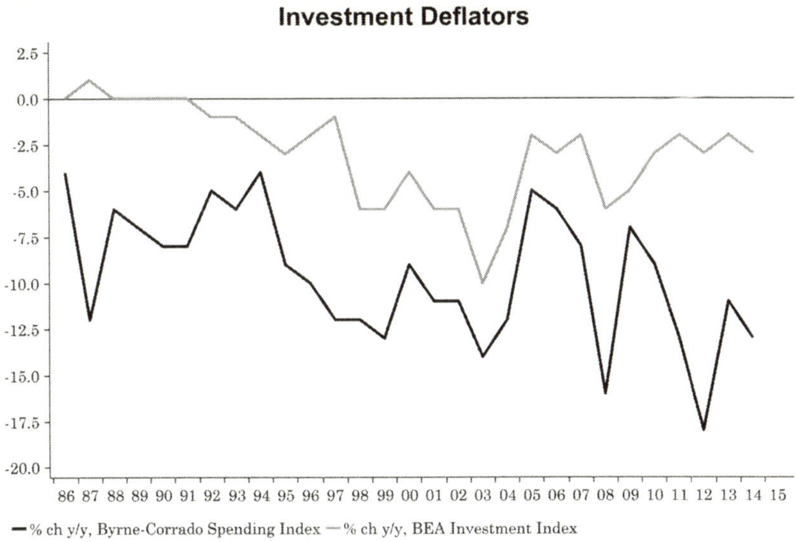

Source: *Recent Trends in Communications Equipment Prices*, David Byrne & Carol Corrado, FEDS Notes, September 29th 2015

Chart 4d

Data Storage Equipment and the State of IT Innovation[47]

Progress in data storage equipment often goes hand-in-hand with innovation in the IT sector. This general-purpose technology stores digital information for repeated use, enhancing productivity. In turn, this increases the value of the "new wave" of IT, including smartphones, tablets and cloud computing. Greater data storage capacity is integral to the new IT applications. It may also spur complementary investment in software and business organisation, supporting labour productivity. Recent "engineering advances" have been significant and "may be expected to underpin declines in quality-adjusted prices".[48]

---

47 See *Prices for Data Storage Equipment and the State of IT Innovation*, David N. Byrne, FEDS Notes, July 1st 2015.

48 Ibid., "In addition to capacity improvements, performance enhancements for storage devices have come from increases in bandwidth and decreases in latency derived from disk configuration improvements and the adoption of better specialized internal processors to manage data requests. Hardware and software schemes have

Alternative Price Indexes for Data Storage Equipment

Year	**FRB** Product Series	**FRB** Industry Series	**BLS** Product Series	**BLS** Industry Series
2002	1010.49	589.60	357.24	160.71
2003	647.48	422.60	274.08	138.74
2004	418.59	298.92	207.02	122.96
2005	288.60	226.19	157.46	114.70
2006	188.63	164.23	122.44	106.02
2007	133.86	125.34	109.18	102.21
2008	100.00	100.00	100.00	100.00
2009	69.72	75.13	88.60	89.75
2010	56.87	62.70	82.04	76.87
2011	43.74	49.99	82.35	75.89
2012	34.94	41.01	94.28	76.77
2013	27.93	33.97	87.12	71.93
2014	20.21	25.64	84.87	70.41
2002-09	-27.80%	-23.00%	-11.30%	-6.60%
2004-09	-30.10%	-24.10%	-15.60%	-6.10%
2009-14	-21.90%	-19.30%	-0.90%	-4.70%

Source: *Prices for Data Storage Equipment and the State of IT Innovation*, David N. Byrne, FEDS Notes, July 1st 2015

Table 5

To capture prices accurately, economist David Byrne argues that it is necessary to control for these valuable features, including capacity, bandwidth, latency and dependability. Mr. Byrne constructs a new matched-model price series using highly granular data from IDC, Inc. (a professional services consulting firm).[49] The new Federal Reserve index

raised dependability through redundant data records, and current storage systems are designed to allow equipment installations to ramp up to a massive scale."

49 Ibid., The matched model approach "credibly accounts for quality improvement in this case because the items are distinguished by price-relevant characteristics, high-frequency price observations are used, and the market is competitive enough that the entry of new products with lower price-performance ratios is likely to drive down the price of incumbent products".

for data storage equipment declines significantly faster than the official BLS series (see Table 5). Between 2002-2014, the Federal Reserve Board product series falls 27.8% (annually), compared with a decline of 11.3% (annually) for the corresponding BLS series.[50]

Data storage equipment investment would rise at a considerably faster rate if the Fed index was employed. Despite a relatively mild slowdown in recent years, the faster rates of price declines suggest IT equipment innovation is advancing at a rapid pace.

High-tech Domestic Manufacturing[51]

The third paper written by David Byrne underlines how much the US manufacturing sector has changed. In 1997, the US captured a significant share of global production in personal and multi-user computers, mobile phones, and data networking equipment. However, nominal output of 'general-purpose electronics' declined 60% between 1997 and 2012.[52] Furthermore, computers and communications equipment formed only

---

50 This new index possesses significant advantages over the BLS's PPI. Unlike the BLS, the Federal Reserve Board collects item weight. This allows the "index to account for a greater share of the substitution among products in response to changing relative prices." Furthermore, whilst explicit quality adjustment is undertaken by the PPI, this is only possible if the "respondents provide sufficient information to price the new features." This may not always be the case. Finally, "The data employed for the research index indicate that on average, capacity for a marketed item increases at an average annual rate of 34 percent over the life-cycle, which indicates that controlling for capacity within item series is critical. The research index addresses this issue by constructing a price per terabyte for each item, whereas the BLS methodology, as discussed above, allows for the use of explicit quality adjustment when respondents provide the marginal price charged for additional capacity. To illustrate the importance of this dimension, a price index was constructed employing price per machine, rather than price per capacity unit, which fell at an average annual rate of 5.7 percent--22 percentage points slower than when capacity was accounted for." On the other hand, the Federal Reserve index is slightly less extensive, and is related to the global market. However, these are likely to have a negligible impact.

51 See *Domestic Electronics Manufacturing: Medical, Military, and Aerospace Equipment and What We Don't Know about High-Tech Productivity*, David Byrne, FEDS Notes, June 2nd 2015.

52 Ibid.

32.5% of total electronics production in 2012, compared with 65% in 1997.[53] Manufacturing of PCs and tablets has been largely relocated to China. There has been a shift from lower-value 'general-purpose' technology to 'special-purchase equipment' (see charts 4e, 4f and 4g). The latter includes medical, military and aerospace, as well as a wide range of sophisticated equipment such as motor vehicle instruments, industrial process control, automatic environmental control, kinematic testing & inspection and geophysical & meteorological instruments. By 2012, manufacturing of special purpose electronics "accounted for two-thirds of domestic electronic equipment manufacturing." (see Table 6).[54] The intrinsic lead US companies have secured in some of these industries may have helped insulate the manufacturing sector from the strong rise in the Dollar over the past two years.

Nevertheless, price declines for special-purpose electronics have been muted. Research on quality-adjusted price indices for this category of electronics is scarce, casting doubt over the reliability of the deflators. Again, the deflators are likely to be overstated, and the innovation in special-purpose electronics not fully appreciated.

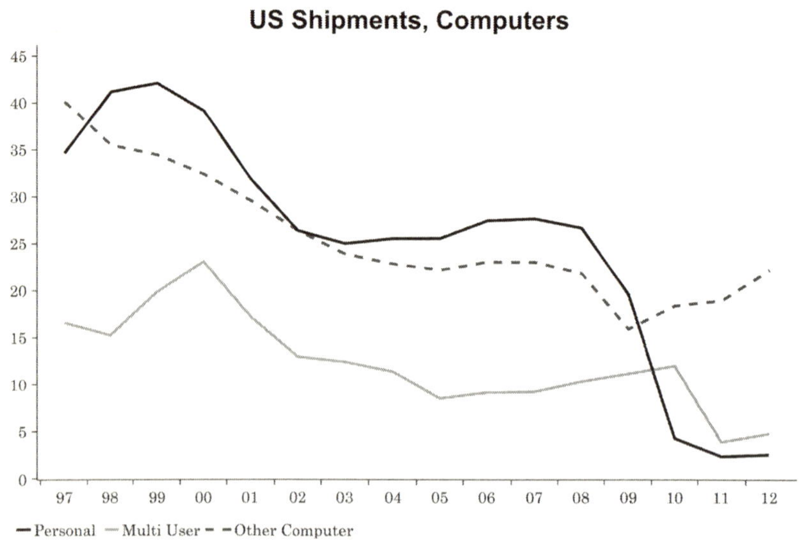

Source: *Domestic Electronics Manufacturing: Medical, Military, and Aerospace Equipment and What We Don't Know about High-Tech Productivity*, David Byrne, FEDS Notes, June 2nd 2015
Chart 4e

53 Ibid.

54 Ibid.

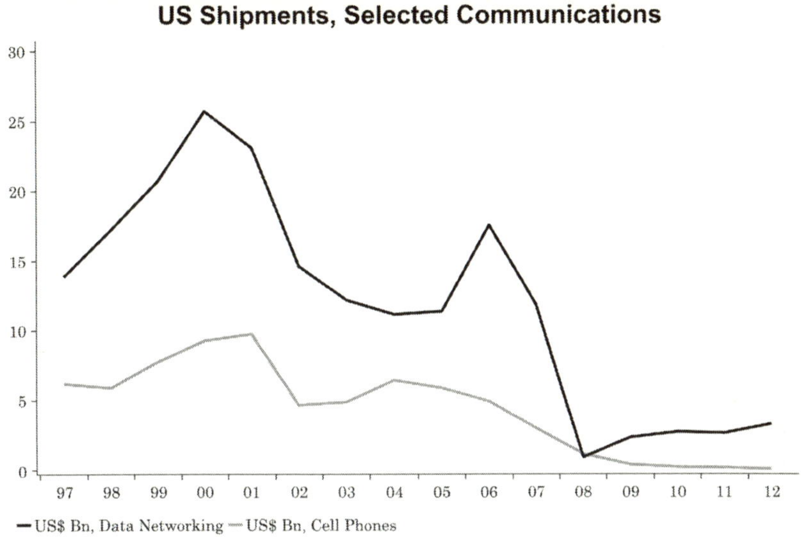

Source: *Domestic Electronics Manufacturing: Medical, Military, and Aerospace Equipment and What We Don't Know about High-Tech Productivity*, David Byrne, FEDS Notes, June 2nd 2015

Chart 4f

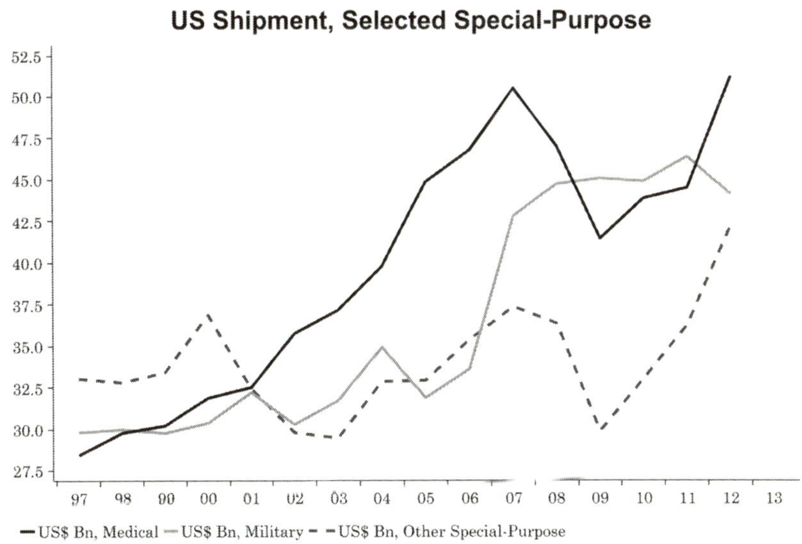

Source: *Domestic Electronics Manufacturing: Medical, Military, and Aerospace Equipment and What We Don't Know about High-Tech Productivity*, David Byrne, FEDS Notes, June 2nd 2015

Chart 4g

Output of General and Special Purpose Equipment

	Value of Production, $ Billion				1997-2012 Growth		Share of Production			
	1997	2002	2007	2012	Total	Per Year	1997	2002	2007	2012
Final Electronics	260.7	188.6	250.2	203.9	-21.80%	-1.60%				
Computing and communications	169.4	92.8	119.5	66.4	-60.80%	-6.10%	65%	49%	48%	33%
Computers and peripherals	91.3	65.7	60	29.6	-67.60%	-7.20%	54%	71%	50%	45%
Communications equipment	78.1	42	59.5	36.8	-52.90%	-4.90%	46%	45%	50%	55%
Special-purpose	91.3	95.8	130.7	137.6	50.70%	2.80%	35%	51%	52%	67%
Medical	20	26.4	44.1	48.6	143.30%	6.10%	22%	28%	34%	35%
Military & aerospace	29.8	30.3	42.8	44.1	48.10%	2.70%	33%	32%	33%	32%
Other special-purpose	41.5	39.2	43.8	44.9	8.20%	0.50%	45%	41%	34%	33%
Memo:										
Computer and Elec. Prod. Mfg. (NAICS 334)	410.4	305	372.7	319.5	-22.10%	-1.70%				
Final Electronics	260.7	188.6	250.2	203.9	-21.80%	-1.60%	64%	62%	67%	64%
Electronic Components	138.8	109	116.8	112.5	-18.90%	-1.40%	34%	36%	31%	35%
Miscellaneous	11	7.3	5.7	3.1	-71.70%	-8.10%	3%	2%	2%	1%

Source: *Domestic Electronics Manufacturing: Medical, Military, and Aerospace Equipment and What We Don't Know about High-Tech Productivity*, David Byrne, FEDS Notes, June 2nd 2015

Table 6

Trade in goods

A new World Trade Organization agreement (*Information Technology Agreement expansion*) signed in December 2015 will remove barriers to trade in high-technology goods.[55] This will include the liberalisation of "new generation multi-component integrated circuits (MCOs), touch screens, GPS navigation equipment, portable interactive electronic education devices, video game consoles and medical equipment, such as magnetic resonance imaging products and ultra-sonic canning apparatus."[56] As stressed above, the US is forging a competitive advantage in high-end manufacturing and new technologies. These are precisely the areas being liberalised. The US is well positioned to benefit from this trade agreement. The ITA eliminates import tariffs for 201 products, either with immediate effect or progressively over three years. The value of the goods in question is around $1.3tr annually (or approximately 7% of global trade).[57]

The economic impact will be widespread. Consumers will benefit from lower prices and access to the latest technology products. Furthermore, by driving down the cost of IT, firms will improve their competitiveness. The ITA Expansion agreement also commits to tackling non-tariff barriers in the IT sector. More broadly, "It will create jobs and help to boost GDP growth around the world. It will improve productivity and market access, and enhance predictability for traders and investors."[58]

At first glance, the benefits to the US economy may seem to be overplayed. Data from the Census Bureau show that the trade balance in advanced technology products has been on a secular decline since records began in 1992.[59]

---

55 See *WTO members conclude landmark $1.3 trillion IT trade deal*, World Trade Organization, December 16th 2015.

56 See *Briefing note: The Expansion of Trade in Information Technology Products (ITA Expansion)*, World Trade Organization, December 16th 2015.

57 Ibid.

58 See *Information Technology Agreement Press Conference*, Director-General Roberto Azevedo, December 16th 2015.

59 Source: U.S. Census Bureau, Commodities, Trade Balance, Advanced Technology Products. The trade balance for advanced technology products hit an all-time low

Source: GFC Economics

Chart 4h

However, the drop is a result of imports outpacing exports. Exports have been strong: since the trough in September 2009, the 12-month moving total for exports has risen 42.1% to $341.0bn as of January 2016 (see chart 4h).[60] Aerospace accounted for 34.5% of total advanced technology exports in January 2016, the single largest component.[61] This was followed by information & communications (28.5%) and electronics (13.2%).

of -$99.69bn in May 2012 (12-month moving total). The deficit was $91.87bn in January 2016, on a similar basis.

60 Source: U.S. Census Bureau, Commodities, Export, Advanced Technology Products.

61 Source: U.S. Census Bureau, U.S. International Trade in Goods and Services, Exhibit 16a. U.S. Trade in Advanced Technology Products by Technology Group and Selected Countries and Areas, January 2016.

Chapter 5
Measuring the US economy

(First published March 10th 2015)

Introduction

The 'economy' is a continuously evolving concept. Rapid technological change and the shift towards a services-based economy pose fundamental challenges for calculating Gross Domestic Product (GDP). The National Income and Product Accounts (NIPAs) must adapt to a changing economic environment. As Ben Bernanke once remarked, "We will be more likely to promote innovative activity if we are able to measure it more effectively and document its role in economic growth."[1]

Statisticians and economists must first define the production boundary (i.e. determine which activities qualify as economic production). Expanding the production boundary could highlight new sources of growth, which will in turn influence what the statisticians decide to measure. This is neatly summarised by Mr. Bernanke, who acknowledged that "what we decide to measure, or are able to measure, has important effects on the choices we make, since it is natural to focus on those objectives for which we can best estimate and document the effects of our decisions."[2]

The practical difficulties of accurately measuring the economy are also significant. The initial data are subject to sizeable revisions. These can occur either because of conceptual changes (in definitions, classifications, or methodology) or as a result of newly incorporated source data. Perceptions of the economy may change due to revisions that are undertaken on a frequent basis.

1 See *Promoting Research and Development: The Government's Role*, Ben S. Bernanke, May 16th 2011.

2 See *Economic Measurement*, Ben S. Bernanke, August 6th 2012.

The Bureau of Economic Analysis (BEA) has accommodated some of the technological advances of the 'information age'. However, it is likely that further methodological changes will be implemented in the future, particularly with regards to the measurement of 'intangibles' and deflators. The current recovery may look substantially different when future revisions take place.

Measuring the economy

The revision cycle

The *advance estimate* of GDP is based on monthly surveys for either two or three months of the quarter.[3] If these source data are unavailable, estimates are based on trends or judgement. By the *second* and *third estimates*, new and revised data are incorporated from monthly and quarterly surveys that become available after the advance estimate. *Annual revisions* include source data based on more extensive surveys, on annual data from other sources and on adjustments to monthly and quarterly source data. They may also reflect methodological changes.[4] These annual revisions generally apply to the previous three years. *Comprehensive revisions* are carried out at five-year intervals and result in changes to the data that extend back many years. These estimates incorporate the best available data and also provide an opportunity to change definitions, statistics and the presentation of the data.[5]

---

3 See *Gross Domestic Product and Gross Domestic Income: Revisions and Source Data*, Alyssa E. Holdren, BEA Briefing, June 2014.

4 Methodological changes refer to the plethora of statistical, classification and definition revisions.

5 See *Gross Domestic Product and Gross Domestic Income: Revisions and Source Data*, Alyssa E. Holdren, BEA Briefing, June 2014. "Comprehensive revision estimates often reflect the introduction of conceptual and major methodological changes and benchmarking to the BEA benchmark input-output accounts in addition to the incorporation of newly available and revised source data, such as data from Census Bureau quinquennial economic censuses."

2013 Comprehensive revision

The BEA has historically adapted to the changing economic environment by updating the way it measures GDP (see table 7).[6] In the 2013 comprehensive revision of the national accounts, the BEA recognised expenditures on research & development (R&D) and entertainment, literary & artistic originals as investments (i.e. a commitment of current resources to gain future profits).[7] Previously, these outlays had been measured as current expenses. Together with investment in software, they formed a new 'Intellectual Property Products' category. This was a positive step. A dynamic economy that embraces technological advances must measure the effects of innovation and intangible investment on economic growth and productivity. Investment in intangibles is an increasingly important component of the economy that can positively affect the long-term growth path.

Private fixed investment in Intellectual Property Products has been particularly strong. As a share of GDP, it hit a new high of 4.15% in Q4 2014.[8] This impressive trend supports the view that investment in 'productive' areas of the economy has been driving the recovery.[9] Looking at the components of Intellectual Property Products, R&D and software investment have also hit a record as a share of GDP, reaching 1.71% and 1.95%, respectively.[10]

---

6 A major classification revision also occurred in 1999 when the BEA began treating business and government expenditures for computer software as investment in order to better capture the effects of new technology. See Table 7 for a timeline of key BEA updates intended for better measurement of 'The Knowledge Economy'.

7 This was in line with recommendations by the System of National Accounts, an internationally recognised framework for measuring the economy.

8 Source: Bureau of Economic Analysis (BEA), Real Private Fixed Investment, Non-residential, Intellectual Property Products and Real GDP.

9 See *The U.S. Economic Recovery*, Graham Turner, GFC Economics, 2QT Publishing, 2014.

10 Source: BEA, Real Private Fixed Investment, Non-residential, Intellectual Property Products, R&D, Software and Real GDP.

Key Updates to GDP

Year	Description
2013	R&D and Entertainment, literary & artistic originals are recognised as investments. These are included in a new 'Intellectual Property Products' category, along with software investment
2005	Improved price index for custom software
2003	Hedonic price index for photocopying equipment
1999	Software expenditures recognised as investment
1996	Introduced new quality-adjusted price indices for semiconductors for chain-type measure of real GDP
1985	In conjunction with IBM, BEA developed more accurate, quality-adjusted computer price indices for computers and peripheral equipment

Source: BEA

Table 7

As a mere accounting exercise, classifying R&D expenditures as investment raised the level of non-residential investment and thus GDP. The historical trend growth rates of GDP and productivity did not alter dramatically. Nevertheless, comprehensive revisions highlight the changing composition of economic activity. Chart 5a shows that the investment-to-GDP ratio looks significantly different if one compares the time series of advance estimates with the view from today.[11] These revised data provide a better insight into the potential for productivity growth in the future.

11 See Bureau of Economic Analysis & Real-Time Data Set, Federal Reserve Bank of Philadelphia.

Source: GFC Economics

Chart 5a

This has ramifications for policy. As economist Athanasios Orphanides notes, the positive output gap during the period of the *Great Inflation* was grossly mismeasured, as is evident when comparing real-time data with the final revised data.[12] This was attributable to the productivity slowdown of the late-1960s and early-1970s, which was not reflected in the national accounts at the time. Specifically, the positive (i.e. inflationary) output gap was wider than estimated. The obverse may be true today. With the recent rise in productive investment, the actual negative (i.e. disinflationary or deflationary) output gap may be larger than current estimates suggest. Nevertheless, this gap might also be closing at a faster rate. The increase of productive investment is generating robust jobs growth in the US labour market, with strong payrolls set to continue in 2015.[13]

---

12 See *The quest for prosperity without inflation*, Athanasios Orphanides, Journal of Monetary Economics, 50, 2003.

13 See *US: What if another 3 million payrolls are added in 2015 and 2016?*, GFC Economics Commentary, March 2nd 2015.

Intangible investment

The 2013 comprehensive revision reflected a broader discussion as to whether investment in intangibles should be included in the NIPAs. Investment is the commitment of current resources to increase future consumption (at the expense of current consumption). Any outlay satisfying this definition should, in theory, be treated as capital investment. From this perspective, investment in intangible capital ought to be capitalised in the national accounts.

Table 8 groups intangible investment into three broad categories: computerised information, innovative property and economic competencies.[14] There are some significant omissions from the national accounts, notably the 'economic competencies' category. This attempts to capture spending on branding and organisation that will contribute to future profits and productivity.[15] The argument for expanding the asset boundary of the NIPAs is compelling, yet remains subject to a lingering criticism: there may be political pressure on statistical authorities to broaden the scope of GDP to provide an 'artificial' boost to the economy. It must also be recognised that this process will never be wholly objective. There are many value judgements involved, stemming from the heterogeneous, complex nature of an advanced economy.

---

14 See *Measuring Capital and Technology: An Expanded Framework*, Carol Corrado, Charles Hulten, and Daniel Sichel, National Bureau of Economic Research, August 2005.

15 See *Brands As Productive Assets: Concepts, Measurement, and Global Trends*, Carol A. Corrado and Janet X. Hao, World Intellectual Property Organization, Economic Research Working Paper No. 13, November 2013. There is some debate as to whether or not some economic competencies, such as marketing and advertising, should be capitalised. Whilst they may yield future benefits for a particular firm, the 'zero-sum' argument claims that at an economy-wide level the net impact is negligible: rather than stimulating overall demand, it leads to substitution between products that are close substitutes. The level of aggregate consumption would remain unchanged. Corrado and Hao discuss four rebuttals to this view. Their most compelling argument is that intangible investment has the capacity to create whole new industries, "each of which, alone and in conjunction with patent protection and business secrecy, convey market power and a degree of protection for the innovator (at least for a time)." In this sense, advertising becomes persuasive, rather than merely informative, altering consumer preferences.

The national accounts are also constrained by data availability. As Nobel Laureate Richard Stone noted in his memorial lecture, the current method "whereby commercial products are valued at market price, government services are valued at cost and unpaid household activities are simply ignored, [is] not a matter of principle but of practical convenience."[16]

Intangible Investment

Name of group	**Type of knowledge capital**	**Specific asset type**	**Included in the NIPAs? (Yes or No)**
Computerised information	Knowledge embedded in computer programmes and computerised databases	1. Software	Y
		2. Databases	Y
Innovative property	Knowledge acquired through scientific R&D and non-scientific inventive and creative activities	3. Mineral exploration	Y
		4. R&D	Y
		5. Entertainment and artistic originals	Y
		6. New product/systems in financial services	N
		7. Design and new product systems	N
Economic competencies	Knowledge embedded in firm-specific human and structural resources, including brand names	8. Brand equity (eg. advertising and market research)	N
		9. Firm specific resources (eg. organisation and employer-provided training)	N

Source: Adapted from *Measuring Capital and Technology: An Expanded Framework*, Carol Corrado, Charles Hulten, and Daniel Sichel, NBER, August 2005.

Table 8

16 See *The Accounts of Society*, Richard Stone, Nobel Memorial Lecture, December 8th 1984. Richard Stone received the Sveriges Riksbank prize in Economic Sciences in Memory of Alfred Nobel in 1984 for "having made fundamental contributions to the development of systems of national accounts and hence greatly improved the basis for empirical economic analysis."

Knowledge creation, R&D, marketing, management, and organisational efficiency are strategic investments that contribute to the long-run growth and success of an enterprise. It is imperative that these components are accurately measured, to ensure the optimal incentive structures are in place to encourage investment in such areas.

The BEA plans to expand and improve its measurement of intangibles.[17] Before this can be done, satellite accounts need be set up in parallel to official statistics. They will provide the opportunity to experiment with new methods and data before incorporation into official statistics.

The only ongoing satellite accounts are in Health Care and Travel & Tourism. Nevertheless, a BEA briefing in 2009 noted that the "BEA is considering an expanded satellite account that would contain experimental statistics for a broader array of intangible assets alongside our existing measures for R&D."[18] An earlier BEA paper outlined a "long-term plan" for expanding measurement of intangibles.[19] Specifically, the BEA plans to expand measurement in the economic competencies category by hoping to develop "measures of of firm-specific investment in their organizational capital, including new business models."[20]

Deflators

Capturing quality change in price indices is notoriously difficult. The issue of devising deflators for intangibles is critical.[21] Furthermore,

---

17 See *Toward Better Measurement of Innovation and Intangibles*, Ana M. Aizcorbe, Carol E. Moylan, and Carol A. Robbins, BEA Briefing, January 2009.

18 Ibid.

19 See *BEA's Role in Accounting for Growth: Measuring Advances in Technology and Knowledge*, J. Steven Landefeld and Sumiye Okubo, BEA paper presented at the American Economic Association Annual Meeting, January 3rd-6th, 2008.

20 Ibid.

21 See *The Role of Hedonic Methods in Measuring Real GDP in the United States*, Dave Wasshausen and Brent R. Moulton, BEA, 2006. Capturing quality changes in price indices can be challenging for statistical authorities. This problem is particularly pronounced in the case of rapid innovation and the introduction of new products in the market. In some cases, 'hedonic' methods have been implemented to address these concerns. In its simplest form, 'hedonics' describe

the heterogeneous nature of innovations implies that it is difficult to determine quality change using routine methods: each case is distinct and should ideally be treated individually. The economist William Nordhaus noted that "in the end quality decisions require the subjective judgement about the extent of quality change, [yet] agencies are reluctant to make subjective judgements."[22] This problem is accentuated in the face of rapid technological change and ground-breaking innovations, so-called "tectonic shifts". History suggests that price indices can fail to capture great advances in quality change. This generates upward biases in the price indices, understating the real figures. Indeed, Nordhaus claimed that "the most revolutionary breakthroughs are most often missed."[23] He considered the price of lighting, a useful example due to its relative simplicity as a technology and because it has also undergone rapid technological change over the years. Using historical data, he found that official statistics *severely* overestimated the price of lighting. Between 1800 and 1992, "the conventional price of light [had] risen by a factor of about 1000 relative to the true price".[24]

To determine real expenditure, statisticians must decompose growth in nominal spending into price and quantity. Methods used to calculate price indices for R&D investment, semiconductor prices, software and healthcare services highlight some of the obstacles faced in generating reliable real GDP data.

Research & Development

In the NIPAs, the nominal value of economic activity is predominantly measured according to market prices. However, much of the investment

the use of regression techniques to decompose the price of a product into its economically meaningful characteristics. For example, the price of a computer can be explained by its processing power, memory, and other features. Once product characteristics are 'controlled' for, the coefficient on a time dummy variable (measuring the change in price attributable to time, taking into account product characteristics) can be used to infer the price change.

22 See *Quality Change in Price Indexes*, William D. Nordhaus, Journal of Economic Perspectives, 12(1), Winter 1998.

23 Ibid.

24 Ibid.

in intangibles is 'own-account' (i.e. not purchased, but undertaken by the company itself): a market price does not exist. In such instances, 'own-account' R&D is derived as the sum of production costs.[25] For own-account R&D, "the annual business R&D price index is a weighted average of the cost components of the scientific R&D services industry (60 percent) and an 'all private industries' aggregate (40 percent)."[26] A similar technique is used for calculating quarterly R&D estimates, with the difference that input costs are confined to wage costs.[27] That said, the figures estimated from production costs do not include a profit mark-up that would otherwise be present in the market. To account for this, a profit mark-up is calculated "based on the net operating surplus of the miscellaneous professional, scientific, and technical services industry" and added to the input costs.[28]

The input cost approach fails to account for changes in productivity. If R&D productivity rises, the price index should be adjusted downward: more could be produced for a given level of input. The obverse holds if productivity falls. This method requires that measures of capital and labour productivity are observed, but this is often not the case. Instead, the Bureau of Labor Statistics (BLS) multifactor productivity measure (private nonfarm business sector multifactor productivity) is used as an estimate of unobserved R&D productivity to deflate own-account R&D.[29] In periods of slow, officially recorded productivity growth (what we see today), the deflators may be too high and real R&D investment too low. Although the official accounts show that R&D investment is at an all-time high as a share of GDP, it may still be underestimated.

---

25 See *Measuring R&D in the National Economic Accounting System*, Marissa J. Crawford, Jennifer Lee, John E. Jankowski, and Francisco A. Moris, *Survey of Current Business*, November 2014.

26 Ibid.

27 Ibid., "The business R&D price index for the current quarterly estimate is derived as the growth rate in a three quarter moving average of a composite average wage index based on data from the BLS CES in which average wages of the scientific R&D services industry receives a 60 percent weight, and the average wages of all private industries receives a 40 percent weight."

28 Ibid.

29 Ibid.

Healthcare

Healthcare spending is increasing as a share of GDP.[30] Nevertheless, healthcare is a particularly difficult component of personal consumption expenditures to measure in real terms. For this reason, the BEA recently introduced a new Health Care Satellite Account (HCSA) to experiment with methodological changes and to evaluate potential sources of new data.

One of the key aims of the HCSA is to move from a services-based framework to a disease-based accounting framework.[31] At a fundamental level, this is intended to improve the healthcare deflator by measuring the price of the service (being treated), rather than the price of inputs (for example, visiting your doctor). It is widely acknowledged that "the extent to which a particular health care expenditure is beneficial depends on the conditions being treated."[32] Early indications show that healthcare prices based on the treatment of diseases rose faster than the BEA officially estimated, which would have led to "slower measured growth in real GDP by about 0.1 percentage point per year."[33] However, it is difficult to reconcile this with the advances in technology and improved healthcare in the developed world.

Medical advances are moving hand-in-hand with technology.[34] The use of robotics is proliferating. Nanorobots can be injected into the patient, targeting specific cells or tissues. Robot-assisted keyhole surgery allows

---

30 Source: BEA, Real Personal Consumption Expenditures, Services, Health Care and Real GDP. In Q2 2014, healthcare was 11.4% of GDP.

31 See *Introducing the New BEA Health Care Satellite Account*, Abe Dunn, Lindsey Rittmueller, and Bryn Whitmire, Survey of Current Business, January 2015. "The principal contribution of the HCSA is that it redefines the commodity provided to patients by the health sector as the treatment of disease (for example, cancer or diabetes) rather than the specific types of medical care that individuals purchase (such as visits to a doctor's office or the purchase of a drug), as is currently published."

32 See *Toward a Health Care Satellite Account*, Ana M. Aizcorbe, Bonnie A. Retus, and Shelly Smith, Survey of Current Business, May 2008.

33 See *Introducing the New BEA Health Care Satellite Account*, Abe Dunn, Lindsey Rittmueller, and Bryn Whitmire, Survey of Current Business, January 2015.

34 See, for example, the *Innovation in Health Care* Special Report series, Financial Times, 11th December 2014.

for greater precision and less trauma to the patient, reducing recovery time and post-operative pain. Three-dimensional (3-D) printing is transforming the world of prosthetics and implants. These could significantly increase productivity of treatment if prosthetics can be produced on-site, whilst also transforming the traditional supply-chain model. Products can be tailored to individual patient-specific needs. Furthermore, bio-printing could change the nature of research and clinical trials, whereby testing is done on tissue created from 3-D printing.

Some of the biggest advances in productivity could occur where healthcare becomes patient-specific. 'Genomics' – the decoding of DNA and subsequent use in healthcare – is a case in point. While the initial breakthrough in 2000 has taken time to yield practical benefits, there have been significant developments in more recent years. Instruments that can read DNA have improved productive capacity and the increase in computing power now allows analysis of much more data. Whereas "The original Human Genome Project took several years and cost more than $1bn … today's machines can sequence a human genome accurately within a day at a cost not far off $1,000."[35]

As patients move to the centre of the decision-making process, traditional models of healthcare may become redundant. Smartphones can allow individuals access to swathes of their own data which, together with help to interpret the information, will guide patients through taking greater control over their own health. In some sense this mirrors the flexible, on-demand economy that technology is generating in other sectors.

This is a small glimpse of the potential impact of technology on healthcare. Given these developments, the price deflators may not be correctly capturing the quality of treatment. Unfortunately, there exists no clear consensus on how this is best achieved, and so price indices are constructed under the assumption of constant-quality. Clearly, this is unrealistic and leaves scope for substantial revisions to the data moving forward.[36]

---

35 See *Advances in decoding aid diagnosis and treatment,* Innovation in Healthcare, Financial Times Special Report, December 11th 2013.

36 This is regarded as in important next step in accurately measuring health care spending. See, for example, *Introducing the New BEA Health Care Satellite Account,*

Software

Constant-quality price indices for information technology are also difficult to measure. As economist Boragan Aruoba notes, consumer durables (particularly related to IT expenditures) have been subject to substantial revisions.[37] Relatively little research has been conducted on software deflators.[38] Copeland (2013) constructed a measure of constant-quality price change for pre-packaged software.[39] He used new industry-wide scanner data, considered superior to BEA data.[40] Copeland also attempted to correct for seasonality issues.[41] According to this study, pre-packaged software prices declined at an annual rate of 15.9% between 1997 and 2004. By contrast, official figures from the BLS estimated an average annual price decrease of 7.7% over the same period.[42] This suggests that personal consumption expenditures on software are not fully captured in the NIPAs. Similar issues may also apply to investment in software.

Abe Dunn, Lindsey Rittmueller, and Bryn Whitmire, Survey of Current Business, January 2015.

37 See *Data Revisions Are Not Well Behaved*, S. Boragan Aruoba, Journal of Money, Credit and Banking, 40(2/3), March-April, 2008.

38 Software can be sub-divided into three categories: pre-packaged, custom and own-account software. "Software is pre-packaged when it is sold or licensed in standardized form and is delivered in packages or as electronic files downloaded from the Internet." See *Seasonality, consumer heterogeneity and price indexes: the case of prepackaged software*, Adam Copeland, Journal of Productivity Analysis, 39(1), February 2013.

39 See *Seasonality, consumer heterogeneity and price indexes: the case of prepackaged software*, Adam Copeland, Journal of Productivity Analysis, 39(1), February 2013.

40 Scanner data are electronic records of transactions that are collected by establishments. For example, bar code scanning accumulates as data for retail stores.

41 Pre-packaged software expenditure is boosted annually in December due to the holiday season. If this seasonality is not captured in price indexes, it can potentially distort the price index in a way that is not reflective of truc movement.

42 This is based on the CPI, computer software and accessories, U.S. city average.

GDP Revisions

Source data

There is a trade-off between timeliness and accuracy of data. Releasing data 'early' allows policymakers to react quickly to developments in the economy. However, more timely data tends to be less accurate. Many different sources are used in preparing the national accounts.[43] *Comprehensive data* provide the most extensive coverage of the population; these numbers can be incorporated into the NIPAs with only minor adjustments. *Adjusted comprehensive data* are also very broad, but require further "substantial adjustments" to conform to national accounts guidelines.[44]

Indicator data are used to infer the movement of a series, rather than the level. For example, less detailed quarterly source data may be used to extrapolate the numbers forward when more comprehensive annual source data are unavailable. *Direct indicator data* are directly related to the numbers in question (for example the Quarterly Services Survey (QSS) is a direct indicator for the Service Annual Survey (SAS)). On the other hand, *indirect indicator data* make use of data that could be considered reasonable proxies. For example, a relevant wage series could be used to infer own-account investment (own-account investment is typically measured on a cost-basis, of which employee compensation forms a significant part). Finally, *trend-based data* are the least reliable and are used when no current data are available. These are based on previous estimates: a trend is observed and then extrapolated. Typically this will involve the use of moving averages and regressions to estimate the data.

---

43 See *Gross Domestic Product and Gross Domestic Income: Revisions and Source Data*, Alyssa E. Holdren, BEA Briefing, June 2014.

44 Ibid., Some tax or regulatory data are "are adjusted to correct for misreporting, differences in coverage, and differences in accounting concepts. For example, data from the Internal Revenue Service (IRS) tabulations of corporate tax returns are incorporated into the second and third annual revision estimates of corporate profits". However, these data must be "substantially adjusted, so that they conform to national accounts concepts."

Shares of Source Data for Successive Estimates of GDP (%)

GDP	Advance	Second	Third	First annual	Second annual	Third annual	Comprehensive revision
Comprehensive data	25.5	36.8	38.5	73.5	84.3	87.6	96.7
Adjusted comprehensive data	0	0	0	0.5	0.9	0.9	0.9
Direct indicator data	12.2	9.7	27.8	15.3	9	9	0
Indirect indicator data	34.4	33.1	21.5	4	2.7	2.5	2.3
Trend-based data	27.9	20.3	12.2	6.7	3	0	0

Source: *Gross Domestic Product and Gross Domestic Income: Revisions and Source Data*, Alyssa E. Holdren, BEA Briefing, June 2014.

Table 9

Revisions are driven by the incorporation of more complete or revised source data. In many instances, the most comprehensive source data are unavailable at the time current estimates are published. It is, therefore, necessary to use less complete figures. In other cases 'judgemental' trends are used. Table 9 highlights how more comprehensive data are incorporated into the NIPAs over successive revisions.

Historical GDP revisions

In 2008, Boragan Aruoba published a statistical analysis of US GDP and its key components.[45] He argued that revisions should satisfy certain

45 See *Data Revisions Are Not Well Behaved*, S. Boragan Aruoba, Journal of Money, Credit and Banking, 40(2/3), pp. 319-340, March-April, 2008. The data used in this study come from the Federal Reserve Bank of Philadelphia's Real Time Database, available at: http://www.philadelphiafed.org/research-and-data/real-

desirable statistical properties that would indicate they are 'well-behaved'. The 'final' revisions should: 1) have mean zero, 2) exhibit small variance compared to the variance of the final value, and 3) be unpredictable at time of initial announcement.[46] Over a 35-year sample period, Aruoba found "strong evidence *against* [author's italics] the three properties outlined above." In particular, the unconditional mean of revisions were positive for most variables; many were also statistically significant (see Table 10).[47] Initial announcements by statistical agencies are biased estimates of final values.

There is significant evidence against the mean-zero hypothesis.[48] Between Q3 1965 and Q4 2002, real output growth was revised up between 17 and 26 basis points (b.p.). This is economically significant given that real output growth has averaged 2.9% over this period.

---

time-center/real-time-data/. This dataset contains successive revisions to GDP and its key components that were originally published by the BEA.

46 Ibid. More formally, revisions can be defined using the following identity: $y_t^f = y_t^{t+1} + r_t^f$, where *f* denotes final value, *t* is the date of the variable in question, and *t+1* denotes the time of the initial announcement. The three desirable properties are: 1) $E[r_t^f] = 0$, 2) $var(r_t^f)$ is small, and 3) $E[r_t^f | I_{t+1}] = 0$.

47 Ibid. These variables are nominal and real output, inflation (output deflator), labour productivity, real final sales, non-farm payroll employment, industrial production (total industry and manufacturing), civilian unemployment rate and capacity utilisation (total industry and manufacturing).

48 Ibid. The revision is defined as $r_t^h = y_t^{(t+1)+h} - y_t^{t+1}$, which measures the revision *h* periods after the initial announcement at y_t^{t+1}. y_t refers to the growth rate of that variable (either quarterly or annual). All quarterly growth variables are annualised. A judgment needs to be made about the final revision. Technically, the final revision may never be observed; for example, historic data are revised with each successive comprehensive revision. It may then seem reasonable to take the latest value for that vintage as the 'final' measurement. However, revisions analysis is concerned with the revision of data due to the incorporation of new information. Indeed, some comprehensive revisions incorporate more complete source data (for example, the Economic Census is used as a benchmark and is conducted every 5 years). However, it would be implausible to argue that revisions made today incorporate new information about, say, the 1970s. Definitional and classification changes certainly change the outlook of the economy. Nonetheless, there is nothing the statistical agencies could have done about this at the time. The authors argue, albeit somewhat arbitrarily, for including "as many revisions as possible in our final revision in order to include all relevant revisions" whilst avoiding "including too many benchmark revisions." In this particular study, the final revision was recorded approximately three years after the initial announcement.

Revisions to Real GDP and its Components

Variable	**Sample size (period)**	**Mean revision (percentage points)**	
		Annual	**Quarterly**
Nominal output	150 (Q31965-Q42002)	**0.31**	**0.47**
Real output	150 (Q31965-Q42002)	0.17	**0.26**
Inflation (output deflator)	150 (Q31965-Q42002)	**0.12**	**0.2**
Labour productivity	134 (Q31968-Q42001)	**0.34**	0.31
Consumption	137 (Q41965-Q42000)	0.14	0.15
Durables consumption	137 (Q41965-Q42000)	**0.5**	0.55
Non-durables consumption	137 (Q41965-Q42000)	0.15	0.27
Services consumption	137 (Q41965-Q42000)	0.04	-0.05
Business fixed investment	137 (Q41965-Q42000)	**-0.66**	0.03
Residential investment	137 (Q41965-Q42000)	0.55	0.54
Government purchases	137 (Q41965-Q42000)	0.08	-0.11
Exports	137 (Q41965-Q42000)	**1.33**	**2.19**
Imports	137 (Q41965-Q42000)	0.14	0.82

Source: *Data Revisions Are Not Well Behaved*, S. Boragan Aruoba, Journal of Money, Credit and Banking, 40(2/3), pp. 319-340, March-April, 2008. Statistically significant figures are in bold.

Table 10

Aruoba also decomposed real output revisions into key components. Statistically significant variables included durables consumption, exports and non-residential private fixed investment. He highlighted the importance of durables consumption: "This result is quite significant given the debate concerning measurement of consumer electronics and similar goods whose quality changes quite remarkably in short amounts of time. Our results are at least suggestive that the revisions to components of output that are arguably harder to measure contribute to the results we find in this paper regarding revisions to output."[49] Furthermore, the above analysis was repeated for two subsamples, and the desirable properties outlined above were rejected on a stronger basis in the latter

49 See *Data Revisions Are Not Well Behaved*, S. Boragan Aruoba, Journal of Money, Credit and Banking, 40(2/3), pp. 319-340, March-April, 2008.

sample. The author concluded that "This finding is consistent with the view that technological progress makes collecting data harder due to the difficulty in adjusting the quality of goods in the economy."[50]

The BEA has also analysed revisions to GDP. From 1993-2012, real GDP growth was revised down on average by 6 b.p.[51] The same authors released a similar paper for the period 1983-2009: in contrast, real GDP growth was revised up 21 b.p. on average.[52] Interestingly, the greatest variability in revisions occurred in durable goods. Whilst the most recent paper is somewhat contradictory to Mr. Aruoba's initial findings, caution must be emphasised. These BEA studies use smaller sample sizes. Furthermore, the BEA takes the most recent estimate of a vintage as its 'latest' value. By contrast, Mr. Aruoba defines the latest estimate approximately three years after the initial estimate. Nonetheless, it is not implausible for the properties of revisions to vary across time.

Short-term revisions

The more recent figures show that investment, rather than personal consumption expenditures (PCE), has been subject to substantial upward revisions (see table 11).[53] Chart 5b shows that in the run-up to the crisis, real non-residential investment was consistently underestimated.[54] After a period of downward revisions, it is now being revised up again on a regular basis.

---

50 Ibid.

51 See *The Revisions to GDP, GDI, and Their Major* Components, Dennis J. Fixler, Ryan Greenway-McGrevy, and Bruce T. Grimm, Survey of Current Business, August 2014. The mean revisions for components of real and current-dollar GDP are small, with mixed signs. Nominal Gross Private Domestic Investment was revised up by 59 b.p, but the real measure was revised down by 66 b.p. Durable goods and structures exhibited the greatest variability.

52 See *The Revisions to GDP, GDI, and Their Major Components*, Dennis J. Fixler, Ryan Greenway-McGrevy, and Bruce T. Grimm, Survey of Current Business, July 2011. Breaking this down further, real PCE rose 20 b.p. on average, whilst investment fell 85 b.p. Again, durable goods (PCE) and structures (investment) exhibited the greatest variability as measured by standard deviation or mean absolute revision.

53 Revisions are defined differently here. Rather than taking the revision with respect to the growth rate of a variable, we are taking it with respect to the level.

54 However, as a share of GDP, non-residential investment was being revised down. In other words, GDP was being revised up at a far greater rate.

Revisions to Real GDP and its Components since Q2 2013

	GDP	PCE	Non-res. Fixed Inv.	Productive Investment (Equipment and IPP**)	IPP**	Equipment
Q4 2014*	-0.11%	-0.01%	0.71%	0.76%	0.86%	0.68%
Q3 2014	0.34%	0.35%	0.80%	0.96%	1.09%	0.87%
Q2 2014	0.15%	0.02%	0.99%	0.78%	0.48%	0.98%
Q1 2014	-0.72%	-0.62%	1.96%	2.21%	0.20%	3.56%
Q4 2013	-0.31%	-0.20%	1.48%	1.82%	-0.38%	3.29%
Q3 2013	-0.06%	-0.18%	0.71%	1.74%	0.39%	2.65%
Q2 2013	-0.27%	-0.29%	-0.21%	-0.23%	-1.07%	0.33%

Source: BEA. * Latest estimate for Q4 2014 is the second estimate.
** Intellectual Property Products

Table 11

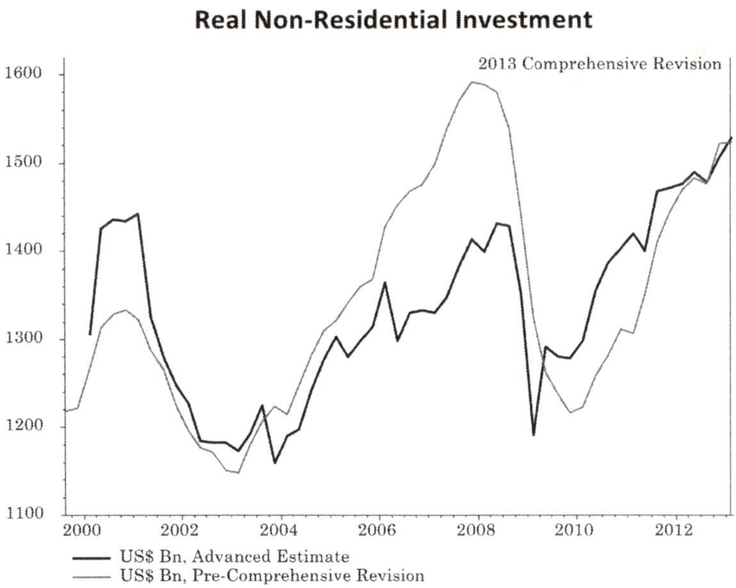

Source: GFC Economics

Chart 5b

Delving further into the nature of the revision process can illuminate potential sources of bias. Indirect indicator data are used extensively in calculating initial estimates of Intellectual Property Products. Annual estimates of investment in R&D are derived from the Business Research and Development and Innovation Survey (BRDIS), conducted by the National Science Foundation (NSF). Quarterly estimates are based on less reliable and detailed source data.[55] For the advance estimate, indirect indicator data are used: investment in R&D is extrapolated using the growth rate of seasonally-adjusted aggregate wages for all private industries (Current Employment Statistics data or CES). Software R&D (included in the 'software' component of Intellectual Property Products) is calculated in a similar fashion. For the second and third vintages, direct indicator data are incorporated. More specifically, the "BEA constructs an indicator based on reported R&D expenses from a matched sample of publicly traded companies' quarterly financial statements."[56]

Software can be classified as either purchased (pre-packaged or customised) or own-account. The advance and second estimates for investment in purchased software are based on receipts from company reports. These are far less reliable and comprehensive than the revenue data from the Quarterly Services Survey (QSS), which forms the basis of the third estimate.[57]

The quarterly estimates for investment in own-account software are slightly more involved, but are essentially an extrapolation based on BLS's CES data.[58] Annual estimates are then calculated as the sum

---

55 See *Measuring R&D in the National Economic Accounting System*, Marissa J. Crawford, Jennifer Lee, John E. Jankowski, and Francisco A. Moris, Survey of Current Business, November 2014.

56 Ibid.

57 BEA Handbook, Principal Source Data, Chapter 3. "Quarterly Services Survey (QSS) is a Census Bureau sample survey that was initiated in 2003–2004 in order to improve the coverage of the service industries in the U.S. economy. The coverage of the QSS has since been expanded several times so that it now covers most of the categories of health care, transportation services, recreation services, communication services, and professional and other services. The QSS data are primarily used in estimating PCE and private investment in intellectual property products. The QSS data are released about 2½ months after the close of the reference quarter."

58 See Private Fixed Investment in NIPA Handbook, technical note. "The estimates of expenditures for own-account software for the current quarters are prepared by extrapolation, using an index of employment in four industries for which computer-

of production costs. For own-account software, this is predominantly employee compensation as well as the costs of some intermediate inputs. A seemingly arbitrary assumption is then made regarding what types of workers are engaged in the software investment process, and what portion of their time is allocated to the development of own-account software.[59]

For services (part of the PCE category), judgmental trends are used in many instances for the advance and second estimates. This is often done by extrapolating using previous trends from QSS data. The QSS data are less timely, and are generally released together with the third estimate of GDP.

Exports have historically been subject to substantial revisions. This is partly because significant judgement is used to estimate data for the third month of the given quarter's advance estimate. Specifically, the BEA's projections for the third month are based on various estimation methods, including averages, regressions, and trend analysis, as well as on available data at the time of the estimate, such as volume data on petroleum products from the U.S. Department of Energy.

Are the data capturing small business activity?

Small businesses are vital to the US economy (see table 12). These firms tend to have higher growth rates and are an important pillar in driving technological innovation and productivity gains. Nevertheless, their size can make them more difficult to measure. Many non-employers and self-employed workers are excluded from official statistics. A significant number of small businesses may also be underrepresented in

---

related occupations account for a relatively high portion of total employment. The index is derived using BLS current employment data for computer systems design and related services; software publishers; data processing, hosting, and related services; and computer and peripheral equipment manufacturing."

59 Ibid., "The estimates of wages for all years are derived by multiplying the number of programmers and systems analysts in selected industries times the wage rate in those industries. Wages are reduced by half under the assumption that these programmers and analysts spend only about half their time working on the development of new or enhanced own-account software."

surveys. A proliferation of smaller enterprises may signal a shift in the traditional workplace landscape that could have significant implications for productivity.

Indeed, work at the beginning of the 20th century was organised differently from today. The economy abounded with agricultural workers and independent workers. The movement out of agriculture and into urban, large-scale production led to a decline in the self-employed and smaller businesses. Workers became more productive in larger groups. They also sought the security of unionised work that larger corporations offered.

Small Business by Firm, Establishment, Employment and Payroll Size (% of total)

Enterprise Employment Size	Number of Firms	Number of establishments	Employment	Annual Payroll
0-4	61.9%	47.8%	5.1%	4.4%
5-9	17.3%	13.5%	5.6%	4.1%
10-19	10.4%	8.5%	6.9%	5.4%
<20	89.6%	69.8%	17.6%	13.9%
20-99	8.6%	9.2%	16.7%	14.5%
100-499	1.5%	4.8%	14.0%	13.5%
<500	99.7%	83.9%	48.4%	41.9%
500+	0.3%	16.1%	51.6%	58.1%

Source: Adapted from Statistics of U.S. Businesses, Census Bureau, 2012.

Table 12

Technology has the ability to influence and change traditional working arrangements. A shift back to small business dominance may be underway. Larger corporations can no longer grant the unionised benefits they once did. Their comparative advantage, which they derived from their ability to profit from 'economies of scale', is in some cases being eroded by technology. Working independently is no longer associated with less interconnectedness or isolation. The opposite may be true. Smartphones and social media have brought people and independent workers together. Technology could have a similar impact at the firm level.[60]

Nevertheless, official data from the Business Employment Dynamics (BED) point towards a decline in small business dynamism. Job creation and destruction in the smallest firms (1-4 employees) has trended down since the *Great Recession* (see chart 5c).[61] By contrast, total job gains and job losses have been growing in larger businesses. Given the importance of small businesses in the US, it is imperative to ask whether their contribution is being captured adequately: these enterprises have historically been the most dynamic and entrepreneurial.

Source: GFC Economics

Chart 5c

The BED data are derived from Unemployment Insurance administrative records for 7.5 million private sector employers. Although the data supposedly cover "98% of all employment", they exclude establishments

60 However, it may also work the other way. Technology may be conducive to monopoly arrangements that threaten competition. See, for example, *Everybody wants to rule the world,* The Economist, November 29th 2014.

61 Source: BLS, Business Employment Dynamics (BDM), 1 to 4 Employees, Employment, Gross Job Gains + Gross Job Losses, Total Private, Level.

with "zero employment".[62] For Q1 2014, this was estimated to be around 1.3 million establishments. This is in addition to the "self-employed" that are excluded from the Quarterly Census of Employment and Wages (QCEW). These figures could be underestimating the business dynamics at the bottom end of the scale. This has happened before: the BLS payroll survey substantially understated job creation in small business in the past.[63] The BLS had to adjust its birth/death model accordingly to factor in the lag between the establishment of an enterprise, and its inclusion in the sample universe.

Gaps in the Economic Census

The US Benchmark Input-Output (I-O) accounts provide detailed statistics on industry activity. These are prepared at five-year intervals to incorporate the latest Economic Census, conducted by the Census Bureau. It is mandatory and provides the most comprehensive source data available, covering all types of businesses, locations and industries. Certain components of GDP, such as personal consumption expenditures and private equipment and software expenditures, are benchmarked to these I-O accounts. However, under-coverage can occur here too.[64]

The most economically significant firms are prioritised. In the Census, "all large- and medium-size firms and all multi-establishment firms [are] sent report forms to be completed for each of their establishments and returned to the Census Bureau."[65] This is not the case for smaller firms, which are sampled. For the smallest firms and non-employers, administrative data from records of other federal agencies are used. With all surveys and near-censuses, a certain degree of sampling and non-sampling error is inevitable.

Under-coverage can also occur for establishments belonging to multi-unit companies. This is because "The Census Bureau does not create

---

62 See *Gauging Employment: Is the Professional Wisdom Wrong?* George L. Perry, Brookings Papers on Economic Activity, 2:2005.

63 Ibid.

64 See Economic Census, sample design and selection: http://www.census.gov/econ/census/help/sector/sources_of_the_data.html

65 Ibid.

a multi-unit company structure in the Business Register for very small employers (less than 10 employees) identified in the Economic Census."[66] The Business Register is the most comprehensive database for US businesses and establishments that is used by the Economic Census.

These preliminary findings are suggestive of a deeper underlying tendency for "federal statistical agencies [to focus] greater attention on larger, more mature business units."[67] Inevitably, "the desire for a cost-effective approach to measuring the level of economic activity leads naturally to a focus on larger, more mature units."[68]

To be quite clear, the statistical authorities attempt to ensure that small businesses are accurately captured in the data. Nonetheless, non-sampling error can occur in many official reports due to under-coverage. For example, in the Quarterly Services Survey, the sample is updated on a quarterly basis to capture firm 'births' and 'deaths'. That said, there is a lag between the moment a business is established and its incorporation into the QSS/ASS sample.[69] It can take on average around nine months for new firms to be added to the sample. Given that the sample is updated on a quarterly basis, nine months should be seen as a lower-bound. This is typical of many surveys and official reports. Furthermore, the sample is restricted to employer companies. Similar issues arise in the more comprehensive Service Annual Survey, which is used in the annual GDP revisions.

The Business R&D and Innovation Survey

The Business R&D and Innovation Survey (BRDIS) collects data on R&D expenditures. This is used to calculate R&D investment in the

---

66 See Economic Census, Business Register, https://www.census.gov/econ/overview/mu0600.html

67 See *Measuring the Dynamics of Young and Small Business: Integrating the Employer and Nonemployer Universes*, Steven J. Davis, John Haltiwanger, Ronald S. Jarmin, C. J. Krizan, Javier Miranda, Alfred Nucci, and Kristin Sandusky, NBER, 2009.

68 Ibid.

69 This is due to the time it takes for the firm to acquire an Employer Identification Number and then undergo the subsequent 'two-phase birth-selection' procedure.

NIPAs. Only firms with five or more employees are eligible, which excludes around 62% of companies in the US (estimated as of 2012).[70] This indicates that a significant proportion of R&D investment may be going unmeasured. Whilst it may be reasonable to assume that the bulk of R&D will be undertaken by firms with five or more employees, small businesses and start-ups are driving the innovation economy. Ground-breaking scientific discoveries may be confined to large corporations and academic institutions, but innovation (defined as the application of invention) can – and does – take place on a far smaller scale. Portable device applications ('apps') epitomise this trend toward smaller innovators.

An outdated NAICS classification system

The changing nature of work also brings with it new difficulties associated with grouping and classifying various industries. The North American Industrial Classification System (NAICS) is currently being used by the statisticians. It was recently updated in 2012. Nevertheless, it can be difficult to account for the types of jobs being created as a result of technology permeating the workplace. Subsequent classification of new enterprises can be challenging. For example, the line between software and hardware is blurred and has become less clear with advances in technology. Despite this, NAICS only allows for single-industry classification: classifications are mutually exclusive. This rigid classification method may soon become anachronistic.

Companies can now transcend seemingly unrelated industries.[71] Google is teaming up with Bosch, Continental and Delphi (the car industry's global suppliers) to develop driverless cars. Traditional car manufacturers are being bypassed as software becomes increasingly integral to the latest vehicles. Technology groups could become car companies. This competition is having an impact on the business practices of other sectors as well. Santander recently announced that it would be offering cloud computing storage services, a direct response to the 'threat' posed

70 See *Survey FAQs*, Business R&D and Innovation Survey. Available at: http://www.nsf.gov/statistics/srvyindustry/about/brdis/faq.cfm

71 See *Software is steering auto industry*, Financial Times, February 18th 2015.

by technology groups.[72] Currently, NAICS assigns categories according to primary function. This is usually based on the activity that generates the greatest revenue. However, NAICS itself is not responsible for assigning NAICS codes – this is done by the various agencies for their own statistical purposes. Furthermore, it is unclear whether or not this classification is updated regularly to reflect the changing business practices of a company.

JOLTS: Possible underestimation?

Job openings reported by the BLS (JOLTS report) have proven an excellent lead for the state of the US labour market. Nonetheless, the measurement of job openings is imperfect.[73] According to the BLS, the JOLTS data do not report job openings for "positions to be filled by employees of temporary help agencies, employee leasing companies, outside contractors, or consultants."[74] Official data on workers employed in "non-traditional employment" or 'alternative' work arrangements are scarce. Until 2005, the BLS published a biennial report detailing the percentage of the workforce employed in 'contingent and alternative employment arrangements'. This included independent contractors, on-call workers and temporary help agency workers. As a combined share of the overall workforce, these groups rose from 9.9% in 1995 to 10.7% in 2005. Anecdotal evidence suggests this upward trend has continued. These shifts pose challenges to the statisticians. Currently, many of these workers are unlikely to be fully captured in official sources of employment data.

The move towards a more flexible, on-demand economy is resulting in more workers being hired as contractors or working as self-employed. In 2005 (the most recent data), the *official* BLS figures showed that there were 10.3m independent contractors (or 7.4% of total employment). However, a recent report indicates that the number of workers in 'alternative work arrangements' has risen strongly in absolute terms and

---

72 See *Santander to offer cloud storage services,* Financial Times, February 2nd 2015.

73 See *US: Labour market stronger than JOLTS data suggest*, GFC Economics Commentary, February 23rd 2015.

74 See *Job Openings and Labor Turnover Survey,* BLS Handbook, Chapter 18.

as a share of GDP.[75] These workers and job vacancies are *not* captured in the official JOLTS figures. There is strong reason to believe that the acceleration in job openings last year *understates* the true strength of the labour market.

Furthermore, JOLTS data is derived from the QCEW, which excludes non-employers (self-employed) from its data. The latest non-employer statistics from the US Census Bureau, derived from tax receipts, corroborate this anecdotal evidence. The most recent data (2012) indicate there were 22,735,915 non-employer establishments, with receipts of around $1.03bn. The number of these establishments has climbed 28.84% since 2002. If the number of self-employed is rising rapidly, then the strength of the labour market may be under-recorded in the JOLTS report.

75 See *Freelancing in America: A national survey of the new workforce*, commissioned by Freelancers Union and Elance-oDesk, 2014.

Measuring the US Economy *update*

Charting further revisions to the data

Since the publication of *Measuring the US economy*, there have been notable revisions to the data. The following charts show how investment and its subcomponents have evolved since Q2 2013 (as a share of GDP) (see charts 5d, 5e and 5f).[76] Initial estimates have significantly understated the role of 'productive' investment in driving the recovery.

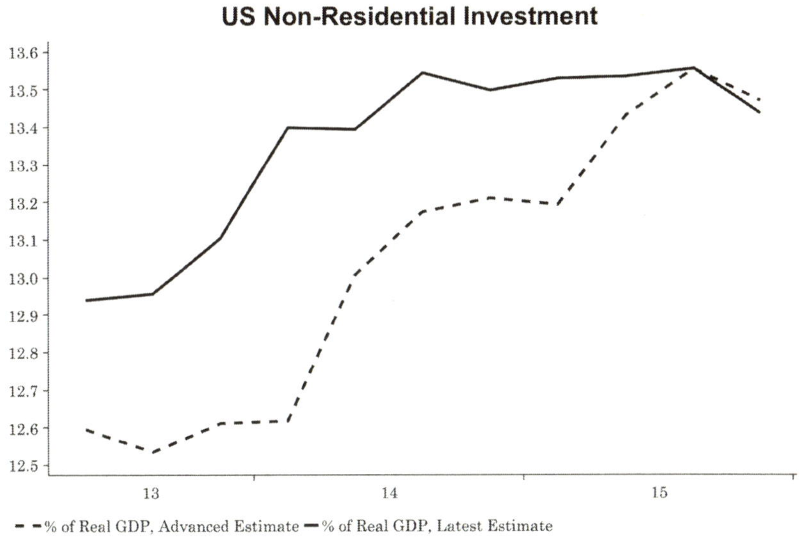

Source: GFC Economics

Chart 5d

76 Source: BEA, Expenditure Approach, Gross Private Domestic Investment, Fixed Investment, Nonresidential, Intellectual Property and Equipment, Constant Prices, Chained.

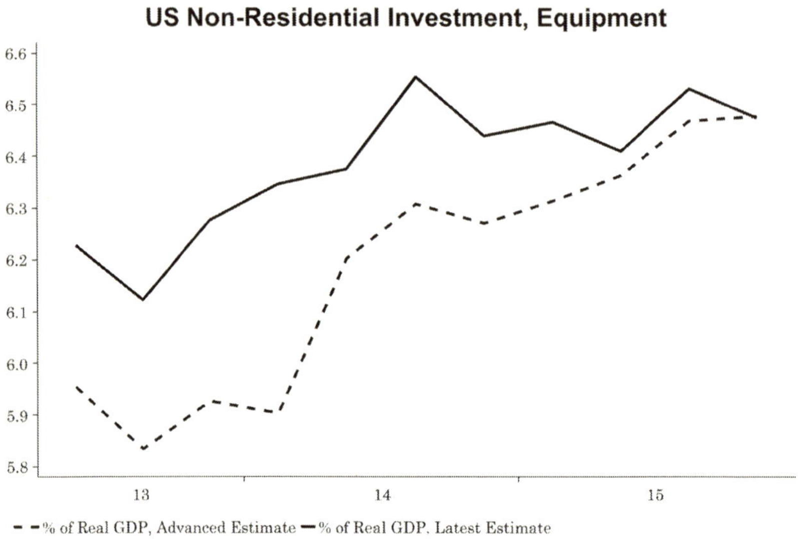

Source: GFC Economics

Chart 5e

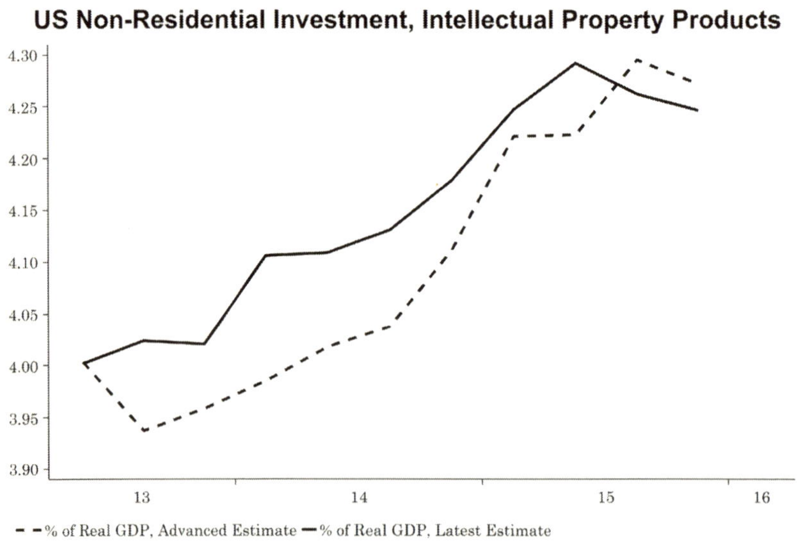

Source: GFC Economics

Chart 5f

Further notes

A more detailed breakdown of intangible capital

Intangible capital is an integral part of modern economies. The Bureau of Labor Statistics provides detailed intellectual property capital measures broken down by sector. This reveals some significant trends.[77] Whereas manufacturing used to dominate intangible investment, the non-manufacturing sector has now taken the lead (chart 5g).

Real gross investment in intellectual property products by manufacturers increased from $94.4bn in 1987 to $223.1bn in 2013 (+136.2%). Over this period, spending on R&D climbed from $88.7bn to $187.8bn (+111.8%), while software jumped from $5.7bn to $35.2bn (+512.6%). Within non-manufacturing, real intangible expenditures surged from $73.9bn to $365.2bn (+394.2%). The rise is even more impressive excluding artistic originals, up from $38.5bn to $287.1bn (+645.7%). Spending on software leapt from $22.0bn to $247.7bn (+1026.0%). R&D was up from $16.5bn to $39.3bn (+138.5%).

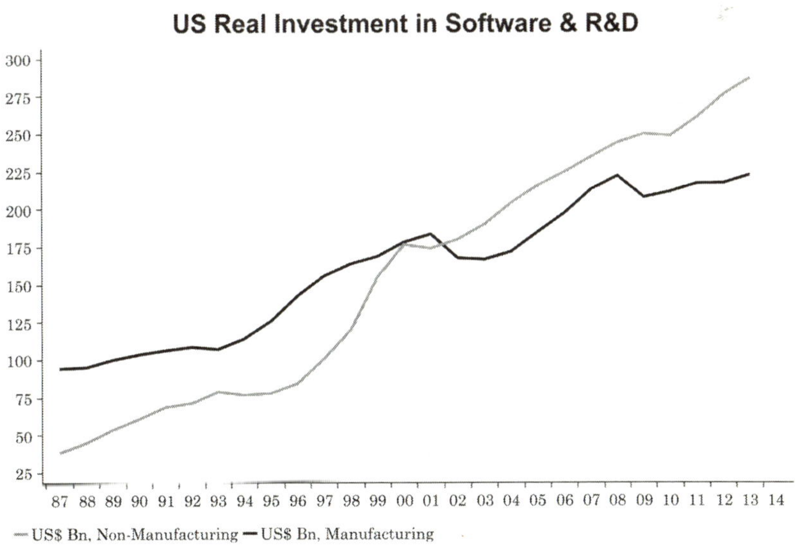

Source: GFC Economics

Chart 5g

77 Source: BLS Multifactor Productivity database, detailed intellectual property capital measures. The latest available data range from 1987 to 2013.

The data can be broken down further by industry to show how the composition of intangible spending has evolved since 1987 (see charts 5h, 5i, 5j, 5k, 5l, 5m, 5n and 5o). Within manufacturing, transportation equipment captured the largest share of intellectual property product expenditures (29%) in 1987. As of 2013, this had been surpassed by 'computer and electronic products' (33%). The top three biggest spenders ('chemical products', 'computer & electronic products' & 'transportation equipment') were the same in both periods.

Non-manufacturing IPP spending is more fragmented. In 1987, 'motion picture & sound recording' was the largest industry as measured by real spending on intangibles (20% of the total). This has since dropped to 10%. By contrast, investment in software and R&D has risen in prominence. By 2013, 'miscellaneous professional, scientific and technical services' accounted for 14% of the total, the largest individual sector.

Some other broad trends are worth mentioning. Manufacturing R&D spending has shifted towards 'computer and electronic products' and 'chemical products' over this period. In 1987, broadcasting and telecommunications comprised 41% of total non-manufacturing R&D spending. By 2013, the biggest single sector was 'miscellaneous professional, scientific & technical services'. Unsurprisingly, almost half of manufacturing software spending is now in the computer and electronic products industry. For non-manufacturing, wholesale trade has expanded its use of software greatly between 1987 and 2013.

GDI vs GDP – which is better at capturing innovation?

The Gross Domestic Product (GDP) data are more widely publicised than Gross Domestic Income (GDI), despite the conceptual equivalence of the two measures. However, a 2010 paper by Jeremy Nalewaik revealed some important statistical relationships which lent support to real GDI as a superior gauge of economic activity. In particular, GDI was shown to be a good predictor of GDP growth, but not vice versa.

Breakdown of IPP

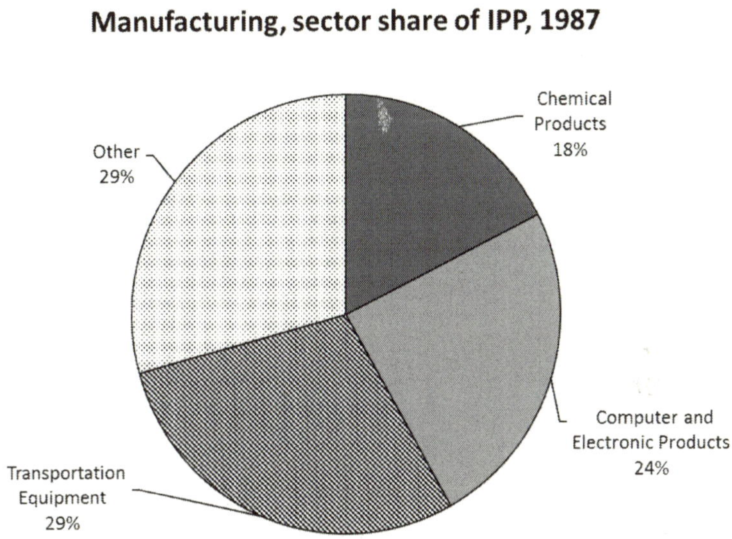

Source: GFC Economics

Chart 5h

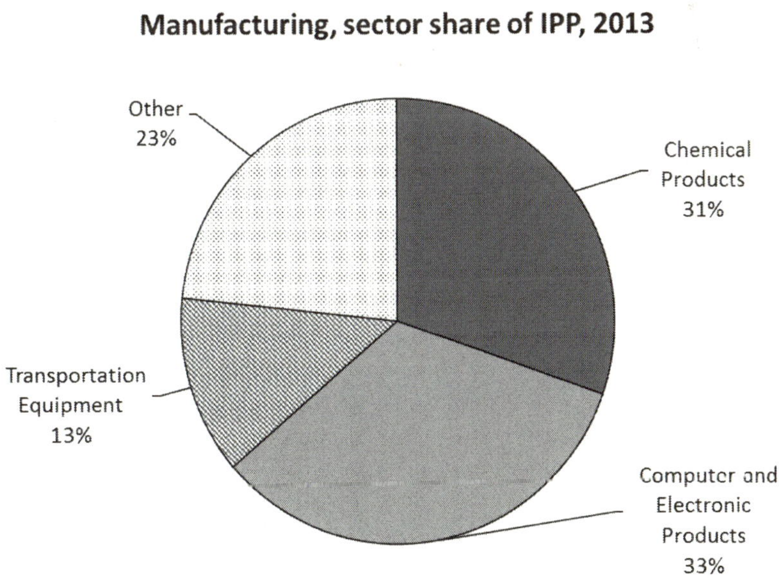

Source: GFC Economics

Chart 5i

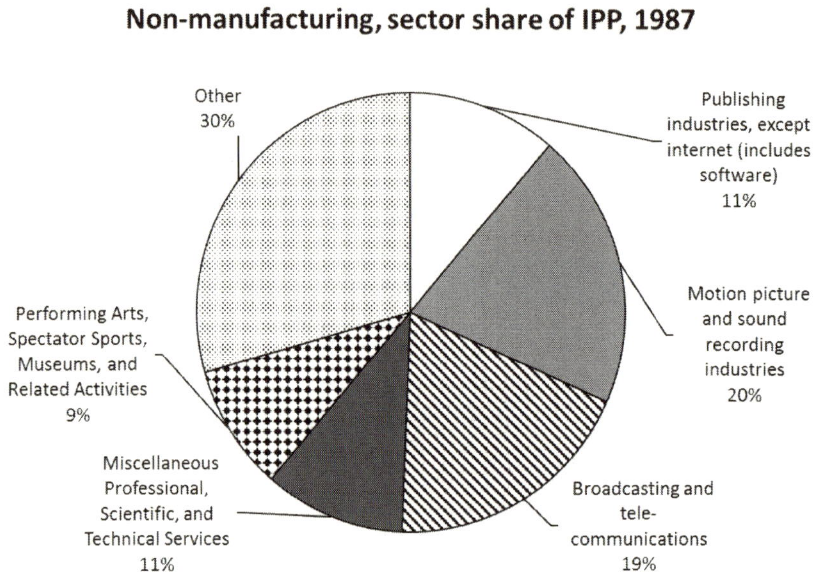

Source: GFC Economics

Chart 5j

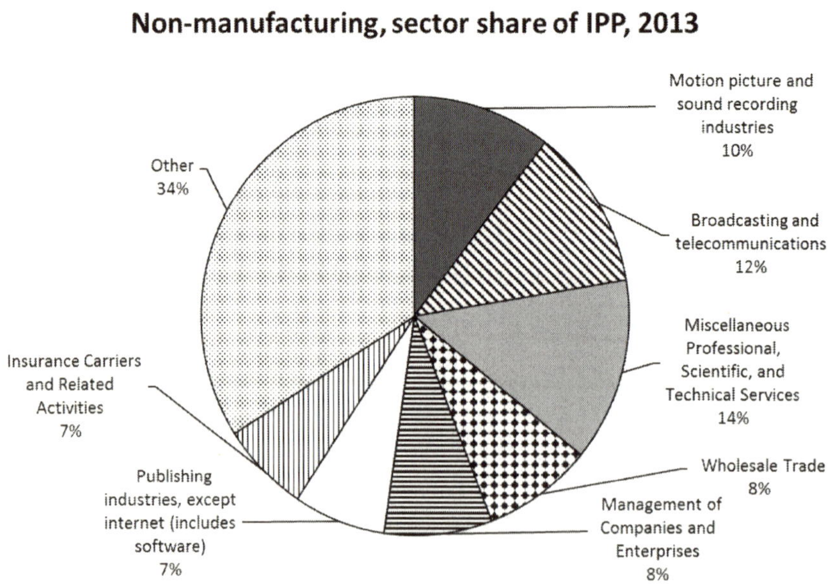

Source: GFC Economics

Chart 5k

Breakdown of R&D

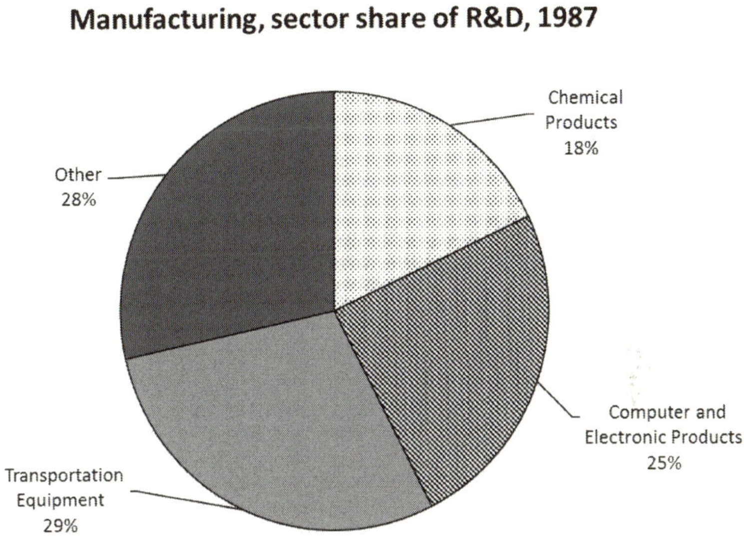

Source: GFC Economics

Chart 5l

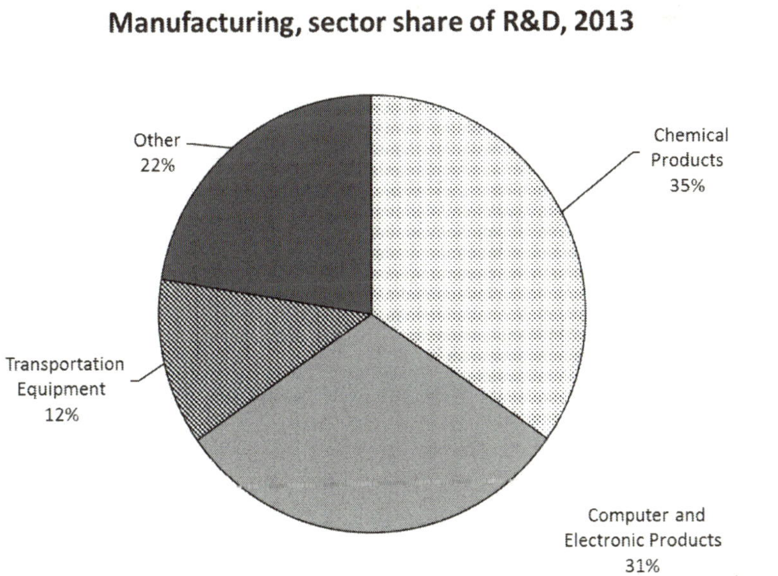

Source: GFC Economics

Chart 5m

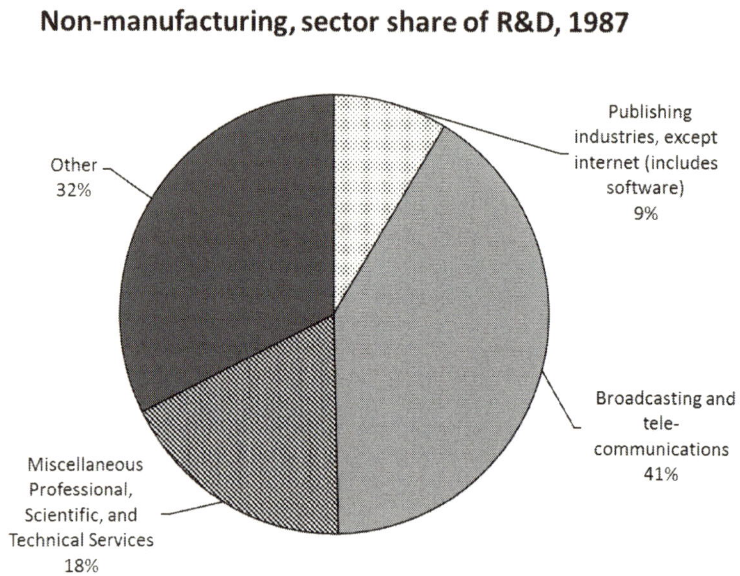

Source: GFC Economics

Chart 5n

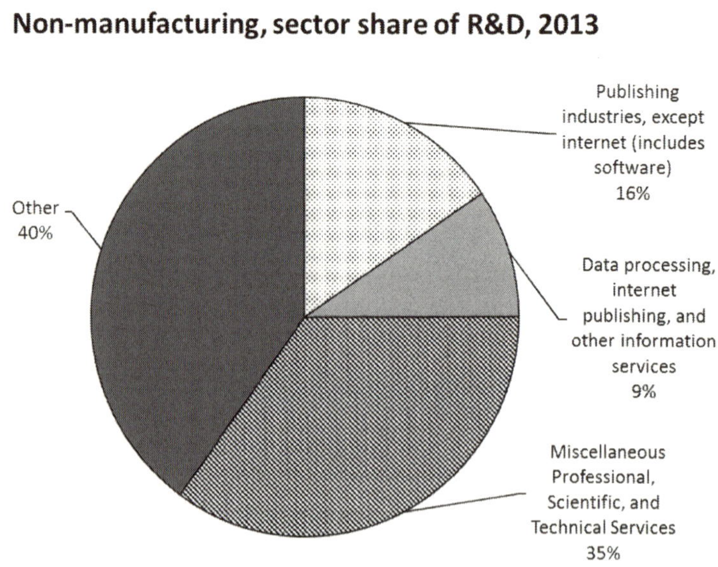

Source: GFC Economics

Chart 5o

Real GDI was also more closely correlated with a variety of key business cycle indicators.[78] In a revised paper the author substantiated his analysis with new data.[79] The BEA now publishes an average GDP-GDI measure, heeding some of the advice from this research.

The two measures vary because they are derived from different underlying source data. Real incomes are also easier to track: GDP and GDI may diverge if expenditures are improperly measured. The measurement of intangible expenditures represents a significant challenge for the statistical authorities. As spending on intellectual property products grows, these issues may become more acute.

Source: GFC Economics

Chart 5p

This is illustrated in the case of R&D, first capitalised in the national accounts in 2013. Whilst market prices exist for "purchased" R&D,

---

78 See *The Income- and Expenditure-Side Estimates of U.S. Output Growth*, Jeremy J. Nalewaik, Brookings Papers on Economic Activity, Spring 2010.

79 See *The Income- and Expenditure-Side Estimates of U.S. Output Growth — An Update to 2011Q2*, Jeremy J. Nalewaik, Brookings Papers on Economic Activity, Fall 2011.

there exists no market value for "in-house" research outlays.[80] Prices are measured on the basis of production costs, an imperfect measure. It can also be difficult to isolate R&D expenditures. In many cases, they are combined with other inputs. Furthermore, it is not always clear which resources have been devoted to the production of R&D.

In the US, the National Science Foundation's Business Research and Development and Innovation Survey tracks R&D spending by businesses. This is the primary source for annual and "benchmark" estimates in the national accounts. It excludes the smallest businesses (<5 employees). There are other "known" sources of measurement error, including "differences in respondent interpretations of the definitions of R&D activities; differences in accounting procedures…; the reporting of R&D activities by companies classified in the R&D services industry…; and differences in how companies count and report numbers of employees in various categories, including whether they work full-time or part-time on R&D."[81]

80 See *Measuring R&D in the National Economic Accounting System*, Marissa J. Crawford, Jennifer Lee, John E. Jankowski, and Francisco A. Moris, Survey of Current Business, November 2014.

81 See National Science Foundation, Business Research and Development and Innovation Survey, About The Survey, http://www.nsf.gov/statistics/srvyindustry/#sd

Chapter 6
Measurement issues in services
(First published August 24th 2015)

Introduction

The largest difficulties in measuring the impact of changes in the economy are probably in consumer spending for services.[1]

The US is predominantly a service economy. However, there exist considerable obstacles in accurately measuring output per unit of input (productivity). Deflators must adjust for quality improvements, but in services this can be ambiguous. Furthermore, advances in technology have facilitated the proliferation of free services. The benefits to the consumer may not be fully captured in the official statistics, raising questions about the reliability of the current data.

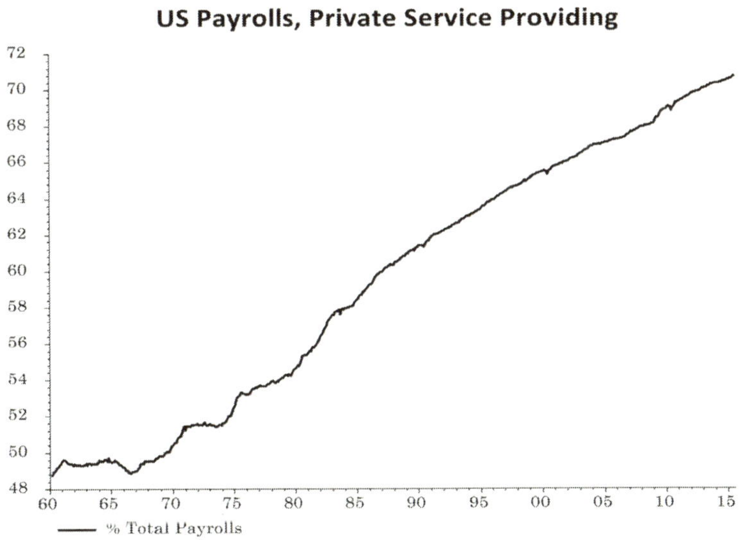

Source: GFC Economics

Chart 6a

1 See *Measuring the New Economy*, J. Steven Landefeld and Barbara M. Fraumeni, Survey of Current Business, March 2001, p. 28.

The incorrect measurement of services inflation will lead to misleading Gross Domestic Product (GDP) and productivity statistics. Estimates of an economy must keep pace with rapid technological innovation. These problems are not new. A 1992 paper by Zvi Griliches raised many issues regarding services output that are still relevant today.[2] In addition, the Boskin Commission was set up in 1995 precisely to deal with some of these concerns. Many of them remained unresolved.

The US is a services economy

The US has been a service economy for half a century or more. The employment data show a marked shift away from the primary sector towards services during the second half of the 19th century and beginning of the 20th century.[3] In 1968, the National Bureau of Economic Research declared that the US had become a services economy.[4] According to the Bureau of Labor Statistics (BLS), the share of employment in private services has continued to rise, from an average of 49.6% in 1968 to 70.8% in July 2015 (see chart 6a).[5]

Services productivity

The first National Income and Product Accounts (NIPAs) were constructed in response to the Great Depression. A dearth of data on the economy hindered efforts in setting an appropriate monetary policy. Statisticians were concerned with the productive capacity of the material economy and far less committed to measuring services accurately. Services have not always been considered a 'productive' activity. Classical

---

2 See *Introduction to "Output Measurement in the Service Sectors"*, Zvi Griliches, in Zvi Griliches (eds.) *Output Measurement in the Service Sectors*, University of Chicago Press, 1992.

3 See *The Service Economy*, Victor R. Fuchs, National Bureau of Economic Research, Columbia University Press, 1968.

4 Ibid.

5 Source: Bureau of Labor Statistics (BLS), Employment, CES, Nonfarm, Payroll, Total and Private Service-Providing.

economists such as Adam Smith sought to distinguish between productive (manufacturing) and unproductive (services) activity.[6]

In 1967, William Baumol hypothesised that a shift towards services would slow productivity growth.[7] This was known as *Baumol's cost disease.* It was, he claimed, harder to boost productivity in services industries compared with goods-producing industries. Part of this was due to the belief that services utilised a "low level of technical and capital intensity."[8] This may have been true in a world that was largely material. However, in an economy where intangible investment plays an increasingly important role, this may no longer be the case. Service industries have overtaken manufacturing to become the largest investors in intangible capital, which includes software and R&D spending.[9] This is the essence of the information age.

Indeed, in 2003, economists Jack Triplett and Barry Bosworth claimed that "Baumol's Disease has been cured."[10] Labour productivity in services accelerated after 1995 to equal the economy-wide average. Subsequent studies also showed that productivity growth at the beginning of the 21st century was being driven by services.[11] That said, a post-recession rebound in productivity has failed to materialise in the major Western economies. Part of the blame has been apportioned to services. A

---

6 See *GDP: A Brief but Affectionate History*, Diane Coyle, Princeton University Press, 2014, p. 84.

7 See *Macroeconomics of Unbalanced Growth: The Anatomy of Urban Crisis*, William Baumol, The American Economic Review, 57, 1967. William Baumol is Harold Price Professor of Entrepreneurship at NYU and Professor Emeritus at Princeton.

8 See *Productivity in services twenty years on. A review of conceptual and measurement issues and a way forward*, Nicola Grassano and Maria Savona, Science and Technology Policy Research Working Paper, University of Sussex, 2014, p. 13.

9 See chapter 5.

10 See *Productivity Measurement Issues in Services Industries: "Baumol's Disease" Has Been Cured*, Barry Bosworth and Jack Triplett, Federal Reserve Bank of New York Economic Policy Review, 2003, p. 23.

11 See *The Early 21st Century U.S. Productivity Expansion is Still in Services*, Barry Bosworth and Jack Triplett, International Productivity Monitor, 2007. See *Services Productivity in the United States: Griliches*, Barry Bosworth and Jack Triplett, National Bureau of Economic Research, 2007.

recent *Financial Times* article claimed that professional services have contributed to weak productivity growth in the UK.[12] This is puzzling given that these sectors employ many high-skilled individuals and invest heavily in new technologies.

Parallels between the 1990s and today

It is not the first time that official services productivity data have been questioned: this topic was a lively source of debate in the 1990s. Alan Greenspan, then Fed chair, recalled discussing the issue at FOMC meetings: "It seemed that the government had been underestimating productivity growth for years. It had not, for example, found *any* efficiency gains in the service economy – in fact, the government's calculations made it appear that productivity there was *shrinking*. Every committee member knew that was absurd on its face: law firms, business services, medical practices and social service organizations had been automating and streamlining themselves along with the manufacturing sector and the rest of the economy."[13]

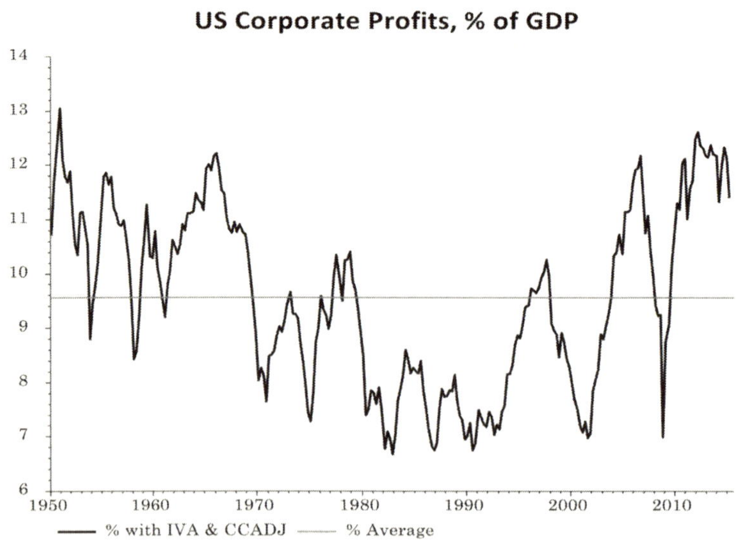

Source: GFC Economics

Chart 6b

12 See *Professional services at heart of UK productivity problem*, Financial Times, April 19th 2015.

13 See *The Age of Turbulence: Adventures in a New World*, Alan Greenspan, Penguin Books, 2008, p. 173.

The services industries (in particular, financial services, wholesale trade, business services, insurance, and communications) were the biggest investors in computers in the 1990s.[14] This generated output that was not reflected in the GDP statistics. For example, ATM machines provided a host of new benefits, including reduced waiting times, weekend transactions and eliminating the need to carry travellers' cheques abroad. However, "Prior to the 1999 revisions to GDP, ATM usage was not reflected in the measure of banking output in the national accounts."[15] Today financial services are investing heavily in 'Fintech', for example. The onus is on the statisticians to ensure these improvements are captured in the data.

Source: GFC Economics

Chart 6c

Mr Greenspan recalls: "Year in and year out, business had been pouring vast amounts of money into desktop computers, servers, networks, software and other high-tech gear... They would order expensive equipment only

---

14 See *Investment in New Structures and Equipment in 1992 by Using Industries*, Belinda Bonds and Tim Aylor, Survey of Current Business, December 1998.

15 See *Productivity in the Services Sector*, Barry Bosworth and Jack Triplett, Brookings Institution, 2000, p. 3.

if they believed the investment would expand their production capacity, or enable their employees to produce more per hour. If the equipment failed to do at least one of these, the managers would stop buying. Yet they'd kept pumping money into high tech. This became evident as early as 1993 when new orders for high-tech capital began to accelerate after a protracted period of sluggish growth. The surge continued into 1994, suggesting that the early profit experience with the new equipment had been positive."[16]

Source: GFC Economics

Chart 6d

It was difficult to *prove* that the official productivity statistics were wrong. Nevertheless, the direction of profits and inflation was telling: "Most companies were reporting rising operating profit margins. Yet few had raised prices. That meant that their costs per unit of output were contained or even falling. Most consolidated costs (that is, for business considered as a whole) are labor costs. So if labor costs per unit of output were flat or declining, and the rate of growth of average hourly labor compensation was rising, it was an arithmetical certainty that if these data were accurate, the growth of output per hour must be on the rise;

16 See *The Age of Turbulence: Adventures in a New World*, Alan Greenspan, Penguin Books, 2008, p. 172.

productivity was truly accelerating. And if so, then rising inflation would be unlikely."[17] In short, the alternative data pointed towards a period of unprecedented innovation.

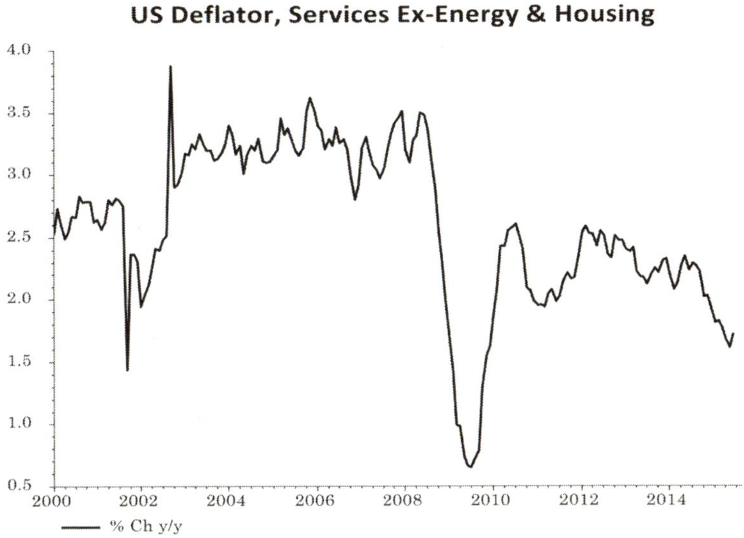

Source: GFC Economics

Chart 6e

In this context, the recent data have been striking. Corporate profits (before taxes) as a share of GDP are near all-time highs, and well above the long-run average (see chart 6b). Some of the most profitable companies are involved in services.[18] Prices have risen ahead of unit labour costs (see chart 6d). Inflation remains subdued: the PCE deflator for services climbed 1.91% y/y in June 2015, down from 2.43% y/y one-year prior.[19] Excluding energy & housing, the services PCE price index was up 1.73% y/y in June (see chart 6e).[20]

Firms could struggle to preserve margins. Technology may intensify competition. Indeed, gains in the S&P 500 are being driven largely by

---

17 See *The Age of Turbulence: Adventures in a New World*, Alan Greenspan, Penguin Books, 2008, p. 172.

18 See *The 15 most profitable business sectors*, Fortune, August 6th 2014.

19 Source: BEA, Personal Consumption Expenditures, Services Price Index.

20 Source: BEA, Real and Nominal Personal Consumption Expenditures, Services, Housing and Household Utilities, Electricity & Gas.

a handful of technology firms.[21] Some of these provide free services. Technology companies are driving down the cost of intermediate inputs, creating further measurement issues: "For both goods and services the problem with the digital economy, including E-business, is that it is mainly business-to-business or intermediate transactions, with only a small share of it, such as household payments to Internet service providers, showing up as final demand."[22] The cost of cloud computing, for example, has declined dramatically.[23] This spending will not show up directly in the GDP data. However, it will reduce business costs. If competition does not force firms to pass lower costs through to the consumer in the form of reduced prices, profits will rise.

Measurement issues in services

The Boskin Commission was established to examine potential deficiencies in the CPI and to suggest improvements. In the final report (1996), the Commission concluded that: "Changes in the CPI have substantially overstated the actual rate of price inflation".[24] Looking forward, the Commission estimated the size of the upward bias to be 1.1 percentage points per annum, with plausible values lying between 0.8 and 1.6 percentage points per year.[25] The Committee identified quality change and new product bias as key issues facing the statistical authorities. These applied to both goods and services. The measurement issues surrounding productivity in services have not been adequately explored since the seminal contributions of Zvi Griliches.[26] Jack Triplett and Barry Bosworth also identified a number of areas where measurement issues are likely to arise.[27]

21 See *The Only Six Stocks That Matter*, Wall Street Journal, July 26th 2015.

22 See *Measuring the New Economy,* J. Steven Landefeld and Barbara M. Fraumeni, *Survey of Current Business* March 2001, p. 28.

23 See *The cheap, convenient cloud,* The Economist, April 6th 2015.

24 See *The Boskin Commission Report: Towards A More Accurate Measure Of The Cost Of Living*, United States Social Security Administration, accessed August 20th 2015, http://www.ssa.gov/history/reports/boskinrpt.html#cpi5.

25 Ibid.

26 See *Introduction to "Output Measurement in the Service Sectors,* Zvi Griliches, in Zvi Griliches (eds.) Output Measurement in the Service Sectors, University of Chicago Press, 1992.

27 See *Productivity in the Services Sector*, Barry Bosworth and Jack Triplett, Brookings

However, there exists no one-size-fits-all solution: the idiosyncratic nature of services demands individual attention and solutions. Jack Triplett and Barry Bosworth noted that "there is no overall theme to measurement problems in services industries. Each appears to be a special case, with specific measurement problems unique to the unique characteristics of services industry output. Each industry problem requires a specific solution, an attack designed uniquely for the special problems posed by the nature of the industry's output."[28]

Furthermore, there are significant 'conceptual' issues regarding *what* precisely should be measured. Resolving such complexities requires thought and experiment with alternative approaches, and not a simple survey. Often, it requires an iterative process of collecting information, analysing the results, consulting with industry representatives and others, and then modifying the survey and collecting a new set of statistics.[29]

Quality change

Far more work has been undertaken to understand quality change in goods. Standard techniques implicitly adjust for quality, but in many cases the resulting price index is still unsatisfactory. Jack Triplett (former Chief Economist at the BEA) noted that "Studies on a number of technologically dynamic products have shown that the matched model method misses price decreases under certain not atypical circumstances".[30] This may also apply to high-tech services that intensively use electronic equipment or components as inputs.[31]

Furthermore, methods for implementing quality-change are non-routine and "heterogeneous in the sense that each quality change is *sui generis* and, like a child, requires individual attention. It is informationally demanding because it may require vast quantities of data that are expensive to obtain

Institution, 2000, p. 8.

28 Ibid.

29 Ibid., p. 5.

30 See *Measuring Consumption: The Post-1973 Slowdown and the Research Issues*, Jack Triplett, Brookings Institution, 1997, p. 50.

31 Ibid., p. 51.

and often do not pass the test of a market transaction. Even though routine procedures are established to handle quality change, in the end quality decisions require the subjective judgement about the extent of quality change, and agencies are reluctant to make subjective judgements."[32]

Imputations

Some transactions occur outside the scope of the market, where prices do not exist. This does not preclude their omission from the GDP statistics. Rather, imputations are carried out for their inclusion. For example, housing is treated as a stock, which provides a flow of services to the owner. Owners of housing "consume" a service in the same way as renters do. This ensures that GDP is invariant between home-ownership and renting.[33] Imputations are also conducted for certain financial services.[34]

The invariance principle states that the accounting aggregates should not depend on institutional differences between countries. Omitting these activities would mean that GDP would differ solely on the basis of institutional arrangements of a given country. "For example, if the same medical services can be provided by either the public or the private sector, overall production should be unaffected by a switch between the two institutional settings. The invariance principle increases comparability, over time and between countries."[35]

The drawbacks of using imputations are data accuracy and coverage. Even for owner-occupied housing services, there exists considerable debate over the correct way to measure prices.[36] Furthermore, it is unclear where the line should be drawn. For example, it could be argued that household production of services deserve inclusion.

---

32 See *Quality Changes in Price Indexes*, William Nordhaus, Journal of Economic Perspectives (12), 1998, p. 61.

33 See *Concepts and Methods of the U.S. National Income and Product* Accounts, BEA, 2014.

34 Ibid.

35 See *Report by the Commission on the Measurement of Economic Performance and Social Progress*, Joseph Stiglitz, Amartya Sen and Jean-Paul Fitoussi, Commission on the Measurement of Economic Performance and Social Progress, 2009, p. 88.

36 See *Accounting for Housing in a CPI*, W. Erwin Diewert and Alice Nakamura, University of British Columbia Discussion Paper, 2008.

Input-cost indices

As early as 1992, Zvi Griliches had identified basic faults with services inflation. In particular, measuring output on the basis of inputs would by definition result in zero productivity growth.[37] This may be having an effect on productivity even today. Indeed, some services are still deflated with input-cost indices. BEA composite indices of input costs are used to deflate 'other components' within 'Financial services furnished without payment', 'Portfolio management & investment advice services', 'Life insurance', and 'other components' within 'Social services & religious activities'. This method virtually assumes that labour productivity is stagnant. To see why consider the following identity for labour productivity:

$$LP = \frac{Q}{L} = \frac{\left(\frac{Y}{w}\right)}{L} = \frac{Y}{w \cdot L} = \frac{1}{S^L}$$

Labour productivity is defined as real output (Q) per unit of unit of labour input (L). If nominal output (Y) is deflated using wages (w), then productivity (LP) is equal to the inverse of the labour share of income (S^L).[38] This will depend on the elasticity of substitution, an exogenous parameter in many models. In any case, this has tended to remain constant over time.

Individual services

Broadband

Internet service provision has improved rapidly over the past couple of decades. Consumers have moved away from dial-up internet connections towards broadband. It is ubiquitous and integral to the functioning of businesses and households. Nevertheless, a broadband price index does

---

37 See *The Search for R&D Spillovers*, Zvi Griliches, The Scandinavian Journal of Economics, 94, 1992.

38 See *Possible Measurement Bias in Aggregate Productivity Growth*, William Gullickson and Michael Harper, Monthly Labor Review, 1999, p. 61.

not exist in the US.[39] Instead, the BEA uses the CPI for internet service providers and electronic information providers (constructed by the BLS) to deflate the consumption of internet access services. This index "combines price data for both dial-up and household Internet-access services, using lagged expenditure surveys to weight price movements. As a result, the price for dial-up service dominates the index for most of the first decade of the millennium, which renders the BLS index almost useless for assessing the effectiveness of US broadband policy." Furthermore, "the BLS index makes no adjustment for increases in quality, such as increases in download bandwidth for either dial-up or broadband services." It also fails to take into account the full improvements "in the quality of Internet access when households switch between dial-up and broadband services".[40]

A recent working paper attempted to construct a price index for broadband services between 2004 and 2009.[41] The authors analysed over 1500 internet service contracts using a combination of matched-model techniques and hedonic price index estimation to control for quality. Whilst the drop in prices is not dramatic, they conclude that there is "some evidence" of modest price declines in quality-adjusted prices in the order of between 3% and 10% in just under six years.[42] Significantly, this exceeded the drop recorded by the BLS price index. Nevertheless, the fall in prices was not as dramatic as recorded for other electronics "such as CPUs, laptops, printers or storage devices, where the quality-adjusted price declines regularly exceed double digits per year." The structure of a particular market plays a key role in price determination, and may even prevent price decreases in certain cases.

Retail

Retail has been innovative. However, there are potential productivity gains that may not be measured: "much of the industry's innovation

---

39 See *Evidence of a Modest Price Decline in US Broadband Services*, Shane Greenstein and Ryan McDevitt, National Bureau of Economic Research, 2010.

40 Ibid., pp. 2-3.

41 Ibid.

42 Ibid., p. 4.

in retail trade is reflected in shifts in the distribution of sales among stores with different formats. Yet, these shifts are explicitly ruled out in the construction of the major price indexes because the survey only tracks the price of a product in a specific store. In effect, the shift of sales from department stores to lower-priced discount outlets is treated as a reduction in quality (and therefore output), not a reduction in price. But the growth in the popularity of discount and outlet stores suggests that they provide a net gain to consumers, and at least a portion of the price reduction should be reflected in increased real output."[43]

Healthcare

Medical care expenditures in real terms have been rising as a share of GDP and are projected to grow further.[44] Personal consumption expenditures on healthcare were 11.47% of GDP in Q2 2015, up from 9.71% in Q1 2000 (see chart 6f). Prices have been rising consistently, albeit at a far slower pace than in the 1980s and 1990s (see chart 6g). Indeed, the deflator for healthcare services has largely tracked the overall PCE inflation rate. This is despite significant advances in science and subsequent applications in medicine.

There are inherent difficulties in measuring quality changes in healthcare. The OECD has acknowledged that "There is growing concern among policy-makers and statisticians that the difficult task of price and volume measurement in health care services needs more attention and that a greater share of statistical resources should be devoted to this task. Reported time series on health care prices are seriously deficient in many instances."[45]

---

43 See *Productivity in the Services Sector*, Barry Bosworth & Jack Triplett, Brookings Institution, 2000, p. 10.

44 See *National Health Expenditure Projections, 2014–24: Spending Growth Faster Than Recent Trends*, S. P. Keehan, G. A. Cuckler, A. M. Sisko, A. J. Madison, S. D. Smith, D. A. Stone, J. A. Poisal, C. J. Wolfe & J. M. Lizonitz, Health Affairs, 34, 2015.

45 See *A System of Health Accounts*, Organisation for Economic Co-operation and Development, 2000, p. 91.

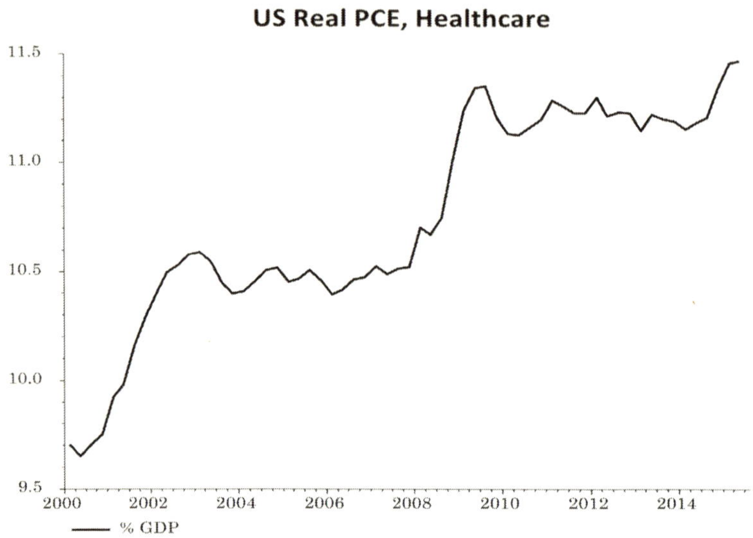

Source: GFC Economics

Chart 6f

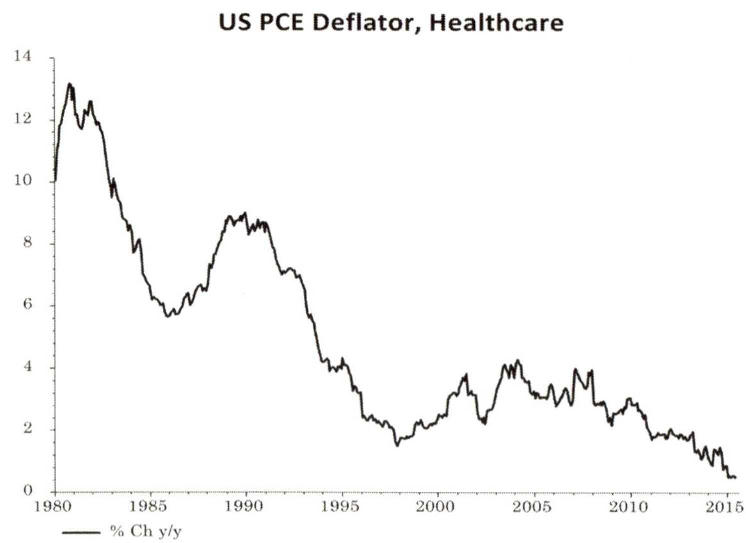

Source: GFC Economics

Chart 6g

Steven Landefeld (ex-Director at the Bureau of Economic Analysis) and Barbara Fraumeni (University of Southern Maine) note that "there are significant benefits in terms of quality of life and length of life that are not reflected in these indexes."[46] If quality changes were measured accurately, real growth in personal consumption expenditures may well have been higher.

However, the concept of output is not clearly defined in medical practice. To deal with this issue, the BEA has set up a new Health Care Satellite Account (HCSA) to experiment with a new definition of an output unit. Using this new methodology, the authors find that PCE deflators currently used in the NIPAs *understated* the extent of price growth, and as a result *overstated* real GDP growth. Despite this counterintuitive result, there is a more promising development: the disease-based price indices "are more amenable to quality adjustment going forward."[47]

Indeed, the current version of the HCSA does "not account for any changes in the quality of health care such as improved health outcomes, fewer side effects, or less risky and invasive procedures."[48] This is partly due to a lack of consensus on how best to approach the subject. The different authorities that recommend adjusting for quality in healthcare in the national accounts have not come to an agreement on how exactly to undertake the task. Without adequate methods "to adjust for quality and to attribute these changes in quality to specific medical interventions, we cannot measure the value of the spending on medical care."[49] Official sources tend to agree that "the measurement of medical output should be adjusted for quality of the treatment, although they do not generally make specific recommendations about what method to use for quality adjustment."[50] The importance of adjusting for quality change has been

46 See *Measuring the New Economy*, J. Steven Landefeld and Barbara M. Fraumeni, Survey of Current Business, 2001, p. 30.

47 See *Introducing the New BEA Health Care Satellite Account*, Abe Dunn, Lindsey Rittmueller & Bryn Whitmire, Survey of Current Business, 2015, p. 3.

48 See *Adjusting the Measurement of the Output of the Medical Sector for Quality: A Review of the Literature*, Anne Hall, US Bureau of Economic Analysis, 2015, p. 8.

49 See *Introducing the New BEA Health Care Satellite Account*, Abe Dunn, Lindsey Rittmueller & Bryn Whitmire, Survey of Current Business, 2015, p. 18.

50 See *Adjusting the Measurement of the Output of the Medical Sector for Quality: A*

stressed in numerous reports: "Perhaps the most important issue [for measuring changes in medical care prices], however, is quality change. The value of medical care changes substantially over time, even if its physical characteristics remain the same. A day in the hospital or an hour in the operating room in 1990, for example, included much more highly concentrated nursing, monitoring, and other services than a day in the hospital in 1980. Even a pint of blood, a seemingly well-defined product, now includes more screening tests for infectious agents and safer packaging than it used to."[51]

Anne Hall (economist at the BEA) finds that "After quality adjustment, the outcomes-based priced index for heart attacks created by Cutler et al. (1998, 2001) and the process-based index for colon cancer created by Lucarelli and Nicholson (2009) showed declines instead of increases." Furthermore, "some research on specific conditions such as heart disease, depression and cancer show that adjusting for quality can make a significant difference to measured inflation in medical care."[52] The growth of healthcare as a share of consumption will ensure the deflators come under closer scrutiny in the future.

While technology may be improving the quality of medical care and treatment, it is legitimate to argue that there are other less favourable trends that also need to be taken into consideration, such as rising obesity.

Competition

In theory, technology may pave the way towards a 'frictionless' economy. Benefits will accrue from new and improved services via "lower search and transaction costs".[53] Nevertheless, it is not always

---

Review of the Literature, Anne Hall, US Bureau of Economic Analysis, 2015, p. 5.

51 See *Are Medical Prices Declining?*, David Cutler, Mark McClellan, Joseph Newhouse &After Dahlia Remler, National Bureau of Economic Research, 1996, p. 2.

52 See *Adjusting the Measurement of the Output of the Medical Sector for Quality: A Review of the Literature*, Anne Hall, Bureau of Economic Analysis, 2015, p. 8 and 27.

53 See *The Second Machine Age: Work, Progress, and Prosperity in a Time of Brilliant Technologies*, Erik Brynjolfsson & Andrew McAfee, W. W. Norton & Company,

clear that technology will enhance competition and reduce prices. In some cases, prices may rise despite major quality improvements due to market structure.

For example, one would expect price comparison websites (PCWs) to intensify competition, putting downward pressure on prices. However, a recent paper found that some websites may be having the opposite effect.[54] Consumers lose out from price comparison websites that are able to forge monopolies.[55] "The analysis presented shows that it is not obvious that PCWs benefit consumers at a fundamental level, and that increasing competition can exacerbate, rather than mitigate the problem. Competition at the aggregate level is only guaranteed to be a remedy if shoppers check all of them, otherwise it can in fact lead to higher prices. When there are many aggregators in the market, a crucial variable is how many of them shoppers check. As a result, regulatory bodies may wish to consider directly limiting the fees charged by aggregators, as well as limiting the number of PCWs in the market and incentivizing consumers to check more."[56] Indeed, some price comparison websites were found to not meet FCA regulations.[57] This lack of competition could hold back productivity.[58] The Competition and Markets Authority in the UK recently found that Pfizer, a pharmaceutical company, had been abusing its dominant position to boost prices for anti-epilepsy drugs.[59]

2014, p. 118.

54 See *Price Comparison Websites*, David Ronayne, PhD dissertation, University of Warwick, 2015.

55 See *Heat is on: Why are energy bills so high?*, BBC News, January 15th 2014.

56 See *Price Comparison Websites*, David Ronayne, PhD diss., University of Warwick, 2015, p. 5.

57 See *Price comparison websites failing to meet FCA expectations,* Financial Conduct Authority, July 16th 2014.

58 See *Focus falls on competition to boost UK productivity,* Financial Times, July 26th 2015.

59 See *CMA issues statement of objections to Pfizer and Flynn Pharma in anti-epilepsy drug investigation,* , Joseph Stiglitz, Amartya Sen and Jean-Paul Fitoussi, Competition and Markets Authority, August 6th 2015.

The 'New Economy'

The 'New Economy' is characterised by a proliferation of free goods and services. Paradoxically, real GDP may fall as more goods and services become available either for free or at a significantly reduced price. In this context, real GDP may not adequately reflect consumer utility.

This is a common criticism of GDP data. Nonetheless, this crude measure of production has always omitted key aspects of the economy. In theory, it has been argued that real output will provide an accurate measure of welfare "When markets are competitive and in the absence of externalities, relative prices of goods and services mirror the relative values that individuals put on these commodities."[60] These assumptions do not hold in practice.

Nevertheless, if the purpose of economics "is to understand and promote the enhancement of well-being", then the economic data must "encompass measures of well being and its determinants."[61] GDP should be scrutinised and its merits debated. The case for other indicators of well-being is compelling. These are summarised in a report by Amartya Sen, Joseph Stiglitz, and Jean-Paul Fitoussi.[62]

How the authorities decide to measure the benefits of free goods and services in this 'New Economy' is important. One of the Boskin Commission proposals was to include a measure of *consumer surplus*. This "compares the amount a consumer would have been willing to pay for something to the amount they actually have to pay."[63] It is an attempt to quantify (i.e. assign a monetary value to) the benefits derived from new technologies. Eric Brynjolfsson and Joo Hee Oh justified measuring consumer surplus

---

60 See *Report by the Commission on the Measurement of Economic Performance and Social Progress,* Joseph Stiglitz, Amartya Sen and Jean-Paul Fitoussi, Commission on the Measurement of Economic Performance and Social Progress, 2009, p. 86.

61 See *Economic Measurement*, Ben Bernanke, August 6th 2012, p. 1.

62 See *Report by the Commission on the Measurement of Economic Performance and Social Progress*, Joseph Stiglitz, Amartya Sen and Jean-Paul Fitoussi, *Commission on the Measurement of Economic Performance and Social Progress*, 2009.

63 See *The Second Machine Age: Work, Progress, and Prosperity in a Time of Brilliant Technologies*, Erik Brynjolfsson & Andrew McAfee, W. W. Norton & Company, 2014, p. 114.

because people using free goods and services give up another valuable 'commodity' – time.[64] McKinsey published a similar study, quantifying the significant value consumers obtain from using the web.[65]

Clearly, ignoring consumer surplus will lead to a downward bias in real consumer spending and real GDP. However, unmeasured consumer surplus from new products will only generate a productivity slowdown if the utility gain from new technologies today outweighed those of the past. It is extremely difficult to substantiate this proposition. In some cases, it is simply not clear: which gave the greater consumer surplus – the CD player, or the MP3?

Is the 'productivity' concept meaningful when looking at services?

Productivity is defined as the ratio of a volume of output to a measure of input. This is a relatively straightforward concept for manufacturing or industry. For services it is less clear. Aggregating multi-inputs and multi-outputs into a single measure can be difficult. Furthermore, "the fact that the typical output of service sectors is intangible to different degrees makes it clearly difficult to count it as a whole or in part and even harder to separate units of output."[66] Additionally, "the production process in the service sector usually involves the contribution of the customer himself."[67] "Intangibility/immateriality, indivisibility and co-production" are properties of services output that may lead to an underestimation of the volume of the service sector's output.[68] This in turn would lead to lower productivity and growth rates.

---

64 See *The Attention Economy: Measuring the Value of Free Digital Services on the Internet*, Erik Brynjolfsson & Joo Hee Oh, 2012.

65 See *The Web's €100 billion surplus*, Jacques Bughin, *McKinsey & Company*, January 2011.

66 See *Productivity in services twenty years on. A review of conceptual and measurement issues and a way forward,* Nicola Grassano & Maria Savona, Science and Technology Policy Research Working Paper, University of Sussex, 2014, p. 8.

67 Ibid.

68 Ibid.

For now, focus on the labour market

Increasingly, there has been a divergence between the real GDP and labour market data emanating from the US and UK. New job openings and employment have risen sharply in both countries, whereas the GDP data have failed to impress. Fortunately, the labour market data are less susceptible to measurement issues (although even here there are difficulties). The unemployment rate and the creation of jobs in services industries point toward economies in the US and UK that are well functioning and dynamic, even if the GDP data do not display this trend. Ultimately, we may need to fall back on more 'stable' or reliable indicators.

Measurement issues in services *update*

An enquiry into the accuracy and suitability of US economic statistics is long overdue. The Boskin Commission attempted to answer this question 20 years ago, and found an upward bias to the deflators. Similar issues plague the data today.

In the UK, an independent review of national economic data was initiated in July 2015 by Chancellor George Osborne, "prompted by the increasing difficulty of measuring output and productivity accurately in a modern, dynamic and increasingly technological economy."[69] An interim report published in December 2015 highlighted, among other things, the need for a more accurate estimate of economic activity and prices in services. The customisation and idiosyncrasy of services present some of the biggest challenges for statisticians.[70] Furthermore, these difficulties "are likely to intensify as the economy evolves. New digital technologies, such as increasingly powerful and portable electronic devices, represent powerful enablers for the provision of services, e.g. the streaming of entertainment services. Moreover technological innovation also increases the scope for mass customisation to fit specific consumer preferences, leading to greater variety across services".[71]

Attention was also drawn to the increasingly academic division between manufacturing and services.[72] In many instances, the distinction between manufacturing and services is being eroded: "Many companies that traditionally focused on producing and selling goods have developed

---

69 See *Independent review of UK economic statistics: interim report*, Charles Bean, December 2015, p. 3.

70 Ibid., p. 21. "But measuring the output and prices of services is inherently more difficult than for goods as, in contrast to goods, the basic unit of production for services is often hard to define. Services are frequently tailored to a particular consumer's requirement and such customisation makes it hard to compare like with like and thus to construct an appropriate price index."

71 Ibid., p. 22.

72 Ibid., p. 22. "Moreover, the separation between services and manufacturing is at best imprecise given that output is classified under the primary activity of the firm. Many businesses that are classified as goods producers also provide a service, such as after-sales care. In some cases, these are a significant source of revenues."

service-type business models. At the same time, companies primarily known for software and online services have branched into designing and producing manufactured goods. Amazon, for example, established a hardware team that developed the Kindle e-reader and Fire TV digital media player, and is developing a smartphone to more effectively deliver its offerings to customers. Google is partnering with contract manufacturers to produce wearable technology products such as Google Glass."[73]

Furthermore, an increasing number of businesses undertake activities in multiple industries: under the North American Industry Classification System (NAICS), Amazon is classified as a retailer. However, the company is at the cutting edge of computer systems design and software programming.[74] Indeed, its cloud business (Amazon Web Services) has generated a significant portion of recent profits.[75] These classification issues imply the structural changes taking place in the economy may not be fully understood.

Trade in services

The concerns raised in the ONS interim report extend to the external sector. It has become more difficult to accurately track trade flows, particularly in services: advances in information technology have facilitated "increased international trade in services and even quite specialised services can now be supplied over the internet from anywhere in the world."[76] The extensive revisions to service exports in the UK underline this point.[77]

---

73 See *Making Value for America: Embracing the Future of Manufacturing, Technology, and Work*, National Academy of Engineering, 2015, p. 15.

74 See *America's Advanced Industries: What They Are, Where They Are, and Why They Matter*, Mark Muro, Jonathan Rockwell, Scott Andes, Kenan Fikri & Siddarth Kulkarni, The Brookings Institution, February 2015.

75 See *AWS Does Amazon's Heavy Profit Lifting*, Wall Street Journal, October 22nd 2015.

76 See *Independent review of UK economic statistics*, Charles Bean, 2015, p. 22.

77 See, for example, *UK Trade: April 2015*, Office for National Statistics, June 9th 2015.

Source: GFC Economics

Chart 6h

These issues may be relevant for US services exports data as well. The US enjoys a significant trade surplus in services (see chart 6h).[78] Despite a strong rise in the Dollar, the 3-month moving average for service exports climbed to $59.4bn in January 2016, marginally below the all-time high of $60.0bn set exactly one year before (see chart 6i).[79] In January 2016, services exports climbed to $59.6bn, up 44.0% since the cyclical trough of February 2009. Over this period, the biggest increase occurred in 'maintenance & repair services' (136.8%), followed by 'telecommunications, computer & information services' (58.6%) and travel (55.5%). 'Other business services' (+42.2%) and 'Charges for the use of intellectual property' (+38.4%) also grew strongly (see chart 6j).[80]

78 Source: Census Bureau, Foreign Trade, Balance, Services, Current Prices. The 3-month moving average for the services balance totalled $18.0bn in January.

79 Source: Census Bureau, Foreign Trade, Export, Services, Current Prices and FX Indices, Federal Reserve, Broad Index, Nominal. The Dollar appreciated 10.9% in the year to December 2015.

80 'Other business services' include 'research & development services', 'professional & management consulting services', and 'technical, trade-related & other business services'. The other components for services are financial services (+36.8%) transport (+34.4%), insurance services (+31.9%) and government goods & services (+6.4%).

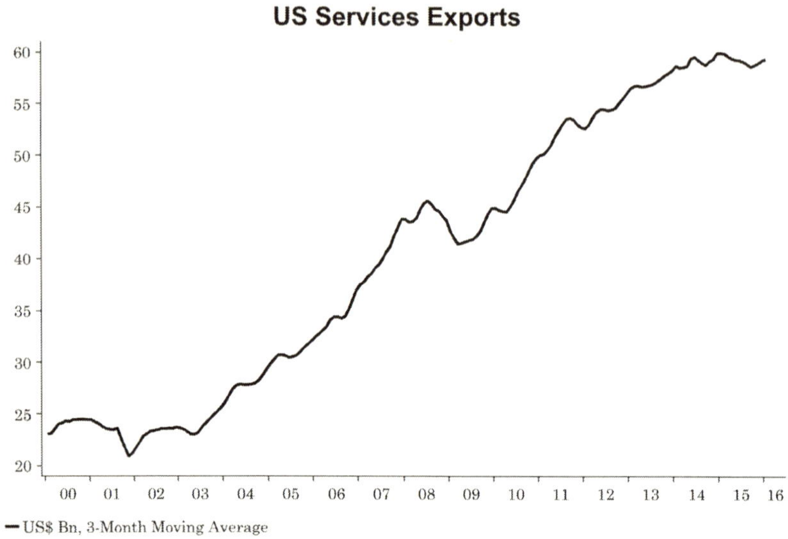

Source: GFC Economics

Chart 6i

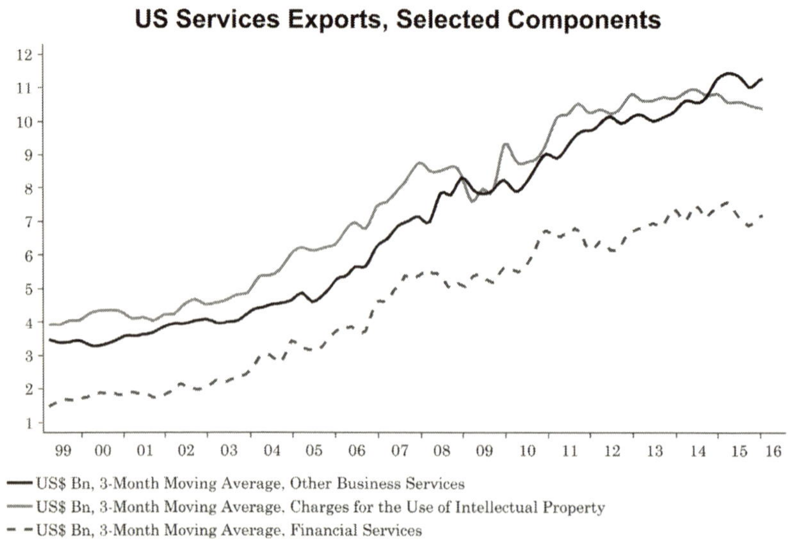

Source: GFC Economics

Chart 6j

Trade has emerged as a highly contentious issue in the run-up to the 2016 presidential elections. The front-runners for both the Republican and Democratic parties have sought to distance themselves from free trade agreements.[81] Some jobs will undoubtedly come under threat from greater foreign competition. However, free trade deals could potentially be a net positive for the US economy.

The Trans-Pacific Partnership (TPP) deal will open up new markets for US exporters.[82] At the same time, domestic businesses will come under pressure to boost their competitiveness. The deal tackles obstacles to trade that are particularly relevant for services.[83] For example, it includes provisions that will facilitate cross-border data flows of information that drive the digital economy. The intellectual property chapter will also "make it easier for businesses to search, register, and protect IP rights in new markets, which is particularly important for small businesses".[84] Indeed, there has been a particular emphasis within the TPP on how small- and medium-sized enterprises can benefit from many of the initiatives to liberalise trade.[85] The benefits are unlikely to be felt immediately: the

81 See *Free Trade Loses Political Favor,* Wall Street Journal, March 9th 2016.

82 See *Summary of the Trans-Pacific Partnership Agreement, Office of the United States Trade Representative,* October 4th 2015.

83 See *The Global Economy Needs More Trade in Services,* Wall Street Journal, July 1st 2015. "While tariff reduction on goods was the main focus of trade deals in the 20th century, the new generation of pacts address 'behind the border' obstacles such as restrictive or biased procurement policies, arcane investment rules and weak intellectual-property protection – all of which stand as barriers to trade in services." See also *Summary of the Trans-Pacific Partnership Agreement,* Office of the United States Trade Representative, October 4th 2015. TPP includes obligations such as "market access, which provides that no TPP country may impose quantitative restrictions on the supply of services (e.g., a limit on the number of suppliers or number of transactions) or require a specific type of legal entity or joint venture; and local presence, which means that no country may require a supplier from another country to establish an office or affiliate, or to be resident, in its territory in order to supply a service."

84 See *Summary of the Trans-Pacific Partnership Agreement, Office of the United States Trade Representative,* October 4th 2015.

85 See *Summary of the Trans-Pacific Partnership Agreement, Office of the United States Trade Representative,* October 4th 2015. These include "export counseling, assistance, and training programs…; information sharing; trade finance" as well as providing "easily accessible information on the TPP and ways small firms can take

integration of supply chains takes time. Nonetheless, it is possible that trade in some services may eventually be as efficient as in manufacturing.

---

advantage of it, including description of the provisions of TPP relevant to small- and medium-sized enterprises; regulations and procedures concerning intellectual property rights; foreign investment regulations; business registration procedures; employment regulations; and taxation information."

Chapter 7
Inequality and the NAIRU
(Published August 24th 2015)

During the years prior to the credit crunch of 2008, it was rare to hear inequality cited as a possible cause of the looming financial crisis. It is now widely accepted that the uneven distribution of wages contributed in part to the record household debt burden and the sharp rise in house prices.[1] The subsequent deep recession aggravated inequality.[2] The forces that drive inequality may also be pushing the non-accelerating inflation rate of unemployment (NAIRU) lower. Inequality and the NAIRU are inextricably linked. Understanding the causes of inequality provides an insight into a possible shift in the trade-off between unemployment and inflation.

Is the NAIRU falling?

The December 2014 labour market report ignited an important and long overdue debate on the NAIRU. The jobless rate fell again to 5.6%, but the annual rate for average hourly earnings tumbled from 2.16% to

---

1 See *Aspects of Inequality in the Recent Business Cycle*, Sarah Bloom Raskin, April 18th 2013, p. 6-7. "The question then arises as to why households with poor income prospects sought out levels of mortgage debt that would ultimately prove so problematic. Putting aside the practice, in the run-up to the crisis, of lenders steering households to mortgage debt products that were more costly than what such households may have otherwise qualified for, one reason may have been that many households in the middle and lower end of the income distribution, whose wage earnings were stagnant, did not recognize the long-run and persistent trends underlying their lack of income growth."

2 See *Perspectives on Inequality and Opportunity from the Survey of Consumer Finances*, Janet L. Yellen, October 17th 2014. Here it is important to emphasise the distinction between wealth inequality (stock variable) and income inequality (flow variable). Wealth inequality fell slightly in the recession, but this has since been reversed.

1.62%.[3] The Job Openings and Labor Turnover Survey (JOLTS) report has underlined the strength of the US labour market. The 3-month average for new job openings hit 4.829m in November 2014, the highest since April 2001 (see chart 7a).[4] Voluntary quits are also trending higher: the 3-month average for quits climbed to 2.688m, the highest since June 2008.[5] In the past, quits have tended to lead wage inflation. However, since the financial crisis of 2008, the lag between these two indicators has lengthened. Furthermore, these two measures are now starting to diverge. Wages would have been expected to accelerate at this stage of the economic recovery (see chart 7b).

Source: GFC Economics

Chart 7a

3 Source: Bureau of Labour Statistics (BLS), Unemployment, Current Population Survey (CPS), 16 Years & Over, Rate and BLS, Current Employment Statistics (CES), National, Average Hourly Earnings of Production & Non-Supervisory Employees, Total Private.

4 Source: BLS, Job Openings & Labor Turnover Survey (JOLTS), Job Openings, Total Private, Level.

5 Source: BLS, JOLTS, Quits, Total Private, Level.

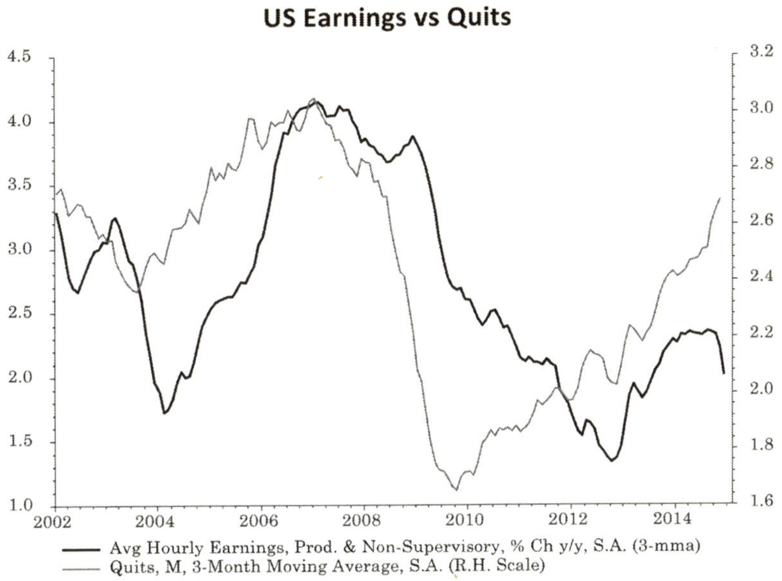

Source: GFC Economics

Chart 7b

Research from the Federal Reserve Bank of Kansas suggests the relationship between wage inflation and quits may not necessarily be breaking down: workers who quit their job voluntarily are seeing a rise in wage rates.[6] Nevertheless, it is likely that the NAIRU has declined faster than Fed members are willing to acknowledge: the jobless rate is just 10 basis points above the FOMC's central tendency for the longer-run unemployment rate, and yet core inflation is dropping again.[7]

It is widely accepted that the NAIRU fell in the 1990s as productivity growth accelerated.[8] This was a reverse of the 1970s, when productivity growth slowed and the NAIRU rose. However, the relationship between productivity growth and the NAIRU is less than straightforward. Faster

6 See *Following the Leaders: Wage Growth of Job Switchers*, Jose Mustre-del-Rio, The Macro Bulletin, Macroeconomic Research from the Federal Reserve Bank of Kansas City, December 19th 2014.

7 See Federal Open Market Committee, Meeting calendars, statements, and minutes, Accessible Materials.

8 See *The NAIRU in Theory and Practice*, Laurence Ball and N. Gregory Mankiw, Journal of Economic Perspectives, 16(4), 2002, p. 115-136.

productivity growth need not cause the NAIRU to fall *per se*. Indeed, the immediate impact of a higher trend rate in productivity – assuming all other variables remain unchanged – would be to push unemployment higher: the same level of output could be attained using fewer workers. Greater productivity merely implies it will require a bigger rise in real GDP before inflation takes root.

Wages and the ability of workers to demand higher pay provide the link between productivity and the NAIRU. In the long run, productivity growth will determine how quickly real wages can rise without hurting profit margins. In the 1970s, productivity growth dipped. The failure of real wages to slow in line with productivity led to a squeeze in margins. The NAIRU climbed and this set the stage for an increase in inflation. In the late-1990s, productivity growth accelerated, but workers had become 'accustomed' to slower real wage gains. This in part reflected the labour market reforms that began in the early 1980s, symbolised by President Reagan's stand against the Professional Air Traffic Controllers Organization. Investment in technology had expanded too. The NAIRU fell.

None of this would seem to support the case for a lower NAIRU *today*. The official data would appear to corroborate the slowdown in productivity growth thesis.[9] The Beveridge curve has shifted outwards too.[10] The view that productivity has slowed is contentious: the potential for GDP revisions should not be ignored.[11] If real GDP does get revised

---

9 Source: BLS, Labour Productivity, Output Per Hour of All Persons, Non-Farm Business. Since 2008, productivity growth has averaged 1.5%. Productivity growth accelerated to 3.2% y/y and 3.3% y/y in 2009 and 2010 respectively. Since then however, productivity slowed, averaging just 0.7% between Q1 2011 and Q3 2014.

10 See chapter 6.

11 See *The Great Recession--Moving Ahead*, Stanley Fischer, August 11th 2014. See also *The Demise of U.S. Economic Growth: Restatement, Rebuttal, and* Reflections, Robert J. Gordon, National Bureau of Economic Research, Working Paper 19895, February 2014. See also *U.S. Productivity Growth: The Slowdown Has returned After A Temporary Revival*, Robert J. Gordon, International Productivity Monitor (25), Spring 2013. See also *Productivity and Potential Output Before, During, and After the Great Recession*, John G. Fernald, National Bureau of Economic Research, Working Paper 20248, June 2014.

up, however, it would be largely immaterial in the context of the NAIRU: revising real GDP and productivity growth higher does not necessarily change the NAIRU, *per se*.

Nevertheless, a faster trend rate for productivity would still be important. When wages increase less quickly than productivity, unit labour costs will fall putting downward pressure on inflation. If wages rise more quickly than productivity, unit labour costs will climb. How fast wages are rising in relation to productivity is critical. A slower gain in unit labour costs compared with prices could lead to higher margins if non-labour costs are not accelerating. Furthermore, this could occur as the rate of inflation falls.

This has essentially been the experience of the US since the crisis of 2008. Unit labour costs (non-financial) have risen 1.2% since Q4 2008, and prices have climbed 6.0%.[12] At the same time, the y/y for prices has slowed from 3.5% to 0.7% over this period. Unit profits from production have jumped by 48.1% to new highs, helped by a very modest increase in unit non-labour costs (0.7%).[13]

Faster productivity would be important for the NAIRU if it was not accompanied by upward revisions to real wages. By implication, profit margins would be higher in this scenario: inequality could also be deeper. Herein lies the link to the NAIRU. At any given unemployment rate, a higher profit margin will increase the cushion employers enjoy against any possible rise in costs, before this in turn leads to higher selling prices by producers. Ben Bernanke made this point in an important speech in 2004.[14]

---

12 Source: BLS, Nonfinancial Corporations, Total Unit Costs and Bureau of Economic Analysis (BEA), Nonfinancial Corporate Business, Gross Value Added, Price per Unit.

13 Source: BEA, Nonfinancial Corporate Business, Corporate Profits with IVA and CC Adj., Unit Profits from Production and BEA, Nonfinancial Corporate Business, Unit Non-labour Cost.

14 See *Monetary Policy and the Economic Outlook: 2004*, Ben S. Bernanke, January 4th 2004. "The high level of markups is an important and perhaps insufficiently recognized feature of the current economic situation. To the extent that firms can maintain these markups, profits will continue to be high, supporting investment and equity values. To the extent that product-market competition erodes these

The trajectories of profits and margins are thus important for the NAIRU. Indeed, given the difficulties posed by estimating the NAIRU, they are a useful additional guide to the growth/inflation trade-off. The absence of reliable productivity data (because of potential revisions to real GDP) also suggests that it is important to focus on the trend for productive investment. An increase in productive investment may indicate that productivity is rising more quickly than indicated by the official data.

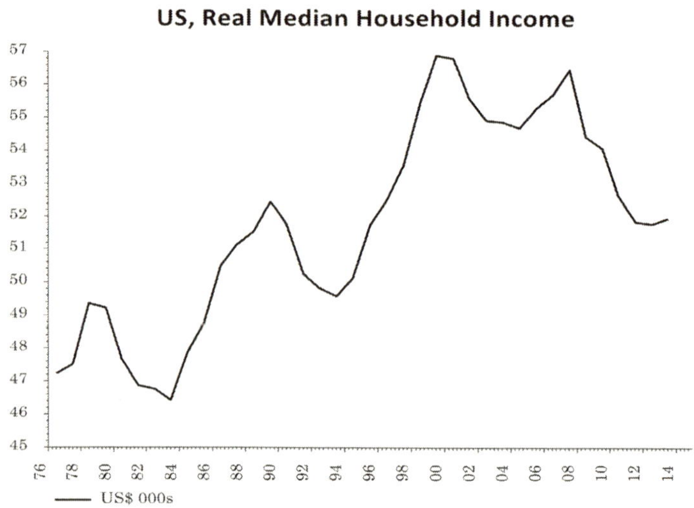

Source: GFC Economics

Chart 7c

For the NAIRU, technological change is critical because of the impact on profit margins. Changes in the distribution of wages as a result of increases in information technology (IT) spending will influence the NAIRU too. The particularly strong rise in IT expenditures since the crisis of 2008 suggests that productivity may be improving more quickly than reported by the BEA. A number of commentators have suggested

---

markups, as is likely to occur over time, downward pressure will be exerted on the inflation rate... As employment begins to pick up and the recovery matures, productivity growth is likely to decelerate, perhaps markedly. Nevertheless, slow growth in wages and the return to normal of price-cost markups should help keep inflation low."

that the payoff from software investment, for example, can be long.[15] In addition, it is possible that some of the future upward revisions to real GDP will be in investment itself. This would boost estimates of productivity. However, it would also imply that the *potential* efficiency gains will be even higher over the course of the economic cycle. In this context, a modest recovery in wages remains consistent with a NAIRU that is a long way below the FOMC's estimate.

Income inequality trends

Income inequality is a major policy concern. As FOMC chair Janet Yellen warned in October 2014, "The distribution of income and wealth in the United States has been widening more or less steadily for several decades, to a greater extent than in most advanced countries."[16] These trends have persisted: "Income inequality narrowed slightly during the Great Recession, as income fell more for the top than for others, but resumed widening in the recovery, and by 2013 it had nearly returned to the pre-recession peak."[17] Janet Yellen also questioned whether this trend of widening inequality was "compatible with values rooted in our nation's history, among them the high value Americans have traditionally placed on equality of opportunity."[18]

---

15 See *Is the Information Technology Revolution Over?*, David M. Byrne, Stephen D. Oliner, & Daniel E. Sichel, Finance and Economics Discussion Series, Federal Reserve Board, March 2013. See also *Patents, Innovation, and Productivity*, Jason Furman, November 7th 2014. "Finally, it is important to recognize that it often takes time for technical breakthroughs to appear in the productivity statistics because current technologies are often deeply intertwined with how we use physical, human and organizational capital… Such a process does not happen overnight. It seems reasonable then to expect that similar processes of industrial reorganization, resulting from revolutions in technologies such as mobile computing, robotics and genomic sequencing, will lead to a lag between the technology's introduction and full realization of its growth-inducing potential."

16 See *Perspectives on Inequality and Opportunity from the Survey of Consumer Finances*, Janet Yellen, October 17th 2014, p. 1.

17 Ibid., p. 5.

18 Ibid., pp. 1-2.

The median income is one possible proxy for assessing inequality. The real median household income in the US trended upwards from around 1967 and reached a peak of $56,895 in 1999. Indeed, it experienced a significant increase for most of the 1990s, rising 14.2% between 1992 and 1999. From 1999 to 2012, the real median household income fell 9.0% (from $56,895 to $51,758). It nudged up to $51,939 in 2013 (see chart 7c).[19]

Nevertheless, since the recession, the median income has fallen by more than the average income, implying that some income groups have been affected disproportionately.[20] Between 2007 and 2013, the real average income for households in the lowest quintile fell 10.2%. By contrast, those in the highest quintile saw their incomes drop 1.9% over the same period.[21] For the top 5%, this figure was just 0.1%. The same pattern has been recorded in the UK.[22]

Critics of unconventional monetary policies claim that quantitative easing (QE) has exacerbated inequality. The Survey of Consumer Finances indicates that the wealthiest 'lost out' disproportionately during the crisis.[23] The subsequent rise in asset valuations has ensured

19 Source: U.S. Census Bureau, Income, Median, Total, Households, All Races, Total, Constant Prices.

20 Source: U.S. Census Bureau, Income, Mean, Households, All Races, Total, Constant Prices. Since the financial crisis hit in 2007, the real median household income has fallen 8.0%. The real average household income has also shrunk, but by 4.4%.

21 Source: U.S. Census Bureau, Income, Mean, Households, All Races, Total, Constant Prices.

22 See *Unfair Shares*, Andrew G. Haldane, May 21st 2014, p. 2. "On standard metrics, the crisis probably reduced wealth inequalities because the collapse of asset values hit hardest existing asset-owners… Meanwhile, the crisis-induced narrowing of wealth inequalities has been at least partially reversed as asset prices have reflated rapidly over recent years." See also m*onetary policy, asset prices and distribution*, Ben Broadbent, October 23rd 2014. Mr. Broadbent argues that there has been an effect on wealth inequality, but no direct effect on income inequality.

23 See *2013 Survey of Consumer Finances*, Federal Reserve. From 2007 to 2010, the median value of before-tax family income fell 7.7%, whereas the corresponding mean figure fell 11.1%. This implies that top incomes suffered larger losses. From 2010 to 2013 however, the pre-crisis trend has continued: median household incomes continued to fall (4.7%) but the mean value rose (3.7%). Nevertheless,

that the trend towards wealth inequality evident prior to the recession of 2008/09 has resumed.

The Federal Reserve has a mandate to hit a 2% inflation target and achieve maximum employment. Nevertheless, a monetary policy that returns an economy to full employment may appear to have exacerbated inequality if it puts the economy back on the 'structural' path it was following prior to the crisis. In the long-run, inequality is determined by technology, institutions and globalisation. The role of QE is limited to reversing the cyclical downward pressure on wages. By returning the economy to full employment, an accommodative monetary policy can reduce inequality in the short-run.[24]

Indeed, FOMC member Daniel Tarullo has suggested that a "stronger labor market can provide a modest countervailing factor to income inequality trends by leading to higher wages at the bottom rungs of the wage scale." A broader wage recovery can be achieved by "reducing labor market slack [which] can help lay the foundation for a more sustained, self-reinforcing cycle of stronger aggregate demand, increased production, renewed investment, and productivity gains."[25] Boston Federal Reserve President, Eric Rosengren, stressed: "The biggest factor that affects inequality is losing your job because if you have no income the income disparity is quite large. So being focused on getting labor markets back to where we think full employment [lies] is I think the most tangible way that monetary policy can impact income inequality."[26]

---

this apparent convergence from 2007 to 2010 is not captured by the Census Bureau. The Census Bureau data are generally considered more reliable on measures of income distribution, whereas Survey of Consumer Finances data are most appropriate when measuring wealth.

24 See *Innocent Bystanders? Monetary Policy and Inequality in the U.S.*, Olivier Coibion, Yuriy Gorodnichenko, Lorenz Kueng & John Silvia, IMF Working Paper 199, August 2012.

25 See *Longer-Term Challenges for the American Economy,* Daniel K. Tarullo, April 9th 2014, p. 11.

26 See *Low for Long: A Q&A With Boston Fed's Rosengren*, Wall Street Journal, October 19th 2014.

Inequality of opportunity

Inequality in outcomes would be even more disconcerting if it were accompanied by inequality of opportunity. In such a scenario, inequality can become self-fulfilling. Indeed, Janet Yellen noted "that economic mobility in the United States has not changed much in the last several decades; that mobility is lower in the US than in most other advanced countries; and ... that economic mobility and income inequality among advanced countries are negatively correlated."[27] The empirical literature suggests that intra-generational mobility has not improved since the 1970s.[28] Indeed, for men there has been a decline since the 1970s, but this has been offset by increased mobility for women.

Miles Corak documents a positive relationship between income inequality and intergenerational income elasticity – a measure of how far the earnings of parents influence their children's potential income.[29] He observes that "Countries with greater inequality of incomes also tend to be countries in which a greater fraction of economic advantage and disadvantage is passed on between parents and their children."[30] The correlation – greater income inequality associated with diminished intergenerational mobility – is referred to as 'The Great Gatsby Curve'.

Some studies have sought to show that an economic 'position' in society has a major bearing on the potential to move up the income ladder. Geography can also have an impact on employment and earnings. A prominent scholar in this field, John Kain, developed the "spatial-mismatch hypothesis".[31] The mismatch refers to low-income households residing in areas which lack job opportunities. In practice, it has been

---

27 See *Perspectives on Inequality and Opportunity from the Survey of Consumer Finances*, Janet L. Yellen, October 17th 2014, p. 8.

28 See *Earnings Inequality and Mobility in the United States: Evidence from Social Security Data Since 1937*, Wojciech Kopczuck, Emmanuel Saez and Jae Song, The Quarterly Journal of Economics, 125(1), 2010, pp. 91-128.

29 See *Income Inequality, Equality of Opportunity, and Intergenerational Mobility*, Miles Corak, Journal of Economic Perspectives, 27(3), 2013, pp. 79-102.

30 Ibid., p. 80.

31 See *The Spatial Mismatch Hypothesis: Three Decades Later*, John F. Kain, Housing Policy Debate, 3(2), 1992, pp. 371-460.

difficult to decipher the direction of causality between geographical area of residence and employment prospects. However, a recent paper has found that "better job accessibility significantly decreases the duration of joblessness among lower-paid displaced workers. Blacks, females, and older workers are more sensitive to job accessibility than other subpopulations."[32]

The 'digital divide' may also be exacerbating inequality. Restricted internet access can have a detrimental impact on education. Online courses have proliferated, and schools now use the internet far more than before. It is difficult to acquire the IT skills that are sought after by employers without proper access to the internet. It can also increase 'matching frictions' because the internet is a major platform for recruitment. In the US, it had been assumed that "the rural make-up of the US was the main factor in a national broadband subscription rate that is just 73.4 per cent, behind other developed nations such as the UK and Germany, which have rates of 88 per cent."[33] However, "new Census Bureau statistics show a huge disparity among US cities and towns, with a gap of 65 percentage points between those with the highest and lowest subscription rates."[34] As such, "The majority of families in some of the US's poorest cities do not have a broadband connection."[35] This is linked to a broader on-going debate surrounding "net-neutrality". President Obama has favoured the reclassification of commercial broadband as a public utility under the Communications Act to make it more affordable. This is being opposed by Republicans. The decision will ultimately lie with the Federal Communications Commission (FCC).

---

32 See *Job Displacement and the Duration of Joblessness: The Role of Spatial Mismatch*, Fredrik Andersson, John C. Haltiwanger, Mark J. Kutzbach, Henry O. Pollakowski & Daniel H. Weinberg, Center for Economic Studies, Working Paper Series, April 2014.

33 See *Digital divide exacerbates US inequality*, Financial Times, October 28th 2014.

34 Ibid.

35 Ibid.

Theories of income inequality

Technology

The 'supply and demand' theory of inequality (the 'canonical' model) places the race between technology and education at the centre of the debate.[36] Technological progress increases the demand for skilled labour. If the supply of skilled labour cannot keep pace, then the premium for skilled labour rises, aggravating inequality. At the same time, innovation or investment in technology may weaken demand for lower-skilled labour and lead to lower unskilled wages.

The 'canonical' model has dominated mainstream academic research on inequality.[37] Rising inequality over the past three decades is seen as a consequence of a slowing rate of accumulation of human capital, which has failed to keep pace with technological change. Technological advances will widen income inequalities unless policies to counter this tendency are implemented. Better education policies are needed to raise the skill set of workers. Investment in human capital can be a major equaliser.

Despite providing a useful framework, the 'canonical' model fails to explain some key observations in the data.[38] More specifically, it implies labour-augmenting technological change will boost real earnings of *all* skill groups. As such, it cannot account for increasing inequality within the top of the income distribution, yet falling inequality at the bottom ('non-monotonic' wage dynamics). Indeed, "The canonical model of factor-augmenting

---

36 See *The Race Between Education and Technology,* Claudia Goldin and Lawrence F. Katz, Harvard University Press, 2010.

37 See *The Rise and Consequences of Inequality in the United States*, Alan B. Krueger, January 12th 2012. Krueger conducted a poll of professional economists asking which of many factors most contributed to rising inequality. The most important factor was skill-biased technical change. See also *Polanyi's Paradox and the Shape of Employment Growth,* David H. Autor, National Bureau of Economic Research, Working Paper 20485, September 2014. A more recent poll of leading academic economists, conducted by Chicago Initiative on Global Markets, found that a plurality of economists have accepted technological advances as the reason for the falling median wage.

38 See *What Does Human Capital Do? A Review of Goldin and Katz's The Race Between Education and Technology,* Daron Acemoglu and David H. Autor, Journal of Economic Literature, 50(2), 2012, pp. 426-463.

technical change robustly predicts that demand shifts favoring skilled workers will raise the skill premium *and* boost the real earnings of all skill groups."[39] However, real wages of low-skill workers have been declining since the early 1980s. Furthermore, the canonical model cannot explain polarisation of earnings or occupational polarisation.[40]

Daron Acemoglou and David Autor focus on a need to capture the multifaceted nature of human capital. In their alternative 'task-based' model, the fundamental units of the production process are job 'tasks' rather than workers' skills: "Workers produce work by performing job tasks, and different tasks require different types of skills. Workers with different types of skills have varying comparative advantages for these tasks. Changes in technology and in the supply of skills affect what types of tasks are in demand and how the available set of skills is assigned to these different tasks."[41] Tasks are characterised as routine/non-routine and cognitive/non-cognitive. Whilst this is a more nuanced approach than the 'canonical' model, inequality is still presented in terms of supply and demand, which may not be wholly capturing the complex dynamics driving inequality.

Globalisation

Globalisation has been cited as one of the main culprits for rising inequality in the industrialised West. Conventional trade theory predicts factor price equalisation in a more integrated world economy. This may lead to lower wages at the bottom as workers compete with cheaper labour in emerging market economies.[42] The free movement of capital, combined with comparatively restricted movement of labour, has further diminished the bargaining power of workers. Some estimates suggest that competition

---

39 See *What Does Human Capital Do? A Review of Goldin and Katz's The Race Between Education and Technology*, Daron Acemoglou and David H. Autor, Journal of Economic Literature, 50(2), 2012, p. 439.

40 Ibid., pp. 440-444.

41 See *What Does Human Capital Do? A Review of Goldin and Katz's The Race Between Education and Technology*, Daron Acemoglou and David Autor, Journal of Economic Literature, 50(2), 2012, p. 428.

42 See *Protection and Real Wages*, Wolfgang Stolper and Paul A. Samuelson, The Review of Economic Studies, 9(1), 1941.

from China can explain about a quarter of the decline in US manufacturing employment.[43] Another paper shows that US manufacturing employment fell significantly following a change in US trade policy that removed the potential for tariff increases on Chinese imports.[44]

Florence Jaumotte and Irina Tytell accept that globalisation has negatively affected the labour share in advanced economies. However, this is one of only several factors. They suggest that "Rapid technological change – especially in the information and communication sectors – has had a bigger impact, particularly on the labor share in unskilled sectors."[45]

Institutions

Other research focusses on the role of institutions.[46] The impact of technology is embedded in a wider institutional story. According to Frank Levy and Peter Temin, "There is no single determinant, whether education, minimum wage, capital or labour mobility, that determines the path of income distribution. Any specific measure therefore can alleviate the distress of some people, but it cannot change the overall distributional trends."[47] The authors constructed a 'Bargaining Power

---

43 See *The Second Machine Age: Work, Progress, and Prosperity in a Time of Brilliant Technologies*, Erik Brynjolfsson and Andrew McAfee, W.W. Norton & Co, 2014, p. 183.

44 See *The Surprisingly Swift Decline of U.S. Manufacturing Employment*, Justin R. Pierce and Peter K. Schott, Finance and Economics Discussion Series, Federal Reserve Board, 2014. See also *Trade and Inequality, Revisited*, Paul Krugman, Vox, June 15th 2007. See also *Trade and Wages, Reconsidered,* Paul Krugman, Brookings Panel on Economic Activity, Spring 2008. Paul Krugman argues that the impact of trade on inequality has risen due to the increase of abundant labour in China and the growing fragmentation of production.

45 See *How has the Globalization of Labor Affected the Labor Income Share in Advanced Countries?*, Florence Jaumotte and Irina Tytell, IMF Working Paper 298, December 2007, p.19.

46 See *Inequality and Institutions in 20th Century America*, Frank Levy and Peter Temin, National Bureau of Economic Research, Working Paper 13106, 2007. See also *The Price of Inequality*, Joseph E. Stiglitz, Penguin Books, 2013, p. 66. "Market forces are real, but that they are shaped by political processes. Markets are shaped by laws, regulations, and institutions."

47 See *Inequality and Institutions in 20th Century America*, Frank Levy and Peter Temin, National Bureau of Economic Research, Working Paper 13106, 2007, p. 41.

Index' to highlight the divergent paths of labour bargaining power and the median income of the top 1 percent of reported incomes.[48]

According to Levy and Temin, "This index can be thought of, roughly, as the share of average output per worker in the economy claimed by the median full-time worker as compensation."[49] Before the 1980s, these two series were relatively constant. Since then, their paths have diverged.

Writing in 1955, Simon Kuznets also suggested that institutions contributed to the decline in inequality during the 1930s and 1940s.[50] He argued that an improvement in "organization and adaptation" and the newly acquired "native" status granted to second and third generations of immigrants allowed them to reap the benefits of industrialisation. Democratic institutions facilitated their emancipation, which "led to a variety of protective and supporting legislation, much of it aimed to counteract the worst effects of rapid industrialization and urbanization."[51]

Daron Acemoglou and James Robinson (2002) are more explicit: "Overall, our theory of the Kuznets curve is that capitalist industrialization tends to increase inequality, but this inequality contains the seeds of its own destruction, because it induces a change in the political regime toward a more redistributive system."[52]

---

48 Ibid., p. 48. The bargaining power index is defined as the 'median annual compensation for full-time workers' over the 'annualised value of output per hour in the non-farm business sector'.

49 Ibid., p. 48.

50 See *Economic Growth and Income Inequality,* Simon Kuznets, The American Economic Review, 45(1), 1955.

51 Ibid., p. 17. See also *Obama set to bring more than 4m unauthorised workers out of shadows,* Financial Times, November 20th 2014. Immigration policy could have a significant effect on inequality. Indeed, President Barack Obama has recently announced plans of an immigration overhaul that would grant legal status to many unauthorised workers. This would give these unauthorised workers greater bargaining powers. In all likelihood, legalising a large portion of this workforce will lower competitive pressures on other workers at the lower-end of the income distribution, raising wages at the bottom and reducing inequality.

52 See *The Political Economy of the Kuznets Curve,* Daron Acemoglou and James A. Robinson, Review of Development Economics, 6(2), 2002, p. 184

The canonical model and the 'tasks' model rest on the hypothesis that workers are paid the marginal product of their labour. However, it is difficult to reconcile marginal productivity theory with the rapid growth of top incomes. FOMC member Daniel Tarullo concedes that whilst "Economists generally agree that technological change and globalization have played a major role [in rising inequality levels]… it is less clear whether technology and globalization are sufficient explanations for the increased share of income going to those at the very top of the income distribution."[53] Indeed, marginal productivity theory would struggle to explain the rise in the share of income taken by the top 1% and 0.1%.[54] Tarullo adds: "Other researchers have noted that a large share of the top earners is found in industries such as finance and law, suggesting that deregulation, corporate governance, and tax policy may have also played a role in the trend towards rising inequality."[55]

Thomas Piketty also argues that "This very sharp discontinuity at the top income levels is a problem for the theory of marginal productivity: when we look at the changes in the skill levels of different groups in the income distribution, it is hard to see any discontinuity between "the 9 percent" and "the 1 percent," regardless of what criteria we use: years of education, selectivity of educational institution, or professional experience."[56] Although "one would expect technological change to have altered the whole top end of the skill distribution in a more continuous way and to have worked its effects in all countries at a similar level of development", this has not been the case.[57] Furthermore, "that the explosion of very high salaries occurred in some developed countries but not others" suggests that institutional differences are likely to play a major role.[58]

---

53 See *Longer-Term Challenges for the American Economy,* Daniel K. Tarullo, April 9th 2014, p. 9.

54 See *The World Top Incomes Database,* Facundo Alvaredo, Anthony B. Atkinson, Thomas Piketty and Emmanuel Saez, http://topincomes.parisschoolofeconomics.eu/, January 14th 2014.

55 See *Longer-Term Challenges for the American Economy,* Daniel K. Tarullo, April 9th 2014, p. 10.

56 See *Capital in the 21st Century,* Thomas Piketty, Harvard University Press, 2014, p. 314.

57 Ibid., p. 330.

58 Ibid., p. 315.

Inequality and the NAIRU

Policymakers estimate the NAIRU using a variety of different techniques.[59] The latest economic projections available indicate that the Federal Reserve Board Members and Federal Reserve Banks Presidents believe the NAIRU lies between 5.2 – 5.5%, consistent with 2% PCE inflation.[60] The latest Congressional Budget Office (CBO) estimate of the long-term natural rate of unemployment is 5.2%.[61] Ultimately, however, the NAIRU is unobserved: there is a great deal of uncertainty surrounding official estimates.

The Boston Fed President Eric Rosengren recently stressed that the definition of full employment "is an empirical not a theoretical concept in many respects, so that if it turns out that inflation is low we should probe on the lower bound of that [unemployment rate]. We do want to get inflation back up to 2% and if we need tighter labor markets than we've historically needed in order to do that then we should allow the unemployment rate to drift further down."[62]

Nevertheless, the FOMC's analysis of inflation leaves much to be desired. In December 2014, Janet Yellen described low inflation as "transitory" given the slide in oil prices and strength of the Dollar. Ms. Yellen implied that the FOMC could still raise interest rates even though the y/y rate for the core consumption deflator was below its 2.0% target.[63] Core inflation on this basis was 1.41% in November 2014 (consumption deflator excluding food and energy) and has remained below the FOMC's target for the 32nd consecutive month (see chart 7d). It is likely to fall further in the coming months. Instead of raising interest rates, the FOMC has been forced to revise down its estimate for the NAIRU

---

59 See *Estimating Potential Output*, Frederic S. Mishkin, May 24th 2007.

60 See Federal Open Market Committee, Meeting calendars, statements, and minutes (2009-2015), Accessible Materials, FOMC December 16-17, 2014.

61 Source: U.S. Congressional Budget Office.

62 See *Low for Long: A Q&A With Boston Fed's Rosengren*, Wall Street Journal, October 19th 2014.

63 The 2.0% target actually refers to the annual change in the price index for *all* personal consumption expenditures (including food & energy). However, given the volatile and transitory nature of food & energy prices, the Fed implicitly targets the core deflator.

(based on the central tendency of its economic projections).[64] Further downward revisions are likely.

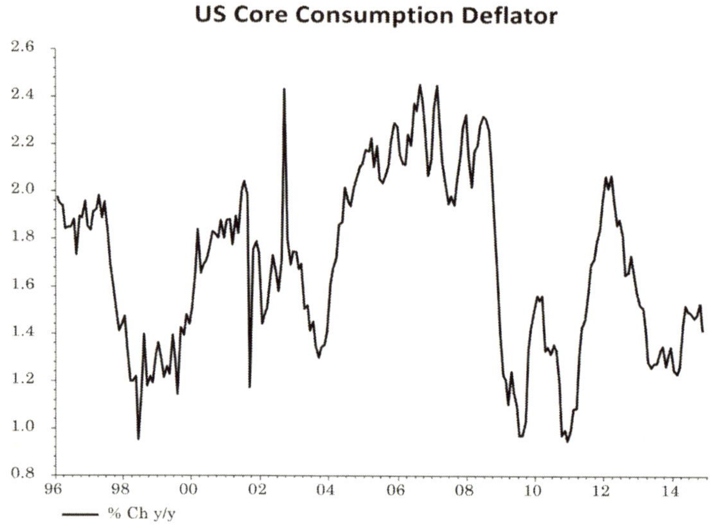

Source: GFC Economics

Chart 7d

There are a number of pitfalls when trying to estimate the NAIRU. Athanasios Orphanides has warned that output gaps were significantly mismeasured in the 1970s: on this occasion, the data overstated the size of the economy.[65] The productivity slowdown at the time was not captured in the data and potential output was lower than assumed. Subsequent revisions to real GDP provide confirmation of this downward bias.

Given the possible mismeasurement of the economy today due to rapid advances in technology (see chapter 3), the series of papers by Orphanides

---

64 See Federal Open Market Committee, Meeting calendars, statements, and minutes, Accessible Materials. The central tendency was revised down from 5.2-5.8% in December 2013 to 5.2-5.6% in March 2014. This was revised down again to 5.2-5.5% in June 2014, where it has remained as of December 2014.

65 See, for example, *Monetary Policy Rules Based on Real-Time Data*, Athanasios Orphanides, American Economic Review, 91(4), pp. 964-985, 2001. See also, *The Quest for Prosperity Without Inflation,* Athanasios Orphanides, Journal of Monetary Economics, 50(3), pp. 633-663, 2003.

are more relevant than ever.[66] The rate of technological progress in semiconductors, for example, may be understated.[67] Furthermore, there is a compelling argument that in many instances spending on 'intangibles' is incorrectly classified as a cost to a firm.[68] Rather, company expenditures on "product design, marketing and customer support, and human capital and organization development are essential inputs to innovation", and therefore constitute important investments, which should be included in the official GDP figures.[69]

To reiterate, faster GDP growth and higher productivity would not automatically imply that the NAIRU was lower. For the unemployment-inflation trade-off to improve, real wages must diverge from productivity. The forces that drive inequality may also be undermining the bargaining power of workers. This is evident from the falling membership rates of unions since the 1970s.[70] However, the role of technology in restraining wage growth has been critical too.

Some economists believe that FOMC estimates of the NAIRU are too optimistic and claim that the unemployment-inflation trade-off has

---

66 See also *Real-Time Properties of the Federal Reserve's Output Gap*, Rochelle M. Edge and Jeremy B. Rudd, Finance and Economics Discussion Series, Federal Reserve Board, 2012. Interestingly, these authors conclude that "the Federal Reserve's output gap is more reliably estimated in real time than previous studies have documented for earlier periods."

67 See *Is the Information Technology Revolution Over?*, David M. Byrne, Stephen D. Oliner & Daniel E. Sichel, Finance and Economics Discussion Series, Federal Reserve Board, March 2013. This paper relates specifically to semiconductors, though the argument can be extrapolated to other areas of technological progress.

68 In the 2013 comprehensive revision of the national accounts, the Bureau of Economic Analysis expanded the classification of fixed investment to include business, academic, non-profit, and government expenditures on research and development (R&D). The BEA is aware of issues surrounding investment in intangibles and such benchmark classification revisions will enable the national accounts to accurately measure the economy as it evolves.

69 See *How Do You Measure a "Technological Revolution"?*, Carol A. Corrado and Charles R. Hulten, American Economic Review, 100(2), 2010.

70 Source: BLS, Union Members. The union membership rate in 2013 was 11.3%, down from 20.1% in 1983, the first year when comparable union data were available.

deteriorated. For example Dave Reifschneider, William Wascher and David Wilcox (2013) examine the supply-side damage to the US economy since the crisis and conclude that "The recent financial crisis and ensuing recession appear to have put the productive capacity of the economy on a lower and shallower trajectory."[71] As a result, "the natural rate of unemployment may have moved up between ½ and 1 ½ percentage points since the onset of the recent recession."[72] In particular, they note that "hysteresis effects associated with the continued high level of long-term unemployment could lead to permanent damage in the productivity or employability of those who remain willing to work, and could lead others to throw in the towel and permanently exit the labor force."[73] The long-term unemployment rate tumbled from 4.398% in April 2010 to 1.804% in November 2014 (see chart 7e).[74] Nevertheless, this remains elevated in relation to previous economic cycles.

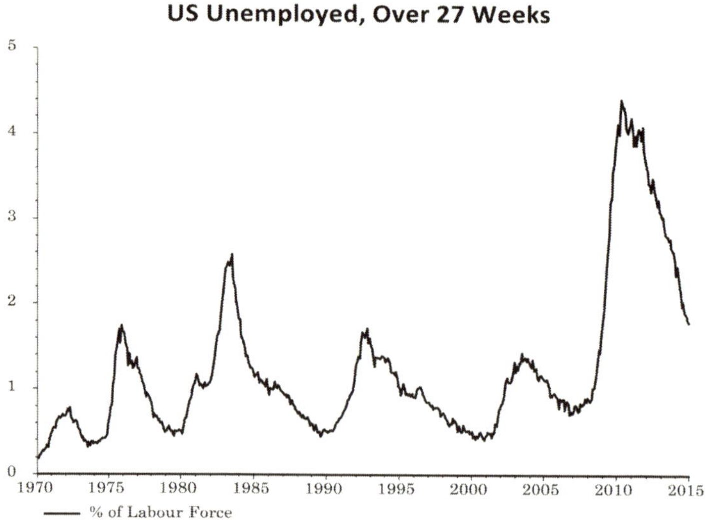

Source: GFC Economics

Chart 7e

71 See *Aggregate Supply in the Unites States: Recent Developments and Implications for the Conduct of Monetary Policy*, Dave Reifschneider, William Wascher, and David Wilcox, Finance and Economics Discussion Series, Federal Reserve Board, 2013, p. 1.

72 Ibid., p. 20.

73 Ibid., p. 21.

74 Source: BLS, CPS, Unemployment, 27 Weeks & Over, Rate.

The shifts in the Beveridge curve in the current economic recovery could be viewed as a reflection of higher structural unemployment. The Beveridge curve plots the job openings rate against the unemployment rate. It typically moves outwards in the early stages of an economic recovery, before looping back in. There has been a decisive shift to the right in this curve, but it has failed to move back in. At first glance, this outward shift implies there has been a decline in the matching efficiency between job openings and hiring. Nonetheless, Peter Diamond and Aysegul Sahin (2014) provide empirical evidence to counter this argument. Historical data shows that "an outward shift in the Beveridge curve does not predict how low unemployment can get during the recovery."[75]

Wages and inequality in an investment-led recovery

The impact of technology on the quantity and quality of jobs being created in the economy could be reflected in 'job polarisation'. The David Autor framework provides a useful explanation:

"Since jobs that are intensive in either abstract or manual tasks are generally found at opposite ends of the occupational skill spectrum – in professional, managerial, and technical occupations on the one hand, and in service and laborer occupations on the other – a straightforward implication of this reasoning is that computerization of routine job tasks may lead to the simultaneous growth of high-education, high-wage and low-education, low-wages jobs at the expense of middle-wage, middle-education jobs."[76]

Job polarisation need not necessarily lead to wage polarisation. There are three potentially mitigating factors: complementarities, income elasticity of demand and labour supply.[77] There is arguably more scope

75 See *Shifts in the Beveridge Curve,* Peter A. Diamond and Aysegul Sahin, Federal Reserve Bank of New York, August 2014, p.4

76 See *Polanyi's Paradox and the Shape of Employment Growth,* David H. Autor, September 2014, pp. 11-12.

77 Ibid., p. 16. 'Complementarities' arise when a new technology serves to increase the value of labour, whilst not substituting directly for it. For example, an excavator will

for complementarities in non-routine, cognitive work.[78] In their book, Erik Brynjolfsson and Andrew McAfee claim that recent technological advances such as big data and analytics, high-speed communications, and rapid prototyping "have *augmented* the contributions made by more abstract and data-driven reasoning, and in turn have increased the value of people with the right engineering, creative, or design skills."[79] David Autor notes that workers in more abstract-intensive occupations (those that require intuition, creativity and problem-solving capabilities) have also benefitted from elastic demand and low labour supply.[80] On the other hand, manual intensive tasks (i.e. tasks requiring "situational adaptability, visual and language recognition, and in-person interactions") provide less opportunity for complementarities.[81] Furthermore, final demand for manual-intensive work tends to be relatively price inelastic, whilst labour supply to these sectors is elastic. These three factors have served to restrict wage gains in non-routine, non-cognitive tasks.

However, there are more intricate dynamics at work. In particular, "as technical advances increase labor productivity, employers can afford to pay more for each worker. In some cases, this is reflected directly in higher wages and benefits. In other cases, the prices of products and services fall, so the real wages of workers increases as they are able to buy more with each dollar. As productivity improves, total amount of output

---

raise the marginal product of a construction worker (compared to, say, a shovel), yet it cannot substitute directly for the construction worker. 'Income elasticity of demand' refers to the responsiveness of demand for certain goods with respect to income. Relatively inelastic final demand, as in the case of food, can lead to a situation where productivity growth in the food sector outpaces final demand, resulting in higher unemployment in that sector. However, as noted by Mr. Autor, most technological improvements have ultimately led to increased consumption rather than greater savings as consumers seek to enjoy the benefits of new technologies.

78 Recall that the task-based framework categorises jobs as routine/non-routine and cognitive/non-cognitive.

79 See *The Second Machine Age: Work, Progress, and Prosperity in a Time of Brilliant Technologies*, Erik Brynjolfsson and Andrew McAfee, W.W. Norton & Co., 2014, p. 135.

80 See *Polanyi's Paradox and the Shape of Employment Growth,* David H. Autor, September 2014, pp. 17-18.

81 Ibid., pp. 18-19.

per person would increase, but the amount earned by human workers could either fall or rise with the remainder going to capital owners."[82]

Capital owners would appear to have the upper-hand. Nevertheless, this need not continue. Paradoxically, the biggest threat to capital comes from capital itself. "In a free market, the biggest premiums go to the scarcest inputs needed for production. In a world where capital can be replicated at a relatively low cost (think of computer chips or even software), the marginal value of capital will tend to fall, even if more capital is used overall. The value of existing capital will actually be driven down as new capital is added cheaply at the margin. Thus, the rewards earned by capitalists may not automatically grow relative to labor. Instead the shares will depend on the exact details of the production, distribution, and governance systems."[83]

Furthermore, "the payoff will depend on which inputs to production are scarcest. If digital technologies create cheap substitutes for labor, then it's not a good time to be a laborer. But if digital technologies also can increasingly substitute for capital, then capital owners shouldn't expect to earn high returns either."[84]

Jeremy Rifkin claims there is a paradox underlying a dynamic and entrepreneurial society. Technology may drive marginal costs down to zero.[85] This is epitomised by the availability of free services on the internet. As a result, the return on technology may fall (in much the same way that an abundance of capital will lead to a decline in the marginal product of capital).

These hypotheses need to be treated with some caution. Capitalism is highly adaptable. The role of advertising on the internet is one clear example. Whilst Google obtains no direct revenues for providing

---

82 See *The Second Machine Age: Work, Progress, and Prosperity in a Time of Brilliant Technologies*, Erik Brynjolfsson and Andrew McAfee, W.W. Norton & Co., 2014, p. 143.

83 Ibid., pp. 145-146.

84 Ibid., p. 146.

85 See *The Zero Marginal Cost Society: The Internet of Things, The Collaborative Commons, and the Eclipse of Capitalism*, Jeremy Rifkin, Palgrave Macmillan, 2014.

its 'search' service, companies bid for its advertising space. Much will depend on the regulation of technology, including who will control the rights to the 'digital economy'. In practice, it seems difficult to maintain a competitive environment, which would drive marginal costs to zero. The internet, for example, is perhaps better suited to support quasi-monopolies, due to 'network' effects. This may in turn support innovation and growth that would otherwise be absent in a competitive market.[86] However, companies such as Google are coming under increasing scrutiny for supposed anti-competitive practices, with the European Parliament recently voting in favour of 'breaking up' Google, though this vote was largely symbolic.[87] Regulators will have a major role to play moving forward.

Fears that jobs are being lost to technology tend to grow in a recession. In reality, it can be difficult to distinguish between cyclical and structural unemployment. Recessions may speed up turnover in the labour market. In Brynjolfsson and McAfee's conversations with CEOs, these revealed "that advances in information technology had rendered many routine information-processing jobs superfluous. At the same time, when profits and revenues are on the rise, it can be hard to eliminate jobs." The same authors argue that "the recession ... made it easier to implement a round of painful streamlining and layoffs. As the recession ended and profits and demand returned, the jobs doing routine work were not restored."[88] Indeed, the previous three recessions have been characterised by jobless recoveries.[89] In particular, job losses have been concentrated in middle-income jobs, which have not returned to their previous levels.

However, over time complementarities will emerge. This will actually increase the value of each input in the production process, including

---

86 See *Everybody wants to rule the world,* The Economist, November 29th 2014.

87 See *Euro-MPs eye action to break up Google,* Financial Times, November 27th 2014.

88 See *The Second Machine Age: Work, Progress, and Prosperity in a Time of Brilliant Technologies*, Erik Brynjolfsson and Andrew McAfee, W.W. Norton & Co., 2014, pp. 139-140.

89 See *The Trend is the Cycle: Job Polarization and Jobless Recoveries*, Nir Jaimovich and Henry E. Siu, National Bureau of Economic Research, Working Paper 18334, August 2012.

labour. In reality, "businesses rarely get significant performance gains from simply 'paving the cowpaths' as opposed to rethinking how the business can be redesigned to take advantage of new technologies."[90] Creativity and organisational redesign are crucial to investments in digital technologies. As a result, "the best way to use new technologies is usually not to make a literal substitution of a machine for each human worker, but to restructure the process."[91]

Indeed, investment can lead to a virtuous, self-fulfilling cycle: "each dollar of computer capital was often the catalyst for more than ten dollars of complementary investments in 'organizational capital', or investments in training, hiring, and business process design. The reorganization often eliminates a lot of routine work, such as repetitive order entry, leaving behind a residual set of tasks that require relatively more judgement, skills, and training."[92]

The rationale is clear, as noted by economists Richard Cyert and David Mowery in 1987:

"By reducing the costs of production and thereby lowering the price of a particular good in a competitive market, technological change frequently leads to increases in output demand: greater output demand results in increased production, which requires more labor, offsetting the employment effects of reductions in labor requirements per unit of output stemming from technological change … Historically and, we believe, for the foreseeable future, reductions in labor requirements per unit of output resulting from new process technologies have been and will continue to be outweighed by the beneficial employment effects of the expansion in total output that generally occurs."[93]

---

90 See *The Second Machine Age: Work, Progress, and Prosperity in a Time of Brilliant Technologies*, Erik Brynjolfsson and Andrew McAfee, W. W. Norton & Company, 2014, p. 138.

91 Ibid., p. 138.

92 Ibid., p. 137.

93 See *Technology and Employment: Innovation and Growth in the U.S. Economy*, Richard M. Cyert and David C. Mowery, National Academies Press, 1987.

More efficient use of labour does not imply lower demand for workers. Initially, rising productivity can serve to lower marginal costs. This will translate into cheaper prices for the consumer, higher profits for firms, or both.[94] If prices fall, then "lower prices [may] lead to greater demand for the goods, which can ultimately lead to an increase in demand for labor as well. Whether or not this will actually happen depends on the elasticity of demand (responsiveness of demand to price changes).[95] Economic theory allows for the possibility that "when demand is very elastic, greater productivity leads to enough of an increase in demand that more labor ends up employed." This may seem paradoxical, "But to economists there is no paradox, just an inevitable implication of elastic demand. This is especially common in new industries like information technology."[96]

94 See *Monetary Policy and the Economic Outlook: 2004*, Ben S. Bernanke, January 4th 2004.

95 See *The Second Machine Age: Work, Progress, and Prosperity in a Time of Brilliant Technologies*, Erik Brynjolfsson and Andrew McAfee, W. W. Norton & Company, 2014, p. 176.

96 Ibid., pp. 176-177.

Inequality and the NAIRU *update*

Real median incomes still under pressure

The real median household income in the US remains well below pre-recession levels. Monthly employment growth averaged an impressive 251,300 in 2014, but the real median wage fell 1.5% y/y.[97] Technological progress is generating a higher demand for a subset of skills that are complementary to innovations, while diminishing demand for others. This may in turn be leading to labour market polarisation, fuelling inequality. The "Income and Poverty in the United States" report is the key source of median income data in the US.[98] The real median household income fell from $54,462 in 2013 to $53,657 in 2014. The real median income remains 6.5% below pre-recession levels (2007) and 7.2% below the 1999 peak.[99]

Labour market polarisation can be judged by the shares of aggregate income captured by different percentile groups.[100] On this measure, labour market polarisation has intensified since 2007. The share of aggregate income captured by the highest fifth of the income distribution rose from 49.7% to 51.2% in 2014. Within this, the top five percent increased their share from 21.2% to 21.9%. All other quintiles now capture a lower proportion of aggregate income. The share of the second highest quintile slipped from 23.4% to 23.2%; the middle quintile dipped from 14.8% to 14.3%; the second lowest quintile fell from 8.7% to 8.2%, while the lowest fifth declined from 3.4% to 3.1%.[101]

---

97 Source: Bureau of Labor Statistics (BLS), Employment, CES, Nonfarm, Payroll, Total and U.S. Census Bureau, Income, Median, Households, Total, All races, Constant Prices.

98 See *Income and Poverty in the United States: 2014, Current Population Reports*, Carmen Denavas-Watt & Bernadette D. Proctor, September 16th 2015.

99 Source: U.S. Census Bureau, Income, Median, Households, Total, All races, Constant Prices. The real median income peaked at $57,843 in 1999, and was $57,357 in 2007.

100 Source: U.S. Census Bureau, Income, Share of Aggregate Income, Households, All Races.

101 However, labour market polarisation did not increase in 2014. The share captured by the top twenty percent slipped from 51.4% in 2013 to 51.2% in 2014, while income accruing to the top five percent dropped from 22.2% to 21.9%. This was offset by a rise in the share of the fourth quintile, from 23.0% to 23.2%. All other quintile groups were unchanged.

The latest Income and Poverty report incorporates the 2015 Current Population Survey Annual Social and Economic Supplement (CPS ASEC). It provides the data for 2014 and is based on a redesigned questionnaire, which has attempted to improve the estimate of the median income. As a result, the 2013 real median income was revised up by 3.2%, from $52,789 to $54,462. The annual increase for 2013 is now 3.5%, compared with the 0.4% rise originally reported.

This revision reflected important changes to the survey methodology. Of the 98,000 addresses sampled, approximately 30,000 were randomly selected to receive a newly designed questionnaire. This new questionnaire was used for the latest annual figure. With the release of the latest numbers (for 2014), there has been a backward adjustment to the 2013 data.

Prior to 2013, the questions on income sources had remained unchanged since 1994. However, the CPS ASEC suffered from deficiencies such as misclassification, under-reporting of income, and under-reporting of enrolment in means-tested government programmes. The redesigned questionnaire attempted to improve – amongst other things – the measurement of retirement income (which tended to be under-reported in the CPS ASEC) and asset income (which was improperly classified and measured).

The questionnaire revealed a significant under-reporting of incomes. The total number of income recipients and aggregate income were both revised higher. As expected, a significant number of people had previously been failing to report various sources of income. For example, the number of recipients of retirement income was shown to be 51.7% higher on the basis of the new questionnaire, pushing up the aggregate income by 22.2%. For those who received income from an IRA (Individual Retirement Account), Keogh, and/or 401(k) (all different types of pension plans), there was a 419.5% rise in recipients, and a corresponding 230.0% increase in aggregate income. Aggregate interest income climbed 111.7% using the revamped CPS ASEC.[102]

---

102 See *The Effects of the Changes to the Current Population Survey Annual Social and Economic Supplement on Estimates of Income*, Jessica L. Semega and Edward Welniak, Jr., Proceedings of the 2015 Allied Social Science Association (ASSA) Research Conference, 2015.

These methodological changes boosted the real median income for 2013. This one-off adjustment will obscure comparisons with earlier years, because the data prior to 2013 were not revised. Critically, the 2014 data suggests that, allowing for this revision, the real median income has continued to trend down.

More on labour market polarisation

The Current Population Survey (CPS) provides information on employment by *occupation*.[103] This is a useful complement to the establishment survey, which produces the industry data.[104] The CPS provides a further insight into the *types* of jobs being created.[105] This survey shows that the US created a combined total of 5.25m new jobs in 2014 and 2015.[106] The vast majority – 4.15m – were in management, professional & related occupations.[107] Low-wage 'service' occupations added just 25k jobs over these two years.[108] It is important to distinguish between service occupations and service industries. Specifically, "Service occupations are defined by the Census Bureau as jobs that involve helping, caring for or assisting others."[109] Service industries, on the other hand, encompass a wide range of businesses involved in, for example, healthcare, finance and communications. These service sector businesses

---

103 The Current Population Survey (CPS) is also known as the 'household survey'.

104 See BLS, Labor Force Statistics from the Current Population Survey, Historical comparability of occupation and industry data from the Current Population Survey. Retrieved from: http://www.bls.gov/cps/cpsoccind.htm. According to the BLS, "The occupational classification reflects the type of job or work that the person does, while the industry classification reflects the business activity of their employer or company."

105 Whereas industry refers to the principle activity of the firm, occupation refers to the specific tasks of the worker. For example, administrative staff will be employed in a range of industries.

106 Source: BLS, Employment, CPS, 16 Years & Over.

107 Source: BLS, Employment, CPS, By Occupation, Management, Professional & Related.

108 Source: BLS, Employment, CPS, By Occupation, Service.

109 See *The Polarization of Job Opportunities in the U.S. Labor Market*, David Autor, The Hamilton Project, April 2010, p. 8.

encompass many different occupations.[110] Service industries are utilising technology to create high-skilled, high-wage jobs. The skewed distribution of job gains towards high-wage occupations underlines the profound changes underway in the US.

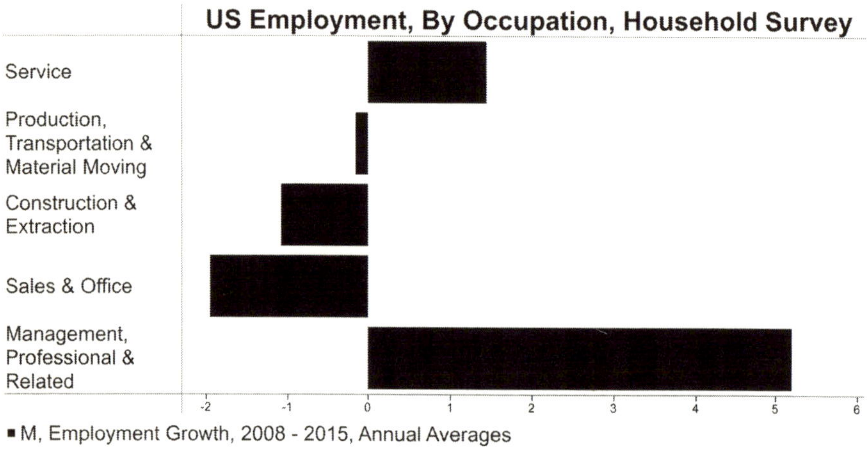

Table 13

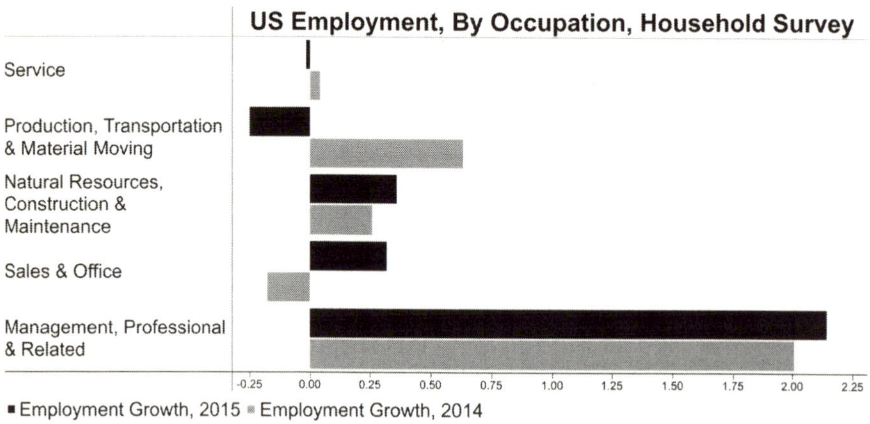

Table 14

110 Source: BLS, Employment, CES, Nonfarm, Payroll, Total and private-service providing and BLS, Employment, CPS, 16 Years & Over and By Occupation, Service. Private-service providing industries accounted for 83.7% of total private non-farm employment in 2015. By contrast, service occupations accounted for only 17.4% of all employment in 2015, according to the household survey.

Wage growth is determined by complementarities, the elasticity of demand and supply. The annual rate for average hourly earnings has been subdued during the economic recovery since 2008/09 (see chart 7f). Nonetheless, this masks a divergence between industries. Consistent with labour market polarisation, wage gains have occurred at both the upper- and lower-end of the income distribution. In the two years to February 2016, the fastest wage growth occurred in the information sector (8.37%). The rise in information pay is linked to greater demand for tech-related employment. Wage growth was also strong in the highly-paid utilities (4.83%) and financial activities (4.96%) industries. However, low-paid jobs in leisure & hospitality (5.95%) and retail trade (5.34%) experienced a significant increase in earnings as well. This contrasts with an overall average pay rise of 4.19% over the two years.[111] Wage growth has been subdued in middle-income jobs found in manufacturing, education & health services, and wholesale trade.[112]

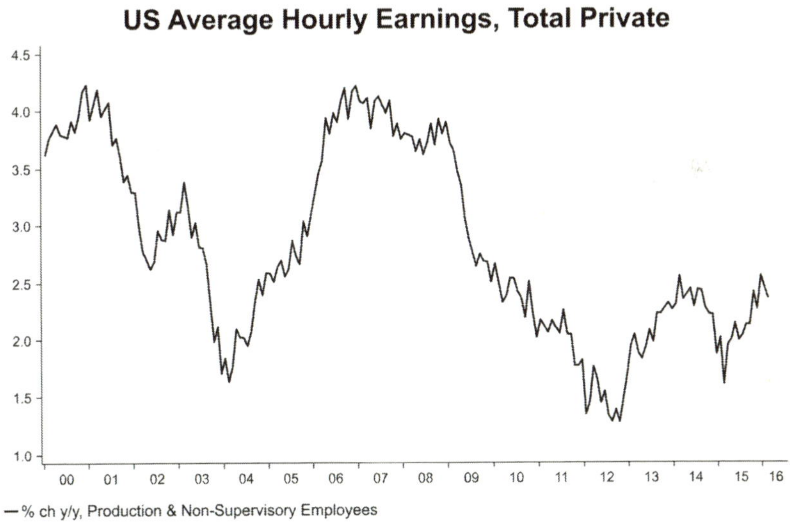

Source: Macrobond

Chart 7f

111 Source: BLS, Earnings, Average Hourly Earnings, All Employees, Total Private.

112 Source: BLS, Earnings, Average Hourly Earnings, All Employees, Manufacturing, Education & Health Services and Wholesale trade. Average hourly earnings for education & health services climbed 3.90% in the two years to February 2016. This was followed by wholesale trade (+3.76%) and manufacturing (+3.52%).

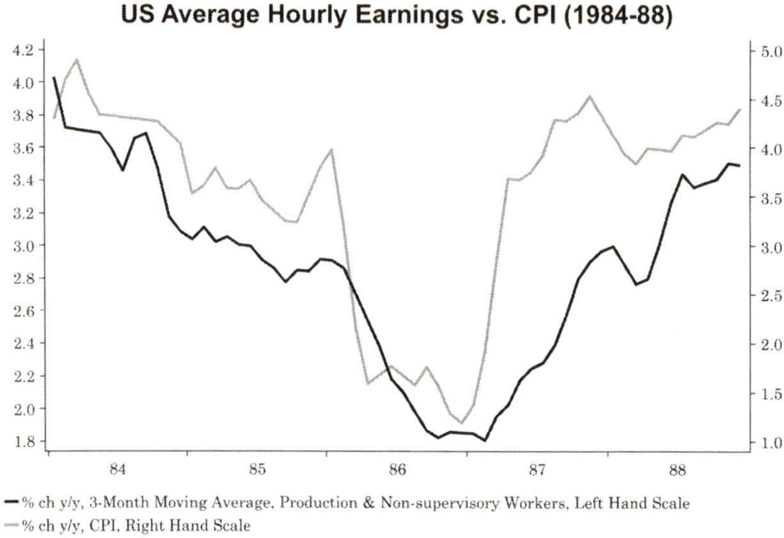

Source: GFC Economics

Chart 7g

What are wages doing?

The steady drop in the unemployment rate has focussed the attention of economists on wage indicators. A pick-up in wages would not necessarily presage a return of core inflation towards the FOMC's 2.0% target. The rise in profit margins witnessed since 2009 may allow firms to absorb wage increases, without having to raise prices.[113] Nevertheless, to reiterate, both measures of average hourly earnings suggested that the rise in wages was still well below the growth rate seen prior to the crisis of 2008.[114] The picture for 2015 was, of course, muddied by the sharp

113 Source: BEA, Price, Costs & Profit per Unit of Real Gross Value Added of Nonfinancial Domestic Corporate Business, Corporate Profits With IVA & CCAdj (Unit Profits From Current Production). Profit margins peaked at $0.161 in Q3 2014, 66.0% above the trough of Q2 2009 ($0.097). By Q3 2015, profit margins had fallen back to $0.150.

114 Source: BLS, Earnings, Average Hourly Earnings, All Employees, Total Private and Production & Non-Supervisory Employees, Total Private. Average hourly earnings for all employees in the private sector climbed 2.64% y/y in December 2015. This was the quickest pace since July 2009, but well below the peak of 3.61% y/y in June 2007. However, the y/y rate slipped to 2.22% in February 2016. Similarly, average hourly earnings for production & non-supervisory workers in the private sector were

decline in oil prices, which pushed inflation lower. In 1986, a large drop in oil prices was also followed by a deceleration in the growth of average hourly earnings (see chart 7g). In real terms, average hourly earnings were rising more quickly during 2015 (see chart 7h).[115]

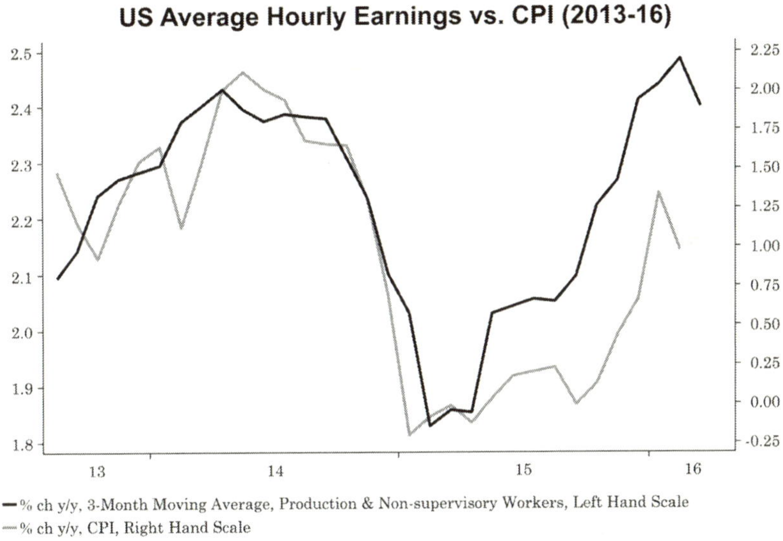

Source: GFC Economics

Chart 7h

The Employment Cost Index (ECI) published by the Bureau of Labor Statistics (BLS) is closely watched by the Federal Reserve. By the fourth quarter of 2015, the ECI showed that wages & salaries in the private sector were increasing at an annual rate of just 2.14% (see chart 7i).[116]

---

up 2.56% y/y in December 2015, before falling back to 2.35% y/y in February 2016. This was also far below the previous cyclical peak of 4.22% y/y in December 2006.

115 Source: BLS, Earnings, Average Hourly Earnings, Production & Non-Supervisory Employees, Total Private, Constant Prices. For production & supervisory workers, the y/y rate for average hourly earnings in real terms averaged 2.53% in 2015. This compares with an average rise of 2.10% y/y in nominal terms.

116 Source: BLS. United States, Productivity, Costs & Hours Worked, Employment Cost Index, Wages & Salaries, Private Industry, All Workers. The ECI for benefits in the private sector increased 1.30% y/y in Q4 2015. The ECI for total compensation in the private sector, a combination of wages & salaries and benefits, climbed 1.88% y/y in Q4 2015. The ECI for total compensation for all civilian workers rose 1.96% y/y in Q4 2015.

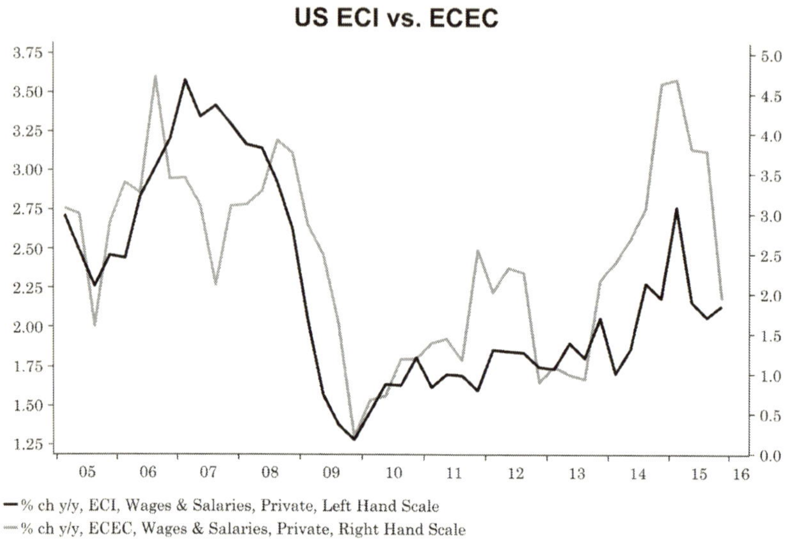

Source: GFC Economics

Chart 7i

The ECI is derived from the National Compensation Survey (NCS) and includes data on total compensation, wages & salaries and benefits. The Employer Costs for Employee Compensation (ECEC) is derived from the same survey. However, unlike the ECI, the ECEC is calculated using the current distribution of employment and is, therefore, affected by changes in employment between industries and occupations.[117] The ECEC measure of wages & salaries had been rising more quickly than other wage indicators. The ECEC accelerated to 4.68% y/y in Q1 2015, but the y/y rate fell back to 1.93% in Q4.[118] The earlier divergence between this measure and the ECI reflected a shift towards higher-paid

117 The ECI uses *fixed* employment weights. The latest ECI data (Q4 2015) were calculated using 2012 employment counts. See *Employer Costs for Employee Compensation – December 2015*, BLS News Release, technical note, March 10th 2016.

118 Source: BLS, Employer Cost for Employee Compensation, Wages & Salaries, Private Industry, Cost of Compensation (Cost per Hour Worked), Professional & Business Services, Information. The acceleration in Q1 2015 was caused by wage growth in high-skilled sectors related to services. The ECEC for wages & salaries for professional & business services surged 8.91% y/y in Q1 2015. Information climbed 6.40% y/y in the same period.

jobs.[119] The ECEC is able to capture the disruptive impact of technology on the labour market structure. Technology is creating a swathe of new services with higher-paid positions, and this initially pushed the ECEC up more quickly than the ECI.

Another estimate of wages is provided by the Federal Reserve Bank of Atlanta (FRBA). This tracks median wage growth in the US using household data.[120] In contrast to the U.S. Census Bureau median household income data, this indicator does *not* estimate the worker in the middle of the income distribution. Rather, it first calculates the annual wage growth for all workers, and *subsequently* takes the median of the wage growth distribution.[121] This was up 3.2% y/y in the three months to February. The Conference Board's 'jobs plentiful' less 'jobs hard to get' index has been an excellent lead for the FRBA wage growth tracker (see chart 7j). The data from the Conference Board have been consistent with a somewhat stronger rise in wages.[122]

---

119 The opposite dynamic occured in the late-1980s and early-1990s. See *Explaining the differential growth rates of the ECI and the ECEC*, Michael K. Lettau, Mark A. Loewesinstein, & Aaron T. Cushner, BLS, Summer 1997. Between March 1987 and March 1996, growth in the ECI for wage & salaries exceeded the ECEC by 0.6 percentage points per year. This difference was due to a shift in employment towards lower-paid industries.

120 Source: Atlanta Fed Measure of Median Wage Growth, Wages & Salaries, Wage Growth, Overall, 3 Month Moving Average. The underlying source data are derived from the Current Population Survey. Earnings are 'top-coded' (i.e. cannot exceed a certain limit), and individuals whose pay is below the current federal minimum wage for tips-based workers are also excluded.

121 The Federal Reserve Bank of Atlanta matches the hourly earnings of individuals compared with one-year prior. It takes the median of the distribution of 12-month wage changes for each month. This 'matched' sample has a slightly greater share of older, more educated workers in professional jobs than the sample of all wage & salary earners: educated workers are more likely to be continuously employed.

122 Source: Conference Board, Consumer Surveys, Consumer Confidence Index, Employment, 'Present Situation, Jobs Plentiful' and 'Present Situation, Jobs Hard to Get'. The 'jobs plentiful' less 'jobs hard to get' index slipped to -2.1 in February. This was down from the high of August 2015 (0.4) and well below the two previous cyclical peaks (11.4 in March 2007 and 46.2 in July 2000). Nevertheless, it was significantly above the trough of -46.1 in November 2009.

Source: GFC Economics

Chart 7j

The Beveridge curve and the NAIRU

Job openings (or vacancies) offered an early warning that the fall in house prices was a threat to economic growth before the Credit Crunch erupted in 2008.[123] These numbers have historically provided a reliable lead for the unemployment rate (see chart 7k). Since the summer of 2009, job openings have risen sharply. By August 2014, the 3-month moving average for vacancies had surpassed the top of the previous economic cycle, and hit a record 5.485m in September 2015.[124] Job openings subsequently levelled out. Nevertheless, the 3-month average for January 2016 was still 14.1% above the last cyclical high witnessed in

123 Source: BLS, Job Openings, Level, Total, Non-farm. Openings hit a high of 4.824m in April 2007, before turning down. The 3-month average peaked in May 2007 at 4.680m. The 3-month average eventually fell to a low of 2.310m in August 2009.

124 Source, BLS, Job Openings, Level, Total, Non-farm. The 3-month average for job openings climbed to 4.774m in August 2014. The previous peak in the 3-month average for job openings was in May 2007 (4.680m).

2007.[125] Openings have been notably strong in professional & business services and education & health services.[126] Furthermore, the number of job openings may be understated, particularly in professional & business services. The Job Openings and Labor Turnover Survey (JOLTS) does not include "temporary help agencies, employee leasing companies, outside contractors, or consultants".[127]

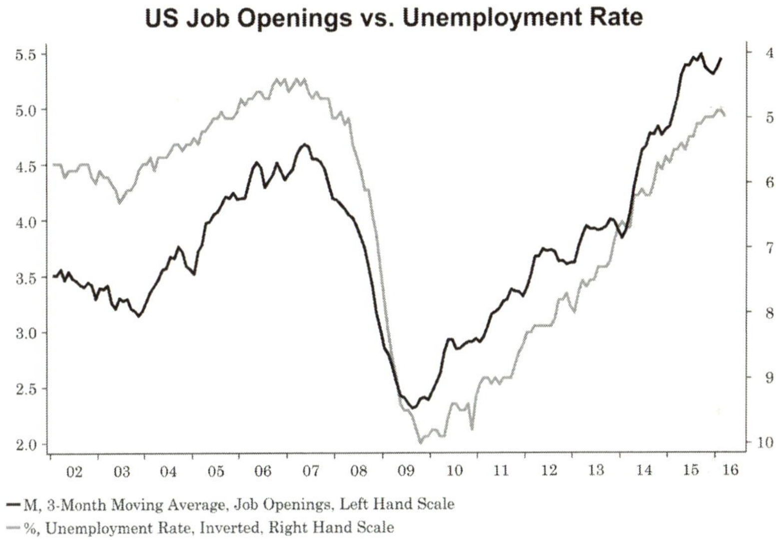

Source: GFC Economics

Chart 7k

---

125 Source, BLS. Job Openings, Level, Total, Non-farm. Job openings averaged 5.340m in the three months to January 2016.

126 Source: BLS, Job Openings & Labor Turnover Survey (JOLTS), Job Openings, Professional & Business Services, Education & Health Services. On a 3-month moving average basis, job openings for professional & business services totalled 1.083m in January 2016. This was 25.8% above the previous peak in January 2006. Openings in education and health services averaged 1.088m in the three months to January 2016, 35.9% above the cyclical high of October 2007.

127 Source: BLS, Job Openings and Labor Turnover – January 2016, Technical Notes, March 17th 2016.

Job Openings

	3-month moving average, million, January 2016	% change since January 2007
Total non-farm	5.340	19.7%
Private	4.862	21.0%
Construction	0.137	-27.7%
Manufacturing	0.297	-7.9%
Trade, transportation and utilities	0.883	11.1%
Retail trade	0.550	26.3%
Professional and business services	1.083	36.5%
Education and health services	1.088	44.6%
Leisure and hospitality	0.729	35.5%
Government	0.478	6.9%

Source: BLS, Job Openings and Labor Turnover Survey

Table 15

By the beginning of 2016, the unemployment rate had fallen to 4.9%. However, this was still *above* the low-point reached during the housing boom, even though job openings have risen to new highs.[128] This partly reflects the persistence of long-term unemployment (see chart 7l). The long-term unemployment rate (out of work for 27 weeks or more) has fallen, but remains high compared with previous economic cycles.[129] By contrast, the short-term unemployment rate (less than 27 weeks) has dropped closer to historic lows (see chart 7m).[130]

128 Source: BLS, Unemployment, CPS, 16 Years & Over, Rate. The unemployment rate dropped to 4.9% in January 2016, and was unchanged in February. In the previous economic cycle, the unemployment rate had fallen as low as 4.4% in October 2006, December 2006, March 2007 and May 2007.

129 Source: BLS, Unemployment, CPS, By Duration, 27 Weeks & Over, rate. The long-term unemployment rate peaked at 4.40% in April 2010. This was well above the previous high of 2.58% in June 1983. This measure dropped sharply to 1.36% in June 2015. However, the decline has stalled since then: the long-term unemployment rate was also 1.36% as of February 2016.

130 Source: BLS, Unemployment, CPS, By Duration, Less Than 27 Weeks, rate. The short-term unemployment rate slipped to a new cyclical low of 3.57% in February

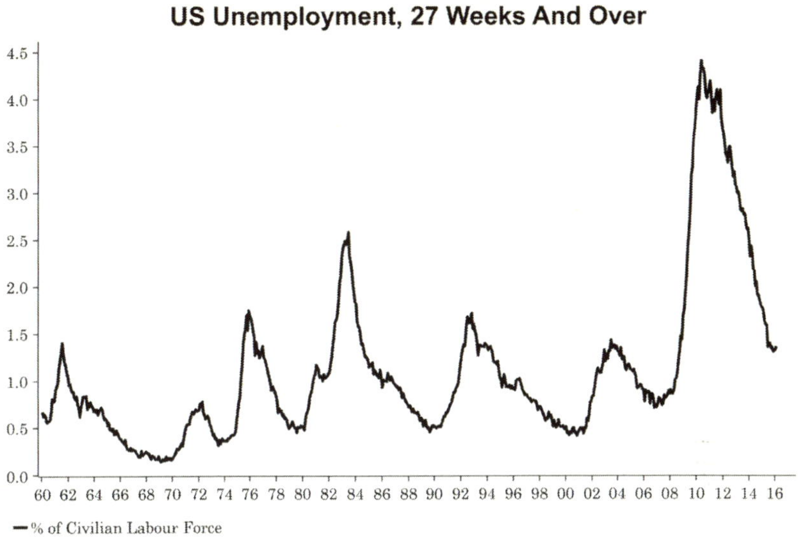

Source: GFC Economics

Chart 7l

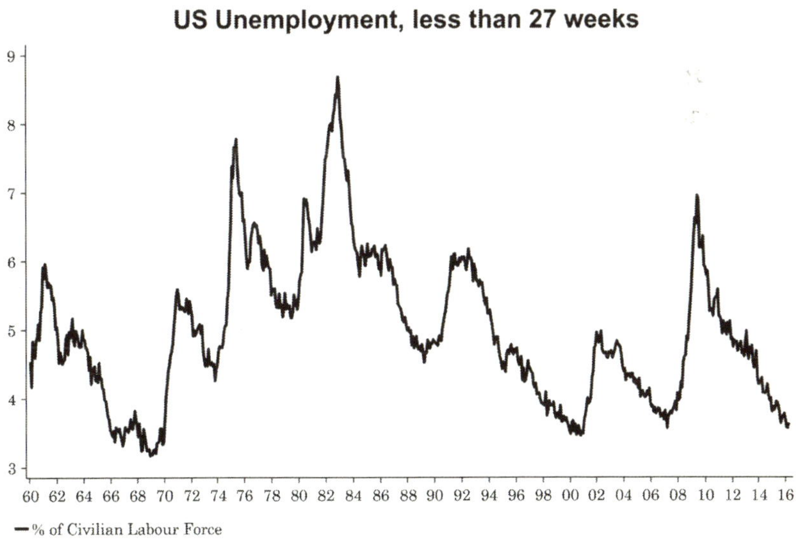

Source: GFC Economics

Chart 7m

2016. This was only a touch above the previous cyclical trough (3.56% in March 2007) and was fast approaching the nadir of the late-1960s (3.17% in December 1968).

The slower decline in long-term unemployment may point to a skills shortage, but it is not clear how much this will contribute to higher wages and a pick-up in inflation. While the rapid changes in technology may render the skills of some workers obsolete, they are also reducing the bargaining power of labour.

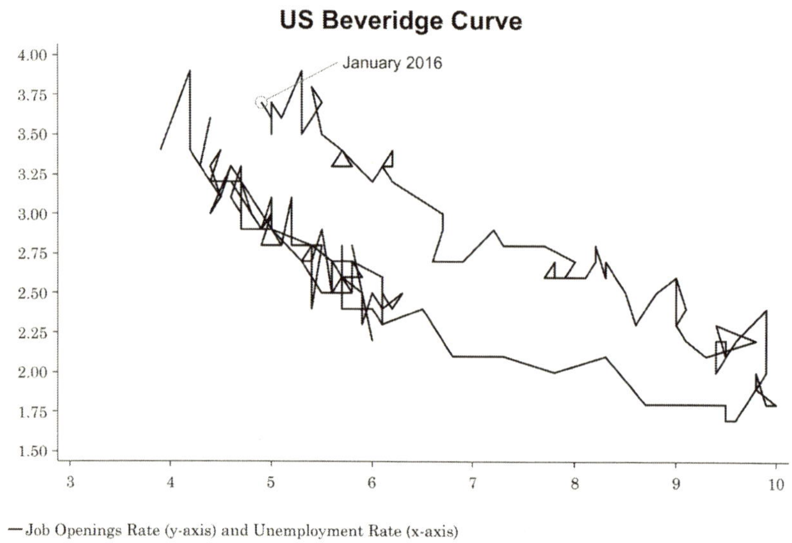

Source: GFC Economics

Chart 7n

As indicated before, the Beveridge curve typically moves outwards in the early stages of an economic recovery before looping back inwards.[131] However, it can also shift over time, reflecting the 'matching efficiency' of the labour market. There are three commonly cited reasons for a fall in matching efficiency: 1) a skills mismatch, 2) house lock or geographical mismatch and 3) disincentives, for example, from an extension of unemployment insurance benefits.[132] Since the Beveridge curve has still not looped back in, it is possible that any one of these factors may have reduced the matching efficiency of the labour market (see chart 7n). This in turn may be pointing to a higher NAIRU.

131 See *Inequality and the NAIRU* in chapter 7.

132 See *Beveridge Curve Shifts across Countries since the Great Recession*, Bart Hobijn, Federal Reserve Bank of San Francisco & Aysegul Sahin, Federal Reserve Bank of New York, November 8–9th, 2012.

Nevertheless, technology may be making it easier for employers and employees to 'match', lowering the NAIRU. The Freelancers Union of America reported that 65% of freelancers had found it easier to find work as a result of the internet: 31% of freelancers had found a job online in less than 24 hours.[133]

Indeed, a rise in job openings in relation to unemployment could be *consistent* with a lower NAIRU. The decline in worker bargaining power raises the incentive for firms to post more vacancies for a given unemployment rate.[134] Lower bargaining power for workers allows firms to offer reduced wages, making it more attractive to hire. The 'job creation' incentive for firms is higher, and this can push the vacancy-unemployment ratio upwards. This generates a strong negative correlation between the change in the labour income share and the vacancy-unemployment ratio.[135] In short, the structural factors lowering the labour share of income may have also pushed down the NAIRU.

The close correlation between job openings and the more flexible measures of wages, such as the ECEC, is also instructive (see chart 7o). Higher job openings are leading to stronger wage growth in sectors that are expanding quickly, underlining the rapid changes in the labour market as a result of technology. Furthermore, these sectors have been very profitable: technology has made it possible for many companies to raise wages without increasing prices to compensate.[136]

---

133 See *Freelancing in America: A national survey of the new workforce,* commissioned by the Freelancers Union of America and Elance-oDesk, 2014. As of 2014, it was estimated that there were 53 million freelancers in the US, approximately 34% of the labour force.

134 According to the International Labor Organization, this decline has intensified since the financial crisis. See *How the Global Financial Crisis Drove Down Collective Bargaining*, Wall Street Journal, October 23rd 2015.

135 See *The Labor Share of Income and Equilibrium Unemployment,* Andrew Figura & David Ratner, FEDS Notes, June 8th 2015: "The labor share [of income] has declined by roughly 6.5 percentage points since the early 2000s and now hovers around 63 percent. Through the lens of a standard labour market model, we argue that if the decline in the labour share has been driven by a reduction in worker bargaining power, the incentive for firms to post vacancies has increased and equilibrium unemployment will be lower as a result."

136 Source: BEA, Corporate Profits With Inventory Valuation Adjustments. Profits

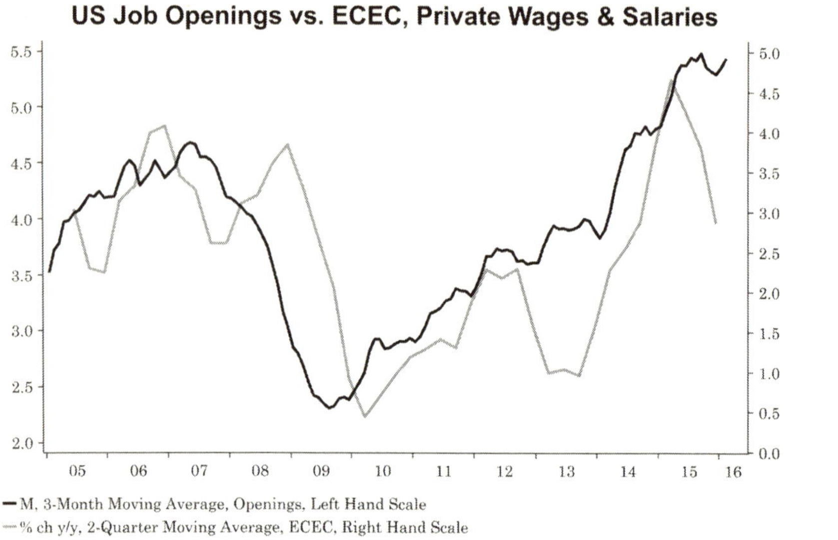

Source: GFC Economics

Chart 7o

Creative destruction and innovation

The widely-held belief that creative destruction is important for economic growth was highlighted by FOMC member Daniel Tarullo in a speech in 2014.[137] A dynamic labour market would, he claimed, be characterised by high levels of "churning of jobs through hiring and separations, as well as firm expansions and contractions". Indeed, "Creative destruction has been shown to improve productivity as jobs that have low productivity are replaced with jobs that yield greater productivity." Declining geographic mobility, as well as the secular drop in gross flows of people between jobs, was seen as "grounds for concern": both point to less creative destruction.

---

with inventory valuation adjustments dropped 6.8% q/q and 2.1% y/y in Q4 2015. However, much of the decline was related to the slide in oil prices. Many of the domestic non-manufacturing sectors posted strong gains: transportation & warehousing was up 66.7% y/y, while information saw an increase of 26.6% y/y. For the whole of 2015, profits climbed 15.2% y/y in wholesale trade, 14.3% y/y in retail trade, 40.9% y/y in transportation & warehousing and 17.2% y/y in information.

137 See *Longer-Term Challenges for the American Economy,* Daniel Tarullo, April 9th 2014.

This apparent decline in US business 'dynamism' has been well documented.[138] This trend appears to have extended to the high-tech sectors of the economy.[139] Less creative destruction would ordinarily be a worry, given that "High-tech firms … play an outsized role in income, employment, and productivity growth overall and are generally focused on the types of cutting-edge technologies that can drive sustained economic growth."[140]

However, much of this discussion misses the point. The argument revolves around the pace of job reallocation, calculated as the sum of total job gains and losses. According to Census Bureau data, this measure of business dynamism has been declining in the post-2000 period.[141] This is corroborated by more timely Business Employment Dynamics data from the BLS. Total job gains and job losses in the private sector averaged 14.071m in the year to Q2 2015, down 16.2% from the peak of Q2 2001 (16.798m).[142]

Theoretically, a degree of churn in the labour market allows better 'matches' between a worker and a firm, raising productivity. Nonetheless, technology will fundamentally alter employer-employee relations. *Human capital* has become an integral component of intangible investment. Many of the skills required in the workforce today are learnt

---

138 See, for example, *Top Ten Signs of Declining Business Dynamism and Entrepreneurship in the US,* John Haltiwanger, Kauffman Foundation, August 2015.

139 See *Declining Business Dynamism in the U.S. High-Technology Sector,* John Haltiwanger, Ian Hathaway, Javier Miranda & Ewing Marion, Kauffman Foundation, February 2014.

140 Ibid., p. 2

141 See, for example, *Top Ten Signs of Declining Business Dynamism and Entrepreneurship in the US,* John Haltiwanger, Kauffman Foundation, August 2015.

142 Source: BLS, Business Employment Dynamics, All Size Classes, Employment, Gross Job Gains & Gross Job Losses, Total Private. The data can be broken down further by firm size: small (1-49 employees), medium (50-249 employees) and large (250+ employees). For small firms, the pace of job reallocation fell 14.4% from 6.995m to 5.990m between Q2 2001 and Q2 2015. Total job gains and losses for medium-sized enterprises dropped by 21.9% from 2.590m to 2.023m. The largest firms saw a decline of 18.7%, down from 4.127m in Q2 2001 to 3.356m in Q2 2015.

"on the job".[143] This will provide greater incentives for businesses to retain their workforce. Given the rising share of intangibles in investment, it would be surprising if labour market churn did not fall.

Another indicator of lower business 'dynamism' is the falling start-up rate, together with the decline in young, high-growth firms.[144] Rather than a sign of faltering innovation, this may be a consequence of technology itself. "Network effects" may generate exponential growth in some sectors.[145] This could be conducive to monopolies, but it need not be a hindrance to innovation. It could facilitate risk-taking behaviour that would otherwise not occur in the presence of greater competition.

Google is a good example. The US company runs a profitable 'core' internet business, which includes an internet search engine, YouTube and Android (the mobile operating system).[146] It has managed to capture a large share of the market, at the expense of competitors such as Yahoo.[147] Nevertheless, the profitable core business has provided the leeway for Google to conduct research in other 'bets', such as driverless cars and 'smart homes'. These are currently generating a loss for the company, and the payoffs are highly uncertain. However, they could well cement Google's position as a 'tech-leader'. Without this 'core' revenue-generating unit, such ventures would be far more difficult for Google to undertake.

---

143 See *Employers Aren't Just Whining – the "Skills Gap" Is Real*, James Bessen, Harvard Business Review, August 25th 2014.

144 See *Top Ten Signs of Declining Business Dynamism and Entrepreneurship in the US,* John Haltiwanger, Kauffman Foundation, August 2015. See also *What Happened to the Breakout Startup,* Wall Street Journal, December 8th 2015. See also *The Missing Startup Recovery*, Wall Street Journal, January 27th 2016. See also *Why It Matters That New Businesses Are Creating Jobs More Slowly Than a Decade Ago*, Wall Street Journal, November 19th 2015. See also *Where Has All the Skewness Gone? The Decline in High-Growth (Young) Firms in the U.S.*, Ryan A. Decker, John Haltiwanger, Ron S. Jarmin, & Javier Miranda, March 2015.

145 See *Where are all the startups? More on America's economic calcification*, American Enterprise Institute, November 19th 2014.

146 See *Alphabet Reports Rising Profits at Core Googles Businesses*, Wall Street Journal, February 1st 2016.

147 See *Yahoo to Cut 15% of Workforce, Explore Strategic Options*, Wall Street Journal, February 2nd 2016.

It is difficult to reconcile the pessimistic argument that innovation is slowing with the strong data on productive investment.[148] Furthermore, an independent report recently showed that of the top ten most 'innovative' companies ranked globally, eight were headquartered in the US.[149] The same report found that eleven out of the top twenty R&D spenders were also US companies. The dominance of US tech companies is striking. This may mean that the rate of start-ups falters, or that labour market churn declines. That said, this need not automatically lead to a drop in innovation or job creation.

Changes in hiring

Technology is changing the labour market in other ways. The growing importance of websites such as *LinkedIn* and other social media platforms are impacting the search for work. The job openings data are derived from a survey of around 16,400 establishments, which submit information on job vacancies on the last business day of each month. This includes positions where the firm is *actively recruiting* from outside, and has taken steps to advertise through at least one of several channels including "posting internet notices".[150] Positions advertised on job portals and websites such as *LinkedIn* are included in the JOLTS report. Technology is also changing *how* people work and the contract between employers and employees. Indeed, it is worth noting that the data contained in the JOLTS report do not include "positions to be filled by employees of temporary help agencies, employee leasing companies, outside contractors, or consultants".[151] By implication, the BLS data may be understating the true strength of the labour market.

The BLS also has difficulty in capturing the economic activity of small businesses. A significant degree of under-coverage can occur. As the BLS has admitted, "hires and separations in the lowest size class may be somewhat understated".[152] Nonetheless, the data still show that small businesses have

---

148 See chapter 3.

149 See *Innovation's New World Order*, PricewaterhouseCoopers (PwC), 2015.

150 See *How does JOLTS define Job Openings*, Data Definitions, BLS, Job Openings and Labor Turnover Survey. Retrieved from: http://www.bls.gov/jlt/jltdef.htm

151 Ibid.

152 Ibid.

been driving the recovery.[153] As of August 2015, job openings amongst smaller enterprises (1-49 employees) totalled 2.083m, 22.3% above the previous cyclical high of June 2007. There were 1.491m vacancies for medium-sized enterprises (50-249 employees) in August 2015, up 8.4% since the high of April 2006. By contrast, job openings for the largest businesses had fallen 1.5% from a cyclical peak of January 2006 to 1.305m.

In contrast to the job openings report, data from the Business Employment Dynamics report show that employment gains in the current recovery have been concentrated in both the smallest and largest firms.[154] In the two years to Q2 2015, the net quarterly employment gain for firms with 1-49 employees averaged 229.8k. This compares with an average of 140.5k among medium-sized businesses (50-249). Larger firms (250+ employees) created the most jobs on average (291.1k) in the two years to Q2 2015.

How much slack to go?

Estimating labour market slack in the US has been one of the more difficult challenges faced by the Federal Reserve. The FOMC's median estimate for the longer-run unemployment rate fell to 4.8% in March 2016.[155] This can be viewed as a proxy for the FOMC's estimate of the NAIRU. Given that the jobless rate was 4.9% in February 2016, this implied that there was very little slack left in the labour market.[156]

---

153 See BLS, Job Openings and Labor Turnover Survey, Experimental JOLTS Estimates by Establishment Size Class. Retrieved from: http://www.bls.gov/jlt/sizeclassmethodology.htm. The Bureau of Labor Statistics collects experimental data which breaks down the JOLTS report by establishment size. These data are available upon request from the BLS.

154 Source: BLS, Business Employment Dynamics, Gross Job Gains less Gross Job Losses, Total Private.

155 Source: Federal Reserve, Federal Open Market Committee, Meeting calendars, statements, and minutes (2011-2016), March 15-16 Meeting, Accessible Materials.

156 As already indicated, it is likely that the NAIRU is lower than the FOMC's current estimate.

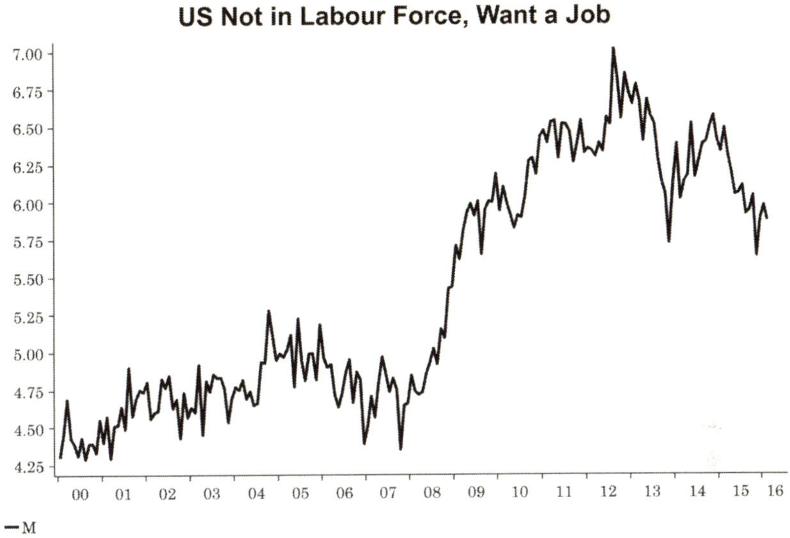

Source: GFC Economics

Chart 7p

Looking at the differential between the unemployment rate and the NAIRU offers a narrow interpretation of labour market slack. Many civilians became discouraged from looking for work following the financial crisis of 2008 and subsequently left the labour force. According to the BLS, there were 5.870m persons who were not in the labour force, but wanted a job as of February 2016 (see chart 7p).[157] This total has declined significantly since peaking at 7.010m in August 2012, but was still 25.0% above the 2007 average of 4.697m. In addition, there were 5.988m 'involuntary' part-time workers at the end of 2015 (see chart 7q).[158] This remained elevated compared to pre-recession levels: it was 36.0% above the 2007 average of 4.402m.

157 Source: BLS, Socio-Demographic Labour Force Statistics, Persons Not in Labour Force, Women & Men, 16 Years & Over, Persons Who Currently Want a Job.

158 Source: BLS, Employment, CPS, Part-Time, Women & Men, All Industries, Economic Reasons.

Source: GFC Economics

Chart 7q

The labour force participation rate also fell to a secular low of 62.4% in September 2015 (see chart 7r).[159] This compared with an average of 66.0% in 2007. Part of this decline will be structural and linked to the ageing population. Nevertheless, the participation rate for 'prime-age' workers has also been trending lower (see chart 7s).[160] To be quite clear, the rise in the total for not in the labour force, but want a job, will be reflected in the drop in the labour market participation rate.

159 Source: BLS, Socio-Demographic Labour Force Statistics, Civilian Labour Force Participation Rate, Women & Men, 16 Years & Over. The labour force participation rate had edged back up to 62.9% by February 2016. The participation rate peaked in January 2000 at 67.3%, and has trended downwards since, albeit with a brief respite in the mid-2000s.

160 Source: BLS, Socio-Demographic Labour Force Statistics, Civilian Labour Force Participation Rate, Women & Men, 25 to 54 Years. The labour force participation rate for the 'prime-age' working population has been declining since the high of January 1999 (84.6%). It dropped to a secular low of 80.6% in October 2013, and again in September 2015, but rebounded to 81.2% in February 2016.

Source: GFC Economics

Chart 7r

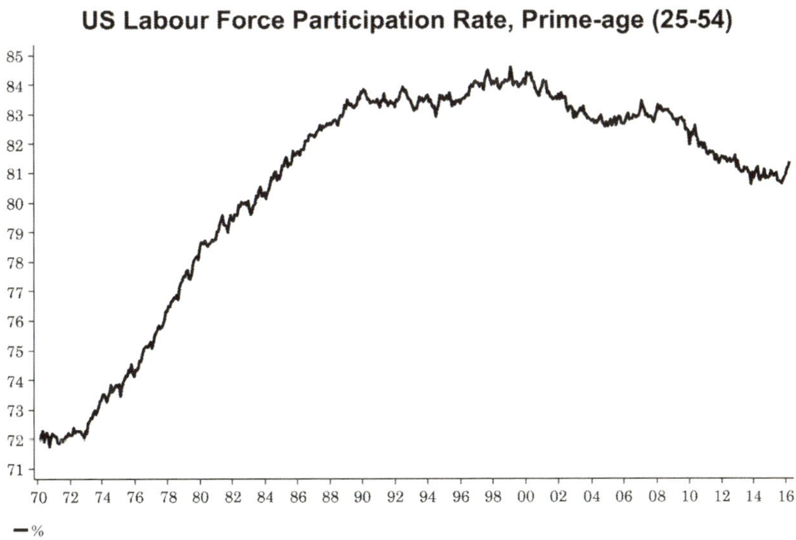

Source: GFC Economics

Chart 7s

A Brookings paper published in 2006 largely predicted the observed pattern in participation rates.[161] In a revised 2014 paper, the authors examined the 2.8 percentage point (p.p.) decline in the labour force participation rate between Q4 2007 and Q2 2014 (3.1 p.p. without adjustments).[162] Nearly half of the drop (1.3 p.p.) was due to ageing, "while ¼ to 1 percentage point may [have been] attributable to a weak labor market". The authors' model pointed to further decreases in the participation rate over the coming decade or so due to the ageing population.[163]

The Atlanta Fed calculates that the US currently needs to create 115k jobs a month to keep the unemployment rate stable at 4.9%.[164] In 2013, the Chicago Fed estimated that this so-called break-even rate was 80,000.[165] It forecast that this break-even rate would drop to 35k from 2016 onwards on the basis that population growth would slow and the labour force participation rate would continue to fall.[166] Whichever of these numbers is correct, it seems likely that the unemployment rate

---

161 See *The Recent Decline in the Labor Force Participation Rate and Its Implications for Potential Labor Supply*, Andrew Figura, Bruce Fallick, Jonathan Pingle, Stephanie Aaronson & William Wascher, Brookings Papers on Economic Activity, Spring 2006.

162 See *Labor Force Participation: Recent Development and Future Prospects*, Stephanie Aaronson, Tomaz Cajner, Bruce Fallick, Felix Galis-Reig, Christopher L. Smith, & William Wascher, Finance and Economics Discussion Series, 2014.

163 Ibid., p. 4. The authors concluded that policymakers "should not expect the participation rate to show a substantial increase from current levels as labor market conditions continue to improve."

164 Source: Federal Reserve Bank of Atlanta, Jobs Calculator. This assumes an average monthly population growth rate of 0.08% (the average of the previous twelve months), and a labour force participation rate unchanged at 62.9%. The rate of population growth is another critical variable, as it determines the rate at which the civilian labour force will grow. Small changes can have big differences, but it is inherently difficult to forecast.

165 See *Estimating the trend in employment growth*, Daniel Aaronson & Scott Brave, Chicago Fed Letter, July 2013.

166 Ibid., See also *Labor Force Participation: Recent Developments and Future Prospects*, Stephanie Aaronson, Tomaz Cajner, Bruce Fallick, Felix Galbis-Reig, Christopher L. Smith & William Wascher, Finance and Economics Discussion Series, 2014. This more timely Federal Reserve paper estimated that the break-even rate lied somewhere between 50k and 75k per month.

will continue to decline if the pace of job creation witnessed in 2015 is maintained.[167]

Of course, if civilians are tempted back into the labour force, a greater number of jobs would be needed to absorb these workers into employment. For example, if the labour force participation rate rose to 63.5% by the end of 2017, then the break-even rate required to keep the unemployment rate at 4.9% would climb to 179k.[168]

Will housing support the recovery in the labour market?

The recovery in the housing market has pushed construction spending higher in the US. Demand for housing has been rising as the economy expands.[169] By January 2016, overall construction spending had climbed 51.2% from the January 2011 trough and was 'only' 5.3% below the February 2006 peak.[170] The number of construction workers had increased 22.2% from the post-recession nadir of January 2011, climbing to 6.631m in February 2016.[171]

A survey from the Associated General Contractors of America (AGCA) found that 86% of construction firms were "having difficulty filling hourly craft or salaried professional positions" in 2015.[172] Indeed, the

---

167 Source: BLS, Employment, CES, Nonfarm, Payroll, Total. Monthly payroll growth averaged 229k in 2015, slightly below the 2014 average of 251k. The 3-month moving average was 228k in February 2016.

168 Source: Federal Reserve Bank of Atlanta, Jobs Calculator.

169 See *Rising Rents Outpace Wages in Wide Swaths of the U.S.*, Wall Street Journal, July 28th 2015. "The cost of renting a home is rising faster than wages across wide swaths of the country....Much of the problem is attributable to simple supply and demand. The job market has improved and millennials are entering the labor pool in force, boosting household formation".

170 Source: U.S. Census Bureau, Construction Investment, All Forms of Ownership, All Forms of Construction, Total.

171 Source: BLS, Employment, CES, Construction, Nonfarm, Payroll, Total.

172 See *Nationwide survey finds 86 percent of contractors have difficulty filing key craft and salaried jobs as demand for construction increases,* The Associated General Contractors of America, September 10th 2015. This worsened from 83 percent in 2014.

unemployment rate in the construction industry has fallen sharply from the peak in June 2010 (22.7%).[173] It dropped to 6.6% in February 2016, not far above the trough in April 2000 (5.4%).

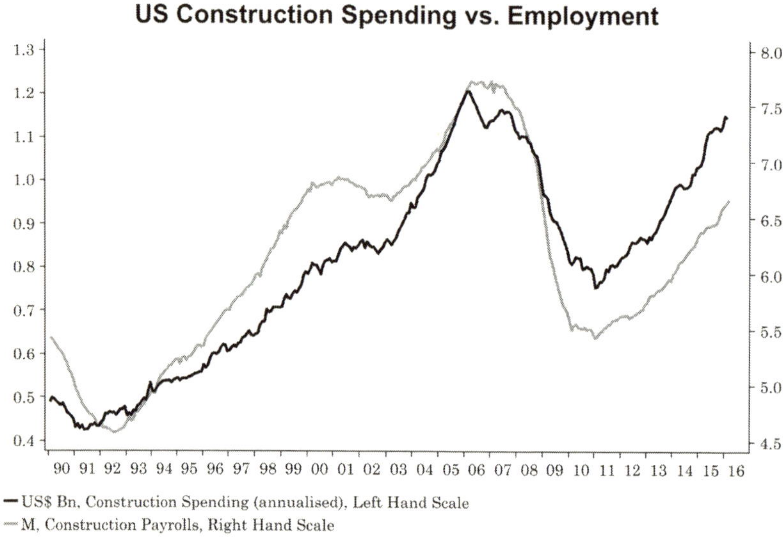

Source: GFC Economics

Chart 7t

Census Bureau data on job flows have tracked the destination of construction workers who lost their jobs in the housing downturn.[174] After a period of unemployment, around 40% found jobs in construction, approximately a third moved into other industries and roughly a quarter left the labour market. The age profile of construction workers has also changed in the aftermath of the housing bubble: this sector now employs fewer young workers, which may be contributing to the 'skills shortage'.

Construction jobs have been a source of relatively high-wage employment. However, the potential for automation cannot be overlooked: development is well under way on "an autonomous

173 Source: BLS, Current Population Survey (CPS), Labor Force Statistics, Unemployment Rate - Construction Industry, Private Wage & Salary Workers.

174 See *Where Did All the Construction Workers Go?,* Hubert Janicki & Erika McEntarfer, U.S. Census Bureau, October 16th 2015.

construction robot capable of laying bricks into pre-programmed structures."[175] Technological progress requires a higher set of skills, and hence the complaints from construction companies that there are skill shortages. But equally, automation may also be putting a natural cap on the pace of wage gains.

175 See *Robot builder designed for construction sites*, Reuters, October 21st 2015.

Chapter 8
The new technologies driving the economy
(First published April 22nd 2015)

Technology and work

Technological progress poses fundamental uncertainty for labour. New technologies will replace some workers, but will create jobs too. The hyperbole surrounding long-term 'technological unemployment' is misplaced. Much of this stems from the 'lump-of-labour fallacy', a belief that there is a fixed pool of work and that labour-saving substitution of capital for labour necessarily leads to a fall in employment.

Technological development has been ubiquitous in modern history. Innovation has progressed, but the shifts in unemployment have been largely cyclical. Such evidence would suggest that workers have nothing to fear. However, short-term unemployment can occur, putting downward pressure on wages. The Luddites feared for their livelihoods: the lack of a social safety net, together with a dearth of opportunities for re-training, rendered their labour services redundant and placed them in a precarious position. Similar anxieties have emerged today. Workers are certainly becoming more aware of the potential impact: in a recent poll, 35% of those categorised as 'unemployed, able to work' cited 'jobs being replaced by technology' as a contributing factor.[1]

In reality, the labour market dynamics are more nuanced. Labour-saving innovations lead to greater productivity, which can feed through to lower prices and stimulate demand. The impact of technology on jobs will depend on complementarities, the elasticity of final demand and labour supply.[2] It must also take into account the potential for innovation to

---

1 See *Kaiser Family Foundation/New York Times/CBS News Non-Employed Poll,* Liz Hamel, Jamie Firth, and Mollyann Brodie, Kaiser Family Foundation, December 2014.

2 This specific three-fold framework of complementarities, elasticity of demand and labour supply is adopted from David Autor's recent paper: see *Polanyi's Paradox and the Shape of Employment Growth*, David H. Autor, August 11th 2014.

drive the production of new goods and services. Increased 'supply' may effectively stimulate higher demand (Say's Law).

Complementarities

Complementarities arise when a new technology increases the value of labour. The precision and flexibility of surgical assistance robots will increase the scope of a surgeon to carry out more complicated operations whilst minimising the impact on the patient. Complementarities may also be embedded *within* a particular technology. Nicholas Carr, a respected commentator on technology and culture, argues the case for "human-centred automation": technology could be designed so that workers are placed at the centre of the decision-making process and are heavily involved in "the continuing process of action, feedback and judgement-making."[3] The value of workers would rise, making it more – not less – profitable for the firm to increase employment.

The greatest scope for complementarities exist in non-routine, cognitive work. In their book, Erik Brynjolfsson and Andrew McAfee claim that recent technological advances, such as big data and analytics, high-speed communications and rapid prototyping, "have *augmented* the contributions made by more abstract and data-driven reasoning, and in turn have increased the value of people with the right engineering, creative, or design skills."[4] Big data allows algorithmic recommendations to be used as inputs to human operators, increasing the value of labour. This will put a premium on workers with high analytical skills.

Algorithms can also be used to offer personalised services across a range of sectors. This will lead to a rise in demand for 'soft' skills. Despite the widespread adoption of automated checkouts, British supermarket chain Wm Morrison recently announced that it was hiring 5,000 shop floor staff. At the same time it cut 720 jobs in its head office. The chief

---

3 See *Automation Makes Us Dumb*, Nicholas Carr, Wall Street Journal, November 21st 2014.

4 See *The Second Machine Age: Work, Progress, and Prosperity in a Time of Brilliant Technologies*, Erik Brynjolfsson and Andrew McAfee, W.W. Norton & Co., 2014, p. 135.

executive emphasised: "We are focusing on the things that matter to our customers… having more of our staff in our stores, improving product availability and helping customers at our checkouts."[5]

Labour supply

Complementarities can only emerge, however, if workers with the requisite skills are available. Big data requires appropriately trained 'data scientists' to extract and interpret meaningful results. Average hourly earnings data from the Bureau of Labor Statistics (BLS) have been subdued, which suggests this is not a pressing concern. However, some evidence of skills shortages is emerging, as seen in the "rising pay for skills *within* many occupations".[6] Indeed, Claudia Goldin and Lawrence Katz have argued that the supply of skilled labour has failed to keep pace with technological change, contributing to rising inequality.[7] An insufficiently educated workforce will fail to reap the full rewards of technology and may well be holding back the pace of innovation.

Technology firms complain that skills shortages are undermining their competitiveness. Silicon Valley has been a vociferous critic of the immigration policy in the US, lobbying for more work permits for recruits born overseas. Although US universities educate many highly-skilled individuals, especially in sought after fields such as computer science, graduates are prevented from staying in the country. Policy will play a critical role going forward. The recently announced 'TechHire Initiative' in the US is aimed at training workers for well-paid professions in technology.[8] This will take place not only through universities and colleges, but also non-standard approaches such as "coding bootcamps" and online courses.

---

5 See *Wm Morrison recruits 5,000 staff but cuts 720 in head office*, Financial Times, April 16th 2015.

6 See *Employers Aren't Just Whining – the "Skills Gap" Is Real*, James Bessen, Harvard Business Review, August 25th 2014.

7 See *The Race Between Education and Technology*, Claudia Goldin and Lawrence Katz, Harvard University Press, 2008

8 See *'FACT SHEET: President Obama Launches New TechHire Initiative'*, The White House: Office of the Press Secretary, March 9th 2015.

Demand elasticity

Technology can generate rapid productivity improvements, cutting costs and pushing prices lower. The elasticity of final demand refers to the responsiveness of demand with respect to a fall in prices. If lower marginal costs are passed on to the consumer through a decline in prices, this may stimulate greater demand for goods and services, increasing output and hence employment. James Bessen notes that the industrial revolution, for all its disruptive force, did not generate longer-term unemployment:

"During the 19th century ... power looms automated 98 percent of the labor needed to weave a yard of cloth. Yet the number of factory weaving jobs increased over this period. Less labor cost per yard meant a lower price in competitive markets; a lower price meant sharply increased demand for cloth; and greater demand for cloth increased the demand for weavers despite the drop in labor needed per yard. Furthermore, while technology automated more and more weaving tasks, weavers' remaining skills, such as those needed to coordinate work across multiple looms, became increasingly valuable. Weavers' wages rose sharply compared with those of other workers during the late 19th century."[9]

Similarly, Henry Ford's assembly line revolutionised manufacturing, generating vast productivity improvements. Again, lower car prices increased demand and employment: this freed up resources, paving the way for whole new industries, such as tourism.[10]

Say's Law

Supply has the potential to create its own demand.[11] Technology can 'reveal' human preferences as well as fundamentally alter them. The Apple 'smartwatch' may seem to some as a superfluous accessory, yet similar comments were uttered about tablets and smartphones. These new technologies are beneficiaries of 'network effects': the greater the

---

9 See *Toil and Technology*, James Bessen, Finance & Development, March 2015.

10 See *The Future of Work in the Age of the Machine*, Melissa S. Kearney, Brad Hershbein, and David Boddy, A Hamilton Project Framing Paper, February 2015.

11 This is known as *Say's Law*, after the work of French economist Jean-Baptiste Say.

number of users, the more valuable the technology becomes. A recent report by Carl Benedikt Frey and Michael Osbourne documents the rapid diffusion of key technologies.[12] The time it took for the number of telephone, radio and TV users (after their invention) to reach 50 million was 75 years, 38 years and 13 years, respectively. In contrast, the Internet reached 50 million users in four years, Facebook after three-and-a-half years and Angry Birds (a gaming 'app') after only 35 days.

New technologies are also particularly adept at nudging consumers towards new products: swathes of data generated from networked devices allow more targeted advertisements. For GSN, a mobile phone games designer, collects data on gaming habits and the 'intensity' of gameplay. This information is then processed, tailoring advertisements to each individual consumer as well as recommending new games at an 'appropriate' time.[13]

Evolving occupations

One recent study has attempted to predict the impact of technology on employment by documenting the susceptibility of today's jobs to computerisation.[14] Using a novel methodology, the authors ranked 702 detailed occupations by probability of computerisation. They concluded that around 47 percent of total US employment was "high-risk", and they expected these jobs to be automated in the near future, perhaps "over the next decade or two". This eye-catching figure would suggest that technologies are becoming more 'disruptive' than ever. Perhaps this time, there is a risk of long-term technological unemployment.

However, this study fails to document where new occupations are likely to arise. The Standard Occupational Classification (SOC)

---

12 See *Technology at Work: The Future of Innovation and Employment,* Carl Benedikt Frey and Michael Osborne, Citi GPS: Global Perspectives & Solutions, February 2015.

13 See *Technology and Persuasion*, MIT Technology Review, 2015.

14 See *The future of employment: how susceptible are jobs to computerisation?*, Carl Benedikt Frey and Michael A. Osborne, Oxford Martin Programme on the Impacts of Future Technology working paper, September 2013.

system sorts workers into occupational categories. Since it was first used in 1977, the number of major occupational groups has increased from 21 to 23, and the number of detailed groups has risen from 662 to 840.[15] According to the BLS, this revision process is "warranted by changes in the economy, technology, and business practices that affect how employers structure work."[16] Indeed, it allows policymakers and analysts to understand what *types* of jobs are being created and subsequently track the jobs growth in particular occupational categories. The latest revision (2010) introduced 24 new occupational categories, including 'web developers', 'information security analysts' and 'magnetic resonance imaging technologists'.[17] Nevertheless, in the absence of an up-to-date classification system, technology could be creating a breadth of new jobs that may not be recognised. Further revisions to the SOC are due in 2018.

In 2013, the BLS published predictions for trends in occupational employment and wages over the coming decade (from 2012-22).[18] While these were only projections, they provide an indication of how occupations are evolving and new jobs are being created as a result of complementarities. In high-tech sectors, 'diagnostic medical sonographers', 'genetic counsellors' and 'information security analysts' are predicted to be among the top-20 fastest growing occupations, with projected growth rates of 46%, 41% and 37% over this period, respectively (the average growth rate for all occupations is 11%). These occupations all have above-average pay.[19]

Official figures for science, technology, engineering and maths (STEM) employment, also published by the BLS, capture trends in technology-

15 See *Revising the Standard Occupational Classification*, Bureau of Labor Statistics (BLS): http://www.bls.gov/soc/revising_the_standard_occupational_classification_2018.pdf

16 See Federal Register notice: http://www.bls.gov/soc/FRn_May_22_2014.pdf

17 See *What's New in the 2010 SOC*, 2010 SOC User Guide, BLS, February 2010.

18 Source: BLS, Employment Projections.

19 According to BLS Occupational Employment Statistics, in 2014 the average annual wage was $47,230 and the median annual wage was $35,574.

intensive occupations.[20] These occupations are projected to grow by 13% between 2012 and 2022. Within STEM occupations, the fastest employment growth is expected for 'information security analysts' (37%), 'operations research analysts' (27%), 'statisticians' (27%) and 'biomedical engineers' (27%). Some of these provide clear examples of the potential for complementarities. The risks of cyber-attacks are growing. Protection is imperative for businesses and jobs growth can be expected to be strong in this area. The rise of 'big data', enabled via networked sensors, the internet and increased storage capacity, has generated opportunities for statisticians. In the broader 'software developers' category, 'developers of applications and systems software' employment is projected to grow by a combined 222,700 (from 1.018m to 1.241m).

The majority of the fastest growing occupations are in healthcare services, including 'personal care aides', 'home health aides' and 'physical therapist aides'. This is due to the ageing population (retirement of the 'baby-boomers'). These jobs demand 'soft-skills', and tend to have lower than average pay. Interestingly, the fastest growing occupation is 'industrial-organization psychologists'.

The same report also included figures for the highest *total* jobs growth projections. Most new jobs were projected to arise in 'personal care aides' (580,000), 'registered nurses' (526,800), 'retail salespersons' (434,700) and 'home health aides' (424,000). While the rise of personal-care robots appears to be an impending threat to these jobs, this need not be the case. Robots may take on the more menial tasks, allowing workers to add value through their 'soft-skills', thus improving the quality of care overall. Indeed, home-health assistance is an example of non-routine work that would be complementary to robotic technology.

However, there will be a premium for high-skilled labour that can complement the technologies in healthcare, and also for managers

20 Source: BLS, Employment Projections. More specifically, "STEM occupations are defined here to include computer and mathematical, architecture and engineering, and life and physical science occupations; managerial and postsecondary teaching occupations related to these functional areas; and sales occupations requiring scientific or technical knowledge at the postsecondary level."

that provide oversight of new technologies. Within the top-20 highest projected median earnings were oral and maxillofacial surgeons (3-D printing), surgeons (robotics), 'prosthodontists' (advanced materials) and 'computer and information systems managers'.

The most recent BLS Occupational Employment and Wages report (2014) provides data on science, technology, engineering and maths (STEM) workers in the US.[21] It found that there were 8.3 million STEM jobs in May 2014. This represents around 6.2% of the US workforce. The industries with the highest concentration of STEM workers were 'computer systems design and related services', 'architectural, engineering and related services' and 'software publishers'. The occupations with the highest STEM employment levels were 'software developers, applications', 'computer user support specialists', 'computer systems analysts' and 'software developers, system software'. Out of 100 STEM occupations, 93 had mean wages above the average for all occupations.

'Disruptive' technology

The following section outlines some of the key technologies that have emerged in recent years and are set to have a 'disruptive' influence in the near future.[22] Particular attention is given to technologies that have the potential to cause substantial dislocation in the labour market, while at the same time delivering significant productivity gains and consumer surplus.

---

21 More specifically, "STEM occupations are defined here to include computer and mathematical, architecture and engineering, and life and physical science occupations; managerial and postsecondary teaching occupations related to these functional areas; and sales occupations requiring scientific or technical knowledge at the postsecondary level." Source: BLS.

22 The categorisation and definitions of the various technologies are taken and adapted from McKinsey Global Institute's 2013 report, unless otherwise stated. See *Disruptive technologies: Advances that will transform life, business, and the global economy*, McKinsey Global Institute, May 2013.

Mobile internet

Definition: Mobile internet is defined as "the combination of mobile computing devices, high-speed wireless connectivity, and applications."[23]

See *Who Needs a Carrier? Go Wi-Fi Only*, WSJ, 3rd March 2015.

- Wi-Fi, which is often provided free-of-charge, is threatening mobile network operators. 'Apps' on electronic devices allow customers to bypass wireless networks. Standard mobile phone functions (calls and messages) can now be undertaken without a network operator – applications for instant-messaging, voice-calling and video-calling are growing quickly.
- The spread of Wi-Fi hotspots is facilitating this trend – Facebook recently announced an initiative to bring the most remote parts of the world into the internet realm using drones that 'beam' down internet (**see *Facebook Creates Team to 'Beam' Internet Everywhere on Earth*, WSJ, 27th March 2015**).

See *There's an app for that*, The Economist, 3rd January 2015.

- Proliferation of 'start-ups' specialising in on-demand labour and services.
- Handy's provides cleaning services in 37 different locations including most major cities in the US, UK and Canada; Instacart employs 'personal shoppers' who buy and deliver groceries from local stores. Services are available across the US, including major cities such as New York and Boston; Washio, based in the US, washes clothes within 24 hours of an order; Uber provides car services and has expanded its operations into 56 countries; Airbnb rents spare rooms or lodgings in over 34,000 cities and 190 countries; Elance-o-desk offers 4 million companies the services of 10 million freelancers.

23 See *Disruptive technologies: Advances that will transform life, business, and the global economy*, McKinsey Global Institute, May 2013.

See *Rise in UK app downloads boosts revenues by a third*, Financial Times, 17th February 2015.

- "The industry employs 110,000 people in the UK, and there are 61,100 developers producing apps for Apple alone. Many are working from their bedrooms; a fifth are under 25 and about 4,000 developers are still at school, according to research group Vision Mobile."
- In the UK, "Revenues generated from app development exceeded £4bn in 2014". Vision Mobile "predicts that the app economy will reach £31bn by 2025. It estimates that 8,000 companies in the UK are working on mobile software, although about a sixth are enterprises where a single person is working on what they hope will be the next Flappy Bird-type sensation."

See *Apple App Store beats sales records*, Financial Times, 8th January 2015.

- It is estimated that customers have spent over $35bn on the App Store since its launch in 2008.
- Apple customers expended nearly $15bn on apps in 2014, up 50% on the previous year.

See *The Mobile Revolution*, The Boston Consulting Group, January 2015.

- The average mobile subscriber cost per megabyte decreased 99% between 2005 and 2013.
- Mobile data transmission speeds have risen rapidly: 4G networks offer 12,000x faster data-transmission speeds than 2G networks.
- Demand for continued innovation: consumers want faster data speeds and longer battery life.
- SMEs that embrace mobile services flourish: around 25% of SMEs that used mobile technology 'intensively' saw their revenues grow 2x faster and jobs 8x faster.

- Mobile value chains generated almost $3.3tr in revenues globally in 2014 and were directly responsible for 11 million jobs.
- High R&D expenditures in mobile tech: companies focussed on mobile technologies invest a larger share of earnings (21 percent) in R&D than any other industry, excluding biotech.

See *US broadband providers wake up to the need for speed,* Financial Times, 6th April 2015.

- Google Fiber, a superfast broadband, is set to challenge the telecoms industry.
- Increased competition from Google has "nudged" other companies to develop faster speeds.
- Comcast (which has roughly 57% of the US broadband market) recently announced Gigabit Pro, "a new residential internet service that offers download and upload speeds of 2 gigabits per second".

See *Tyred and wired,* Financial Times, 4th-5th April 2015.

- 'Connected' cars – "the average premium car today has more than a mile of cables, between 50 and 70 control units and the computing power of 20 advanced PCs."
- "Intelligent transport systems" warn drivers of hazards or traffic jams.
- Car makers can monitor the inner-workings of a car via a 'telematics' unit – this refers to any device that combines telecommunications and informatics, such as GPS systems.
- This allows faults to be spotted early; software glitches can be fixed via an over-the-air update.
- 'Black-box' telematics devices in cars monitor user performance – insurance companies can assess riskiness of driver and set their policies accordingly.

Automation of knowledge work

Definition: "the use of computers to perform tasks that rely on complex analyses, subtle judgements, and creative problem solving. Knowledge work automation is made possible by advances in three areas: computing technology (including processor speeds and memory capacity), machine learning, and natural user interfaces such as speech recognition technology."[24]

See *Right, Left, Right: At UPS, The Algorithm Is The Driver*, WSJ, 18th February 2015.

- Algorithm maps 'best' route for parcel delivery service, based on a trade-off between efficiency and consistency.
- Small efficiency gains can translate into large savings. These may be small at the margin, but can quickly add up: UPS has an expansive network of 55,000 delivery routes in the US alone.
- The Orion algorithm continuously updates 'best' routes based on new information. This has facilitated the implementation of 'My Choice' – a self-service platform that allows customers to change time and place of delivery. My Choice membership has grown steadily.
- The company expects to save \$300-\$400m per year once Orion is fully implemented.
- The company is already saving "\$50 million a year by reducing by one mile the average aggregated daily travel of its drivers."

See *This Wasn't Written by an Algorithm, But More and More Is*, WSJ, 15th December 2014.

- 'Narrative Science' started out using algorithms to generate sports stories. It has since added more clients including financial services companies, retailers and government intelligence services.
- The *LA Times*, for example, has developed a computer programme that writes news articles.

---

24 See *Disruptive technologies: Advances that will transform life, business, and the global economy*, McKinsey Global Institute, May 2013.

- Credit Suisse now uses algorithms to generate summaries of stock activity. However, this is not necessarily labour substituting – rather, it complements the analysts by allowing them to focus on writing more detailed reports for the larger companies.

See *DeepMind algorithm beats people at classic video games*, Nature, 26th February 2015.

- A single computer algorithm has learnt to play 49 different computer games – in half of those, the computer fared better than a human player.
- It is the first Artificial Intelligence (AI) system that can learn a variety of tasks from scratch using the same, minimal starting point.
- Before, one system could learn one game – now, one system can learn several games.
- "Companies such as Google have an immediate business interest in improving AI… Applications could include how best to place advertisements online or how to prioritize stories in news aggregators."

See *Game Theorists crack poker*, Nature, 8th January 2015.

- One particular version of poker (Texas Hold'em with a two-player limit) has been 'solved' – a computer algorithm cannot be beaten with statistical significance.
- Impressive given that the computer does not know the hand that has been dealt to other players – it is a game of 'imperfect information'.
- This is "especially interesting for economists and game theorists, because it includes practical problems such as finding optimal strategies for auctions and negotiations." It could also impact on other fields such as medicine and cybersecurity.

See *The Learning Machines*, Nature, 9th January 2014.

- "Deep learning has the property that if you feed it more data, it gets better and better."
- First deep learning programmes were not particularly successful. They needed examples to learn from, but were constrained by data availability.
- Since the 2000s, however, increases in computing power, together with an abundance of digital data, has led to a new push in deep learning technologies.
- Lends credence to hypothesis of 'exponential' technological progress.

The "Internet of Things"

Definition: "The Internet of Things refers to the use of sensors, actuators, and data communications technology built into physical objects to be tracked, coordinated, or controlled across a data network or the internet."[25]

See *The Economics of the Internet of Things*, MIT Technology Review, July/August 2014.

- "Network effects" – each additional user makes a product more valuable.
- Platform business model: you create the platform, set the 'rules-of-the-game' and let others add value.
- Clearest example of this is Apple's app store: "People have combined the functions of the iPhone into hundreds of thousands of apps that Apple never even conceived of."

See *Car-to-Car Communication: A simple wireless technology promises to make driving much safer, 10 Breakthrough Technologies 2015,* MIT Technology Review.

- Car-to-car communication allows vehicles to broadcast their position, speed, steering, brake status and other data to nearby vehicles.

---

25 See *Disruptive technologies: Advances that will transform life, business, and the global economy,* McKinsey Global Institute, May 2013.

- This allows other cars to build up a picture of surrounding dangers and give warning signals to drivers.

See *Expressways and wifi-connected roads to ease Britain's congestion*,- Financial Times, 20th March 2015.

- Wi-fi can beam information to cars; digital sensors can monitor congestion.
- The network of sensors will send information to a central traffic control system, which will direct traffic, easing congestion.

Cloud technology and Big Data

Definition: "Cloud computing is a model for enabling ubiquitous, convenient, on-demand network access to a shared pool of configurable computing resources (e.g., networks, servers, storage, applications, and services) that can be rapidly provisioned and released with minimal management effort or service provider interaction."[26]

See *Mapping Information Economy Business with Big Data: Findings from the UK*, National Institute of Economic and Social Research, Discussion paper No. 442, 27th November 2014.

- The authors "define 'big' datasets as those that a) are available at massive scale, often millions or billions of observations; b) can be accessed in real time, or close to it; c) have high dimensionality, including phenomena previously hard to observe quantitatively, and d) are much less structured than 'conventional' sources, such as administrative data or surveys."
- Challenges in measuring the 'information economy' – "Data coverage is often imperfect, industry typologies can lack detail, and product categories do not closely align with sector space."
- New dataset combines public administrative data, observed information, and modelled variables from unstructured sources, some developed using machine learning.

---

26 See *The NIST Definition of Cloud Computing*, Peter Meil and Timothy Grace, National Institute of Standards and Technology, NIST Special Publication 800-145, September 2011.

- The authors "find that the 'ICT production space' is around 42% larger than SIC-based estimates, with at least 70,000 more companies." Employment shares in the 'digital economy' also approximately doubled according to these new figures.

See *Supply Chain Management*, BCG Perspectives, 27th January 2015.

- Using big data, advanced analytics and cloud computing provides a visualisation of delivery routes. Companies can identify savings opportunities equal to 15-20% of transportation costs.
- Also allows dynamic rerouting of trucks to meet real-time changes in demand.
- Better demand forecasting allows companies to cut out inventory costs and meet consumers' needs more flexibly.

See *Cloud Technology*, Disruptive technologies: Advances that will transform life, business, and the global economy, McKinsey Global Institute, May 2013.

- Small- and medium-sized enterprises stand to benefit most from cloud technology – they often "find it difficult to build and manage extensive IT infrastructure."
- The "rapid obsolescence" of IT means it is difficult for smaller companies to make the most of the latest technologies.
- Cloud computing cuts costs and helps companies to sustain higher levels of productivity.

Advanced robotics

See *Amazon tests delivery drones at secret Canada site after US frustration*, The Guardian, 30th March 2015.

- Delivery drone capabilities include: sensors that can detect and avoid obstacles in a drone's path; link-loss procedures that control the aircraft should its connection with base be broken; stability in wind and turbulence.
- Designed to deliver packages around the world in less than 30 minutes.
- US regulations were too restrictive for Amazon, so it has moved

some of its testing operations to Canada.[27] However, a recent ruling has given Amazon the green light to test in the US which may speed up the initiation of this technology.

See *Google and J&J aim for cutting edge of healthcare with robotic surgeons*, Financial Times, 28th March 2015.

- Robotic technology has become popular in operating theatres – smaller, less painful incisions.
- Google is focusing on 'informatics' – providing more information, rather than just physical assistance. For example, software helps to highlight blood vessels or nerves that are difficult to see with the naked eye.

See *Japan aims to turn robotics into profit*, Financial Times, 8th October 2014.

- 'Robotics' is a key pillar of Shinzo Abe's economic growth strategy.
- Huge potential for nursing and care robots due to Japan's ageing population – "the government estimates the market for care service robots will reach $3.7bn by 2035 from an estimated $155m in 2015."
- "Panasonic… hopes to increase sales of service robots and its nursing care business to Y200bn by 2025".

Cyberdyne[28]

- Cyberdyne, a Japanese robotics company, has developed exoskeletons for medical use, particularly in cases of lower limb disability. These disabilities often arise when neural pathways that connect the brain to the muscle are impaired.
- Cyberdyne's 'lower limb type' product assists functionality by reading "bio-electric signals" that are sent from the brain to the

---

27 The following link displays the Amazon letter asking for the necessary regulatory support for testing its drones: http://g-ecx.images-amazon.com/images/G/01/rowland/AmazonPetitionforExemption_July92014.pdf

28 See Cyberdyne website, available at: http://www.cyberdyne.jp/english/products/LowerLimb_medical.html

muscles. In doing so it "moves the wearer's legs in accordance with the wearer's intentions", helping people to walk again.

- This technology can also be used to ease the strains of manual labour, not just in healthcare.

Autonomous vehicles

See *Software is steering auto industry*, Financial Times, 18th February 2015.

- Google has partnered with auto industry suppliers Bosch, Continental and Delphi, as opposed to "original equipment manufacturers" such as Ford and GM, to build driverless cars.
- Software and communications are integral to 'connected' and driverless cars.
- Companies such as Bosch – whose mobility division employs 34,000 engineers, of which one-third work on software – are building an increasing share of each car.
- "A premium class car now contains 100 microprocessors and runs on 100m lines of software code."

Healthcare and biotech

See *Internet of DNA: A global network of millions of genomes could be medicine's next great advance, 10 Breakthrough Technology 2015*, MIT Technology Review.

- Thousands of human genomes have been sequenced. Millions more will be sequenced in the future. Patients stand to benefit from this, if the information can be made available to doctors around the world on a large database.
- The number of sequenced human genomes is growing rapidly (largest labs can sequence two per hour – contrast this to the first which took 13 years).
- "Today scientists are broadly engaged in what is, in effect, a project to document every variation in every human gene and determine what the consequences of those differences are."

See *Surgeons embrace 3D printed body parts to save health service time and money*, Financial Times, 22nd November 2014.

- Models can be used for practice – reducing operating times.
- Use of 3-D printing for complex orthopaedic and facial reconstruction procedures – for example, printed implants "help reconstruct the faces of patients with craniofacial tumours. The implants are typically made out of peek – a biocompatible polymer – or titanium."
- Other examples include titanium 3-D printed hip implants. Patients who have had multiple hip operations through the NHS have seen their bone worn down. With custom-made implants, the patient is less likely to need further operations. More expensive in the short-run, but in the long-run, likely to save money.
- "Other collaborative ventures, such as Replica 3DM and Southampton University are seeking government funding to build a 3D bone printer. It would print a porous coral-like scaffold structure of hydroxyapatite, and could be used in areas such as cleft pallet surgery."

See *Your Smartphone Will See You Now*, WSJ, 12th January 2015.

- A patient with a visible ailment can photograph it with a smartphone and process the image with a specific app. An algorithm can then provide a diagnosis and guide the patient on the next stage of treatment.
- Smartphones can also be used for blood-pressure readings and electrocardiograms. They can also measure blood-oxygen, glucose levels and heart rhythm. Data can be processed, stored and shared.
- Video consultations may become the norm (rather than visiting the doctor). Deloitte estimates that as many as one in six doctor visits were virtual in 2014.
- Wristwatch sensors put the patient under constant surveillance within the confines of their own home – this reduces risk of infections and other complications.

- Other products being developed include necklaces which monitor heart activity, contact lenses which monitor glucose levels and head bands which capture brain waves.
- Smartphone sensors are being developed to capture exposure to radiation, air pollution or pesticides in food.

See *Big pharma turns to small biotechs for edge in cancer treatment*, Financial Times, 7th April 2015.

- Immuno-oncology enhances the ability of immune system to fight cancer,
- Disease-fighting T-cells do not attack tumours due to body "immune checkpoints" that are there to prevent the immune system from killing healthy cells.
- Drugs such as Keytruda from Merck and Opdivo from Bristol-Myers Squibb remove this "invisibility cloak".
- Some analysts think this drug category could be worth $40bn within a decade.

See *Investors back £100m plan for UK proton-beam cancer centres*, Financial Times, 3rd April 2015.

- Three clinics offering proton-beam therapy – a targeted form of radiotherapy – to be opened in 2017.
- Investors have pledged £100m.
- Currently, the "NHS spends tens of millions of pounds a year sending hundreds of patients for treatment at proton-beam centres overseas... which costs often above £100,000 per person."

Energy

See *Electricity storage: Pumping heat*, The Economist, 7th June 2014.

- Currently, grid managers do not have a way of storing generated electricity – they need to match demand at any given time.
- Power from renewables (such as wind and solar energy) is intermittent. Despite a significant reduction in the cost of renewables, this hampers more widespread implementation.

- 'Pumped heat electricity storage' is a technology being developed that essentially stores thermal energy, which can be used to generate electricity on demand.

See *The Lowly Thermostat, Now Minter of Megawatts*, MIT Technology Review, July/August 2014.

- Nest Thermostats use the 'Internet of Things' to control thermostats according to residents' habits and preferences.
- Designed to maximise energy savings and in doing so reduces costs of having to build expensive back-up generators.
- This "demand management could reduce peak demand by 2 to 4 percent and cut overall demand by 1 to 2 percent. This would allow utilities to avoid building potentially billions of dollars' worth of additional capacity and infrastructure."[29]

3-D printing

See *Why Advanced Manufacturing Will Boost Productivity*, BCG, 30th January 2015.

- General Electric (GE) is using additive manufacturing (3-D printing) "to build fuel nozzles for LEAP turbofan engines, which are being developed for next-generation single-aisle manufacturing. In additive manufacturing, the nozzles are built by a computer-guided laser from layers of metal and powder."
- GE reports that "The new nozzle is 25 percent lighter than the machined component and is as much as five times more durable than the current nozzle made from 20 different parts."
- The company recently reported it would spend $32 million to build a new research-and-education centre focused on additive technologies.
- Related to 3-D printing, Ford Motor Company is using Integrated Computational Materials Engineering (ICME), which creates computer models of products and simulates their properties digitally.

29 See *Disruptive technologies: Advances that will transform life, business, and the global economy*, McKinsey Global Institute, May 2013, p. 56.

- It is greatly reducing the time and cost of developing aluminium castings for engines: "digital models of castings are tested virtually, and a prototype is built only after engineers are convinced that they have created the best design."
- "Ford invested $15 million over 5 years ... it has generated cost savings of more than $120 million – a 700 percent return on investment – while development times have been cut by 15 to 25 percent."

See *Chipmakers go 3-D to boost performance*, Nikkei Asian Review, 11th August 2014.

- Effort to make semiconductor devices smaller using conventional techniques is hitting a wall.
- 3-D printing enables manufacturers to stack layer upon layer, creating a 3-D chip.

See *How 3-D Printing Is Going Out of This World*, WSJ, 12th April 2015.

- Engineers and designers "are experimenting with a 3-D printer that would make bricks suitable for airtight buildings and radiation-proof shelters using the grit that blows across Mars's red surface."
- The first 3-D object (a ratchet wrench) was successfully printed in orbit – an engineer "designed the wrench on Earth, converted the blueprint into computer code, and then emailed it to U.S. Navy Cap. Wilmore in orbit. There, the astronaut printed the tool on the company's experimental 3-D microgravity printer in three hours, building it up in layers each about 7 millimeters thick from an ink composed of a heated commercial plastic."
- Together with advanced robotics, the effects could be exponential – self-replicating 3-D printers that can construct replicas of themselves are being developed at the University of Bath, UK.

Advanced materials

See *Nano-Architecture: A Caltech scientist creates tiny lattices with enormous potential*, MIT Technology Review, 2015.

- Developing nanomaterials that are strong and light.
- One possible application is to greatly increase the energy density of batteries – the amount of power they can hold for a given size.
- "Also working with biologists to see whether the nanostructured ceramic could serve as a scaffold for growing bones – such as the tiny ones in the ear whose degeneration is one cause of deafness."

See *Graphene's leading lights unveil mass market bulb*, Financial Times, 28th March 2015.

- Graphene was isolated in 2004 and graphene lightbulbs will go on sale later this year. Its application in a commercially viable product has been remarkably quick: according to Professor Colin Bailey, it can sometimes "take 20 years to get a new discovery out there".
- It is the first 2-D material – excellent conductor of heat and electricity and will reduce the cost of lighting.
- Chancellor George Osborne recently opened the £61m National Graphene Institute in Manchester.
- Possible uses for the material are to make lighter aircraft, flexible display screens and lighter batteries.

Fintech

Definition: Fintech is a generic term that refers to 'innovation of financial services'. Technology has the potential to transform the financial arena. New technologies include mobile banking, peer-to-peer lending & crowdfunding and digital currencies.[30]

---

30 See *So what is FinTech?*, NDRC, http://www.ndrc.ie/2014/03/fintech/.

See *The Future of Fintech and Banking: Digitally disrupted or reimagined?*, Accenture, 2015.

- Fintech expenditures grew 201% globally in 2014 (to $12.21bn); compared to overall growth in venture-capital investment of 63%.
- Investment in Fintech start-ups has also been strong – first round investments grew by 48% in 2014.
- As a proportion of global investment, the US had largest share. However, Europe experienced higher level of growth (215% y/y). UK and Ireland made up 42% of European fintech investment.

See *Alibaba eyes small business loans*, Financial Times, 29th January 2015.

- Alibaba, China's largest online commerce company, has begun issuing credit ratings to small businesses as it moves into financial services. Alibaba's private bank is due to begin operations this year.
- This could unlock flows of credit to small businesses, which have trouble borrowing from more traditional lenders.
- Alibaba hopes to use its online platform to gather data on 300m individuals and 37m small businesses that use its servers. This accumulated data will allow for better credit assessment.

See *Apple Pay set to trigger rush of deals among rivals*, Financial Times, 30th January 2015; see also *Samsung buys mobile payments group LoopPay to compete with Apple*, Financial Times, 29th February 2015; see also *Digital payments rise but cash is still king*, Financial Times, 14th April 2015.

- Apple Pay enables the purchase of goods with a touch of a handset.
- An iPhone or Apple Watch is placed in front of a wireless reader and the transaction is completed.
- Widespread use of the technology – "Apple Pay now counts for

two of every three dollars spent via contactless payment on the three largest US card networks".

- Although only some retailers have the necessary readers, Samsung recently announced its purchase of mobile payments group LoopPay, which is estimated to work in 90 per cent of US outlets.
- In the UK, spending via mobile devices is projected to reach £54bn a year in the coming decade.

The economic impact of new technologies

Table 16 is an attempt to classify the economic impact of different technologies. It evaluates eleven key areas of innovation using five economic concepts: consumer surplus, productivity/producer surplus, complementarities, demand elasticity and Say's Law. In some cases, there is substantial overlap. The distinction between consumer and producer surplus is not always clear-cut. A new technology may lead to a better service and by implication deliver a consumer surplus. However, the productivity gains – and implicit cost savings – from the adoption of a new technology will also generate a producer surplus. Indeed, productivity improvements may benefit the producer *first*, before competition erodes margins. The producer surplus may drop; the consumer surplus would subsequently rise. The framework set out below looks simply at the *initial* impact.

Complementarities reflect the impact of new technologies in raising the potential value or contribution of workers: this may require higher skills or 're-training' of the workforce. Complementarities exist across most categories and Table 16 is simply a guide to possible areas where the benefits may be particularly great. There will be an overlap between complementarities and Say's Law. A new technology increases the embedded value of a worker. However, it may also create opportunities to provide new goods and services.

Similarly, there will be an overlap between complementarities and demand elasticity. Productivity may lower a firm's marginal costs, but the extent to which a firm finds it more profitable to employ more workers will be limited by demand. If the demand elasticity is sufficiently high, then this provides the scope for complementarities to emerge.

Key Technologies and their Economic Impact

Technologies (key words)/Key Issues	Consumer Surplus	Productivity/ Producer surplus	Complementarities	Demand elasticity	Say's Law
Mobile Internet (smartphones, apps, wireless)	High			High	High
Automation of knowledge work (AI, machine learning, voice recognition, machine vision)		High	High		High
The "internet of things" (sensors, internet, connectivity)			High		
Cloud technology		High			
Advanced robotics		High			High
Autonomous vehicles (driverless cars, drones)		High			High
Healthcare (genomics, 3-D printing, apps, sensors)	High		High	High	High
Energy (Renewables, energy storage, oil and gas exploration)				High	
3-D printing (healthcare, manufacturing, supply chain)		High			High
Advanced materials (nanomaterials, semiconductors, graphene)		High	High		
Fintech (company financing, crowdfunding, digital currencies, mobile banking)	High		High		

Table 16

The new technologies driving the economy *update*

3-D Printing

- 3-D printing is already being used to manufacture tools in space, to save costs and delay of transporting equipment from Earth. Engineers are "experimenting with a 3-D printer that would make bricks suitable for airtight buildings and radiation-proof shelters using the grit that blows across Mars's red surface".[31]
- 3-D printing is also accelerating the growth of digital manufacturing.[32]

5G

- Previous generations of mobile have been about making the internet faster. 5G will go one step further. It is expected "to make the internet fast enough to make possible a whole host of new applications from connected vehicles to the connective devices that will enable the internet of things". Companies including Vodafone, BT, Huawei, Ericsson, Nokia and Samsung are "working flat out to produce the precious global patents that will underpin the future of mobile connectivity".[33] Most hope to have some form of the technology in testing by 2018.

Algorithms

- "Computer modelling could replace much of the early-stage laboratory work to find molecules that work as medicines".[34]
- Algorithms can be used to teach "the secrets of song composition to a computer".[35]

---

31 See *3-D printing is going out of this world*, Wall Street Journal, April 14th 2015.

32 See *Makers follow the techies to create a 'nurture' space of their own*, Wall Street Journal, December 17th 2015.

33 See *Huawei, Ericsson and Nokia race to develop 5G mobile technology*, Financial Times, May 3rd 2015.

34 See *US biotech group Verseon to list on Alternative Investment Market*, Financial Times, May 7th 2015.

35 See *Jukedeck's computer composes music at touch of a button*, Financial Times,

- Instead of attending public auctions, investors in the US are relying on algorithms "that evaluate home values, proximity to schools and crime rates to outrace rivals for any remaining bargains offered by real-estate agents".[36]
- Algorithms are also being introduced into hiring selection by companies looking to improve staff retention rates.[37]

Artificial Intelligence / Machine Learning

- Competition in artificial intelligence intensifies as more companies are making proprietary machine-learning technology available under an open-source license. The decision by IBM, Facebook, Google and others to open-source their machine learning code should accelerate innovation in artificial intelligence: "IBM is one of the three companies this year to make available proprietary machine-learning technology under an open-source licence. Facebook Inc in February, released portions of its Torch software, while Alphabet Inc's Google division earlier this month open-sourced parts of its TensorFlow system."[38]
- Machine learning will expand the potential for big data to drive down costs: "artificial intelligence's potential has exploded as the cost of computer power drops and as the ability to collect and process data soars."[39]
- A computer has comprehensively beaten a human champion playing Go, the board game which has been dubbed the world's most complex, "achieving a historic milestone in artificial intelligence" according to the scientific journal Nature.[40]

December 7th 2015.

36 See *Racing to buy homes sight unseen*, Wall Street Journal, April 13th 2015.

37 See *Let algorithms show if they can make better hiring choices*, Financial Times, June 17th 2015.

38 See *IBM turns up heat under competition in Artificial Intelligence*, Wall Street Journal, November 24th 2015.

39 See *Artificial intelligence experts are in high demand*, Wall Street Journal, May 1st 2015.

40 See *Google computer triumphs in complex board game*, Financial Times, January 27th

Battery Assisted Bikes

- Rechargeable, battery-powered push bikes. The Gtech eBike has a lithium battery pack that is "cunningly disguised as a frame-mounted water bottle, providing 30 miles of zap and recharging to full in three hours".[41]

Big Data

- "Cross-device tracking technology" will deepen analysis of online habits of consumers.[42]
- Using data to support and drive sales is hardly a new concept. Nevertheless, "the combination of predictive smarts and automation promises to push sales into a new era of data-driven efficiency".[43]
- Furthermore, "firms are keeping head counts low, and even eliminating management positions by replacing them with something you wouldn't immediately think of as a drop-in substitute for leaders and decision makers: data". [44]

Blockchain

- Blockchain is a distributed, electronic ledger of digital events. Each participant must approve a transaction before it is recorded in a 'chain' of computer code. Cryptology is used to secure the transactions and the details are public. In its simplest form, blockchain is a method for having a shared and reliable database for the exchange of assets.[45]

2016.

41 See *The battery-assisted Gtech eBike takes the effort out of uphill slogs*, City AM, September 8th 2015.

42 See *Beware the electronic gossips eavesdropping in our homes,* Financial Times, December 23rd 2015.

43 See *The data-driven rebirth of a salesman*, Wall Street Journal, September 17th 2015.

44 See *Data is the new middle manager*, Wall Street Journal, April 19th 2015.

45 See *Why Blockchains could transform how the economy works*, WSJ, November 20th 2015.

- Blockchain could be used for "central clearing, back office operations and cross-border payments and vastly simplify compliance with anti-money laundering measures."[46]
- Blockchain could "revolutionise the way in which charities operate by cutting transaction costs".[47]
- Chain.com, a privately owned company that itself specialises in blockchain, has issued shares on Nasdaq "to a private investor using the US Exchange's new Linq system that is based on the digital ledger technology. The exchange group said the transaction had created a digital record of share ownership - 'significantly reducing settlement time and eliminating the need for paper stock certificates'. It also allowed the issuer and investor to complete and execute share subscription documents online".[48]
- The Australian stock market, ASX, is planning to use blockchain, claiming that the "technology allows a significant reduction in operational cost, reduces the likelihood of errors or 'fails', reduces capital requirements and allows a for reduction in settlement times".[49]
- Technology could speed up slow and inefficient back offices and save billions in the amount of collateral that is currently required by the global financial system. "The technology aims to prevent fraud by using a public digital database that is continuously maintained and verified by the other computers in a chain of transactions".[50]

---

46 See *Blockchain believers seek to shake up financial services*, Financial Times, December 14th 2015.

47 See *Charities weigh up gains in accepting bitcoin donations*, Financial Times, December 16th 2015.

48 See *Nasdaq claims to break ground with blockchain-based share sale*, Financial Times, December 30th 2015.

49 See *Blythe Masters' blockchain start-up raises $50m and inks ASX deal*, Financial Times, January 22nd 2016.

50 See *Blockchain backers urged to consider protecting users from fraud*, Financial Times, January 25th 2016.

Data Storage

- A number of well-funded start-ups are investing in data storage, putting intense pressure on established companies, including IBM, Hewlett-Packard and Dell. New systems store data on "flash memory rather than hard drives, which have spinning disks and electrical motors that are prone to mechanical failures and consume more energy than semiconductors. Data stored on such chips can be retrieved about 20 times faster than from drives".[51]

Digital Learning

- Personalised learning model combining computer-based and in-person instructions has "held down costs, sustained above average test scores and put students in greater control of their learning".[52]
- Indeed, "it is a waste of time to ask teachers to deliver information and test students on it when that task can be reassigned at least in part to software. Countless start-ups are working on this problem".[53]

Driverless Cars / Automation

- US company Faraday Future has unveiled a 'concept car', which embeds a smartphone in the steering wheel "to give the vehicle a 'sixth sense', personalised to its driver's preferences but also capable of piloting itself".[54]
- A number of companies have rolled out automated systems that "ease some of the more tedious aspects of piloting big rigs (trucks) while helping reduce accidents and save fuel".[55]

---

51 See *Startups dash into hot data-storage sector*, Wall Street Journal, September 4th 2015.

52 See *Ohio school district bets on technology in creating new learning model*, Wall Street Journal, June 7th 2015.

53 See *How humans can win the race against machines*, Wall Street Journal, September 27th 2015.

54 See *CES 2016: Faraday reveals sixth sense concept car*, Financial Times, January 5th 2016. See also *Faraday unveils amped-up 'concept' electric car*, Wall Street Journal, January 4th 2016.

55 See *Truckers gain an automated assist*, Wall Street Journal, August 7th 2015.

- The Obama administration has proposed spending "nearly $4billion over a decade to accelerate the acceptance of driverless cars on US roads and curb traffic delays and travel delays".[56]

Drones

- "Europe is turning to a new tool to catch ship operators skirting pollution limits: emissions-sniffing drones".[57]
- Amazon is using drones for deliveries.[58] Facebook is buying 11,000 drones to facilitate internet access and "is in negotiations to buy a drone manufacturer with the aim of using its high-altitude autonomous aircraft to beam internet connections to isolated communities in Africa".[59]
- China's SZ DJI Technology Co, the world's top consumer-drone maker, has launched a crop sprayer, testing whether farming is fertile ground for drone technology by unveiling an "eight-rotor drone priced at roughly $15,000 that is designed to spray pesticides on crops".[60]
- The world's largest drone maker, SZ DJI Technology Co opened its first retail store in Shenzhen in December 2015.[61]

FinTech

- Smartphones can be used to assess the credit rating of potential borrowers. A number of Silicon Valley start-ups have developed apps that can "dramatically reduce the cost of lending" by using "huge amounts of data - texts, emails, GPS coordinates, social -media posts, retails receipts and so on - indicating thousands

---

56 *See US proposes spending $3 billion to encourage driverless cars*, Wall Street Journal, January 14th 2016.

57 See *Europe tries out sniffer drones for policing ship emissions*, Wall Street Journal, November 26th 2015.

58 See *Amazon's delivery drones: where will they land?* Wall Street Journal, November 30th 2015.

59 See *Facebook buying 11,000 drones to connect Africa*, The Telegraph, March 4th 2014.

60 See *Chinese drone maker plows into agriculture*, Wall Street Journal, November 26th 2015.

61 See *Chinese drone maker DJI to open first flagship store*, Wall Street Journal, November 16th 2015.

of subtle patterns of behavior that correlate with repayment or default." Indeed, "even obscure variables such as how frequently a user recharges the phone's battery, how many incoming text messages they receive, how many miles they travel in a given day, or how they enter contacts into their phone - the decision to add last name correlates with creditworthiness - can bear on a decision to extend credit".[62]

- Digital wallets, or paying with smartphones, will "revolutionise the high street and how we pay for things".[63]
- Financial services will face further disruption from a new breed of companies. Aside from peer-to-peer lenders, "robo-advice businesses, which use sophisticated algorithms rather than highly paid humans to manage their customers' investments across geographies and asset classes, are attracting significant venture capital".[64]
- The number of contactless payments soared by 250 per cent in the twelve months to June 2015: "Almost 460,000 terminals across all of the UK are now ready for face-to-face contactless and mobile payments".[65]

Flexible Pricing

- Flexible or 'dynamic' pricing is being extended to a wider range of goods and services, depending on the timing of purchase by consumer. Price changes will be more rapid as sellers take advantage of software that analyses consumer habits. "Backed by vast amounts of data and powerful software, more businesses are varying prices by the day, the hour, or even the minute".[66]

---

62 See *Lending startups look at borrowers' phone usage to assess creditworthiness*, Wall Street Journal, November 30th 2015.

63 See *Digital wallets will change the way we shop, play and pay*, City AM, September 8th 2015.

64 See *Banks need to adapt to new breed of rival*, Financial Times, December 6th 2015.

65 See *Visa contactless payments grow by 250pc in UK*, City AM, January 26th 2016.

66 See *Now prices can change from minute to minute*, Wall Street Journal, December 14th 2015.

Food Technology

- According to the Centers for Disease Control and Prevention "one in six people in the U.S. experience food poisoning every year, and 128,000 are hospitalised for it". However, the "power to scan our environment at a molecular level, with devices no bigger than our smartphones, is coming".[67] A number of companies are offering devices that will warn consumers of potential contamination.

The Future of the Internet

- The conventional website is "space-organised". The cybersphere of the future will "resemble an electric power network, with information thundering through at tremendous volume and speed. Computers will become 'step-down transformers' to convert high-voltage information from the Internet into a useful, lower-voltage form. Flowing information will power your life".[68]

Gene Editing

- A fast and accurate method of gene editing has emerged, "which biotechnologists believe is the biggest technical advance in their field so far this century. It promises to accelerate genetic engineering across the board". It will also make possible the "extensive DNA rearrangements involved in the emerging science of "synthetic biology". Most of the excitement revolves around Crispr: "This enables researchers to manipulate specific genes, adding, subtracting or changing DNA, far more quickly and precisely than ever before".[69]
- "For decades, rare diseases were all but ignored by the pharmaceuticals industry. The science was difficult and the economics even harder. A third of all medicines approved by the US Food

---

67 See *Startups take bite out of food poisoning*, Wall Street Journal, December 14th 2015.

68 See *The future of the Internet is flow*, Wall Street Journal, October 2nd 2015.

69 See *Excitement rises over gene editing tool, but ethical doubts remain*, Financial Times, December 6th 2015.

and Drug Administration in the past five years have been for rare diseases – including a record 17 in 2014. This rush of R&D is delivering fresh growth to the pharmaceuticals industry – and raising new hope for patients previously stranded on the margins of medical science."[70]

Human Cloud

- "Employers are starting to see the human cloud as a new way to get work done. White collar jobs are chopped into hundreds of discrete projects or tasks, then scattered into a virtual 'cloud' of willing workers who could be anywhere in the world, so long as they have an internet connection". Critics fret this will set off a race to the bottom and "a wild west of unregulated virtual sweatshops". Others more optimistically suggest it will result in people "taking ownership again of the means of production, because you just need a computer, your brain and a wifi connection to work". [71]

The Hyperloop

- Referred to as supersonic transport pods, the hyperloop involves a "low-pressure tube in which levitating capsules carry passengers at about 760 miles per hour". The transportation system uses magnetic levitation. Hyperloop firms aim to cut costs "by using permanent magnets that use much less energy".[72]

A Material Revolution

- Titanium power will allow 3-D printing to lower the cost of producing titanium parts on an industrial scale for the auto and aerospace industries. Titanium power is produced through electrolysis with a 50% reduction in the "heat and energy needed for conventional titanium".[73]

---

70 See *Genomic advance lifts patients' hopes*, Financial Times, September 28th 2015.

71 See *The human cloud: A new world of work,* Financial Times, October 8th 2015.

72 See *Hyperloop races picks up speed*, Wall Street Journal, January 21st 2016.

73 See *Material revolution*, Financial Times, December 9th 2015.

- Graphite is used in electric batteries for its conductivity. Rising demand from electric vehicles, mobile technology and utility storage devices (i.e. renewables) will push graphite prices higher. However, battery producers are "also working on replacing graphite with other materials such as silicon, which could be capable of storing more energy."[74]
- Lithium and cobalt are also used in electric batteries. Cobalt is used as a compound with lithium in the cathode of lithium-ion batteries. Prices for these two materials have been rising, but scientists are "working on using fewer materials for the cathode in lithium-ion batteries" to reduce costs.[75]

Medical Research

- Smartphones will facilitate a "technological revolution in medical research". Researchers have benefitted from a decision by Apple to provide a no-cost development framework – ResearchKit – allowing scientists to produce apps that can gather more data. This in will sharply reduce the cost of clinical trials. Indeed, "The future of research is going to be in these types of studies that are casting broader nets over more diverse people, not constrained by geography". In short, the "scope for discoveries will become greater and the cost lower".[76]

Mining Technology

- New mining technologies, including bigger haul trucks, shovels and other equipment have "enabled the building of facilities that could produce two or three times the copper or iron ore of the previous big generation mines." Hauling rock around accounts for half of Cerro Verde's mining costs, so the company bought trucks and programmed software to run a relatively small number of trucks more frequently. Furthermore, "monitoring software quickly spots problems in trucks and shovels, allowing them to be repaired before they have to be replaced, saving money".[77]

---

74 See *Material revolution*, Financial times, December 9th 2015.

75 Ibid.

76 See *Medical researchers herald an app-driven revolution*, Financial Times, November 11th 2015.

77 See *Supermines add to supply glut of metals*, Wall Street Journal, January 4th 2016.

Music Streaming

- "Streaming music revenue has passed annual sales of digital downloads at a major music label for the first time this year, underlining a seismic shift in the music industry fuelled by the rise of services such as Spotify".[78]

Robots

- Humanoid robots are meeting strong demand; "The first batch of a model called Pepper, developed in the Far East and able to detect emotion, sold out immediately".[79]
- Newer robots are "more flexible, much easier to program and safer for humans."The new YuMi robot "can help assemble such products as smartphones, table computers and laptops that have been assembled largely by hand by workers in lower-cost countries like China".[80]

Satellites/Space

- Ranchers in Australia have embraced satellite technology to track their herds: "satellites take images of every 820 square feet of the ranches daily. On the ground, automatic weighing stations measure cattle each time they come to the water trough. The data is crunched and sent to farmers."[81]
- European rock provider Arianespace SA has notched "a new company record for the number of satellite launches in a year, as management continues to stress reliability and slash expenses to compete with lower-cost rivals."[82]

---

78 See *Warner music's streaming revenues top digital downloads for first year*, Financial Times, December 10th 2015.

79 See *Rise of the Robots: Advanced robotics spark an investment book as experts predict a robot-led industrial revolution is coming*, City AM, January 18th 2016.

80 See *New robots designed to be more agile and work next to humans*, April 13th 2015.

81 See *In Australia, cowboys use satellites to home in on the range*, Wall Street Journal, January 24th 2016.

82 See *Europe's Arianespace sees satellites take giant leap into small steps*, Wall Street Journal, December 18th 2015.

- The UK-based defence and aerospace group BAE Systems is to become a strategic investor in Reaction Engines. The "Sabre design for a reusable hybrid rocket/jet engine promises to transofrm the economics of space", with "a revolutionary engine that could propel aircraft into outer space and back at five times the speed of sound."[83]
- Airbus group SE has taken a big step toward establishing a global high-speed data-relay system in space aimed at eventually "using lasers to rapidly distribute spy photos and other data from satellites and drones".[84]

Sharing Economy

- Renting a holiday home with Airbnb, or hailing a ride with Uber, represent two high profile examples, but "the traditional bureau de change will be the next victim of the 'sharing economy'".[85]
- "Ride-sharing companies, like many other firms in the 'sharing economy', allow for a new kind of employment—sometimes called fractional employment—in which people can take on extra work when and if they need it. The key to fractional employment is flexibility for both these companies and their workers".[86]

Smart Devices

- A connected home service brings together "central heating, home security and energy management under a single internet-based platform".[87]
- A rising generation of start-ups are using Internet of Things to cut business costs. These start-ups are offering companies "inte-

---

83 See *BAE systems to pay £20.6m for 20% of space engine group*, Financial Times, November 1st 2015.

84 See *Space-based laser data-relay system advances*, Wall Street Journal, January 31st 2016.

85 See *Travel money swap shot seeks to ride peer-to-peer wave*, Financial Times, August 7th 2015.

86 See *How everyone gets the 'sharing' economy wrong*, Wall Street Journal, May 24th 2015.

87 See *CES 2016: 02 to launch smart-home platform in UK by summer*, Financial Times, January 5th 2016.

grated combinations of hardware, software, and services delivered over the Internet".[88]

- Soon smartphones will not only take snapshots and videos but also recognise the objects pictured. "With built-in image recognition, smartphones could identify objects in real time for a variety of applications, like identifying people to authorize transactions, aiding blind people and translating signs."[89]

Smart Medicines

- GPS technology can be used to "pinpoint the locations of emergency responders". When an emergency medical call is received, the nearest volunteer can be automatically dispatched to the scene through a smartphone app.[90]
- "Smart medicines that tell doctors when patients have taken them have moved a step closer" after the digital pill was approved by US regulators. The pill "will help ensure patients stick to their prescriptions and so reduce wasteful spending on drugs that are not taken properly".[91]

Virtual Reality Headsets

- It could take a decade, but "virtual reality headsets may become cheap and portable enough to replace smartphones as the technology industry's dominant computing platform".[92]
- Virtual reality can be used to simulate ageing, "the unforgettable and at times distressing, experience shed light not just on ageing, but also how virtual reality equipment can teach empathy and shape our perceptions of the world around us".[93]

---

88 See *Smart-device startups target business customers*, Wall Street Journal, December 8th 2015.

89 See *Google to make smartphones that recognise faces*, Wall Street Journal, January 27th 2016.

90 See *Faster medical attention with app*, Wall Street Journal, December 25th 2015.

91 See *US regulators accept 'chip in a pill' application*, Financial Times, September 10th 2015.

92 See *Oculus founder takes long-term view of virtual reality*, Financial Times, January 4th 2016.

93 See *Getting old? This high-tech suit simulates aging*, Wall Street Journal, January 7th 2016.

- "Virtual reality gets the buzz, but its less-immersive cousin – augmented reality – is also attracting investment and spawning new products". Indeed, "two small Silicon Valley companies are releasing electronic glasses that show workers a digital display in their field of view".[94]

Wireless Headphones

- Wireless headphones are in their infancy, but the technology is improving and a number of products have been launched. The market is likely to grow rapidly, "especially if smartphone makers save space by nixing traditional headphone jacks".[95]

Apple

- Apple has purchased the startup Emotient, which developed a software that reads people's emotions by analysing facial expressions. Apple also bought VocalIQ in October, a firms that develops computers' ability to understand natural speech.[96]
- Apple is racing against Google, Amazon, Microsoft and Facebook to develop personal assistants that delivers information before users ask for it. Apple's proactive assistant is using real time traffic data to suggest when to leave for an appointment.[97]
- The Apple Watch is also opening the door to new services. IBM's Watson software is using the Apple watch to store health data in order to facilitate personalised treatment. This has the potential to reduce healthcare costs.[98]
- Apple is also in discussion with US banks to develop a payment

94 See *Augmented reality moves forward with investments, products*, Wall Street Journal, January 5th 2016.

95 See *Review: Truly wireless headphones arrive, but with a few strings attached*, Wall Street Journal, January 13th 2016.

96 See *Apple Buys Artificial-Intelligence Startup Emotient*, Wall Street Journal, January 7th 2016.

97 *See Tech giants are racing to predict users' needs*, Wall Street Journal, August 5th 2015.

98 See *IBM strikes digital health deal with Apple, Medtronic and J&J*, Financial Times, April 13th 2015.

service that would allow users to exchange money from their phones.[99]

- The rapid diffusion of technologies allows companies to quickly grab market share in new sectors. For example, Apple music streaming services (Apple Music) surpassed 10m subscribers in only six months, twelve times as quick as Spotify. Apple Music has "the potential to be the leading music subscription service by 2017.[100]

Google

- Google and Lenovo are developing a 3-D mapping smartphone, expected to be released this summer.[101]
- Google is working on a quantum computer D-wave system able to solve problems 100 million times faster than traditional machines.[102]
- It is also testing a high speed fibre-optic internet. Google Fiber provides speeds of one gigabit per second, about 100 times faster than the current average.[103]
- Google is also in the process of refining its search engine algorithm, which could have a negative impact on Google's biggest rivals, such as Microsoft.[104]
- Google Maps (Driving Mode) uses stored data and recent online search to suggests a location without users selecting a place to go. For example "if a user searched for a local hardware store

---

99 See *Apple, banks in talks on mobile person-to-person payment services*, Wall Street Journal, November 11th 2015.

100 See *Apple Music attracts 10 million subscribers in just six months*, Financial Times, January 11th 2016.

101 See *Google tangoes with Lenovo to bring 3-D mapping to smartphones*, Wall Street Journal, January 7th 2016.

102 See *Google's tough search: a quantum leap in computing power*, WSJ, December 10th 2015.

103 See *Alphabet considers sending Google Fiber to cities with tech cred*, Wall Street Journal, October 28th 2015.

104 See *Google's 'mobilegeddon' overhaul set to result in demotion for EU's website*, Financial Times, April 20th 2015.

[online] and then launched Maps [...] Google would show the way to that establishment and estimate how long it will take to get there".[105]

- Google Ventures (GV) has backed more than 300 companies since its creation in 2009.[106]

Tesla

- In October 2015, Tesla unveiled its latest car software (Version 7). The software uses predictive algorithms to give the cars auto steering, enabling them to take different visual or road cues on where to drive, and allowing the car to pick lanes. The company delivered 17,400 cars in Q4 2015, the biggest q/q volume and up 75% y/y.[107]
- Tesla is also leading research on home batteries: its Powerall batteries system can store power generated at off-peak times to make it available for peak-time use. [108]

Amazon

- Amazon has launched a drone prototype that uses artificial intelligence to identify and avoid objects in the air. Amazon expects to cut delivery times to 30 minutes or less. [109]
- Indeed, Amazon's expansion is having a disruptive impact on intermediary companies. Amazon is developing its own delivery services, lowering demand for UPS.[110]

---

105 See *New Google Maps feature suggests destinations*, Wall Street Journal, January 13th 2016.

106 See *Tech start-ups waiting 'way too long' for IPO*, Financial Times, December 6th 2015.

107 See *Tesla delivers 17,400 vehicles in fourth quarter*, Wall Street Journal, January 3rd 2016.

108 See *Battery storage is set to transform renewables industry*, Financial Times, November 3rd 2015.

109 See *Amazon Touts New Drone Prototype, Plans Multiple Designs*, November 29th 2015.

110 See *Amazon seeks to ease ties with UPS*, Wall Street Journal, December 22nd 2015.

- Amazon is also tapping into home devices (ultra-high definition TV, tablets), challenging Apple and Samsung.[111]
- Tech companies have become more willing to share artificial intelligence services, in an attempt to foster innovation. Amazon introduced Amazon machine learning last summer, a free software.[112]
- Amazon will launch five cloud computing regions in 2016 including Canada, India, China and the UK. Amazon Web services unit is now expected to become bigger than the retail unit by 2017.[113]

Facebook

- Facebook is developing drones and lasers able to beam the internet to the most remote locations. This service, Internet.org, started in India in November.[114]
- Facebook is also using big data to develop a virtual assistant (called M). Unlike Apple or Microsoft software, M uses a constant flow of new data to improve functionality and automate more tasks.[115]
- Facebook is also working on a stand-alone video app that would support 360-degrees video.[116]

Uber

- Uber is working on an update of its software that will allow car-pooling. The company is trying to catch up with China

---

111 See *Amazon takes aim at Apple in battle for the living room*, Financial Times, September 17th 2015.

112 See *Amazon cloud introduces artificial intelligence service*, Bloomberg, April 9th 2015)

113 See *Amazon's cloud puts retail unit in the shade*, Financial Times, January 27th 2016.

114 See *Facebook's Latest Announcement for India*, Wall Street Journal, November 24th 2015.

115 See *Facebook 'trainers' lend AI a helping hand*, Financial Times, November 17th 2015.

116 See *Facebook Looks to Bring Virtual Reality to Mobile Devices*, Wall Street Journal, September 13th 2015.

ride-hailing Didi Kuaidi, which already provides this service. Car-pooling has the potential to run "the whole city with 20% of the cars we have today".[117]

- Uber sealed a deal with Facebook to allow users to order a ride via Messenger, increasing its pool of potential customers.[118]

117 See *Uber and rivals see promise in ride-sharing*, Financial Times, October 4th 2015.

118 See *Facebook Messenger in transport move with Uber ride ordering deal*, Financial Times, December 16th 2015.

INDEX